The modernist period saw a revolution in fictional practice, most famously in the work of novelists such as Joyce and Woolf. Dominic Head shows that the short story, with its particular stress on literary artifice, was a central site for modernist innovation. Working against a conventional approach and towards a more rigorous and sophisticated theory of the genre, using a framework drawn from Althusser and Bakhtin, he examines the short story's range of formal effects, such as the disunifying function of ellipsis and ambiguity. Separate chapters on Joyce, Woolf and Katherine Mansfield highlight their strategies of formal dissonance, involving a conflict of voices within the narrative. A chapter on Wyndham Lewis explores the use of the form to enact the aesthetics of Vorticism, resulting in the impasse of isolationism in its view of the individual. By contrast, Malcolm Lowry's stories are shown as offering a means of transcending this, in their very different treatment of the individual's experience. Finally, Dominic Head's challenging conclusion takes the implications of his study into the age of postmodernism.

THE MODERNIST SHORT STORY

THE MODERNIST
SHORT STORY

A study in theory and practice

DOMINIC HEAD

School of English
Birmingham Polytechnic

CAMBRIDGE
UNIVERSITY PRESS

CAMBRIDGE UNIVERSITY PRESS
Cambridge, New York, Melbourne, Madrid, Cape Town, Singapore, São Paulo, Delhi

Cambridge University Press
The Edinburgh Building, Cambridge CB2 8RU, UK

Published in the United States of America by Cambridge University Press, New York

www.cambridge.org
Information on this title: www.cambridge.org/9780521104210

First published 1992
Reprinted 1994
This digitally printed version 2009

A catalogue record for this publication is available from the British Library

Library of Congress Cataloguing in Publication data

Head, Dominic.
The modernist short story: a study in theory and practice / Dominic Head.
p.   cm.
Includes bibliographical references and index.
ISBN 0 521 41236 6 (hardback)
1. English fiction – 20th century – History and criticism.   2. Short stories, English –
History and criticism.   3. Modernism (Literature) – Great Britain.   4. Short story.
I. Title.
PR829.H43   1992
823′.01091 – dc20   91-30945   CIP

ISBN 978-0-521-41236-0 hardback
ISBN 978-0-521-10421-0 paperback

For my parents, Peggy and Victor, and for Tricia

Contents

Preface   *page* x
Acknowledgements   xii

1   The short story: theories and definitions   1

2   James Joyce: the non-epiphany principle   37

3   Virginia Woolf: experiments in genre   79

4   Katherine Mansfield: the impersonal short story   109

5   Wyndham Lewis: the Vorticist short story   139

6   Malcolm Lowry: expanding circles   165

7   Conclusion: contemporary issues   185

Notes   206
Bibliography   225
Index   237

Preface

At a time when the theory and criticism of literature has achieved an extraordinary level of complexity and specialization, it is curious to find a major literary genre – the modern short story – that has *not* been subjected to the systematic attentions of literary theory. A welcome recent development has been the increase in outlets (including specialist journals) for articles on the genre, but book-length surveys remain scarce, and relatively unsophisticated: where the theory of the novel runs to countless volumes, short story theory comprises no more than a handful of occasional works from which no developing aesthetic emerges. What *does* emerge from existing short story theory, such as it is, is a static notion of the genre's unity – its supposed reliance on certain unifying devices, such as a single event, straightforward characterization, a coherent 'moment of revelation' – from which an easily identifiable 'point' can be recognized.

This book argues, to the contrary, that the short story incorporates *disunifying* devices which are seminal features of the literary effects produced in the genre; a theoretical frame drawn from the work of (particularly) Althusser and Bakhtin is used to suggest a way of accounting for the formal and narrative disruptions discoverable in the short story.

The apparent perversity of this approach – this taking issue with the existing poetics of a literary genre – appears in a very different light when one considers the nature of the modernist project, and its seminal role in the development of the modern short story: as successive chapters argue, the formal conflicts and dissonances essential to the innovations of the major modernist writers are equally crucial to their short stories, stories which have had a formative influence on the genre in its modern phase. The reverse side of this observation receives emphasis too: the short story shows itself, through its formal capacities, to be a quintessentially modernist form. Ultimately, the extended argument of this work has two (related) foci: a plea for a more rigorous theorizing of the short story, and the claim that the genre ought to be seen as centrally involved in the modernist revolution in fictional practice.

Acknowledgements

My thanks are due to a number of people: particularly to John Goode, for his encouragement and shrewd advice. Frank Doherty and John Rignall offered valued criticisms and suggestions, and I am grateful, also, for help and advice from Tony Bareham, Michael Bell, Bernard Bergonzi, and Pamela Dunbar. I would like to offer a special note of gratitude to my colleagues and founder-members at the Warwick University Arts Graduate Forum – Fiona Becket, Gerry Carlin, Mair Evans, Tim Middleton, Antony Shuttleworth and Anne Surma – for providing an invaluable atmosphere of debate and friendship. I am grateful to the editors of the *Journal of the Short Story in English*, for permission to reproduce, in my conclusion, some text that first appeared in that journal. An earlier version of my chapter on Lowry first appeared in the collection *Malcolm Lowry Eight Years On*, edited by Sue Vice (Macmillan, 1989).

Tricia Head read through the entire manuscript, in an earlier form, and made many helpful suggestions. I also received much useful advice from the referees approached by Kevin Taylor at Cambridge University Press, whose skilful management of the project was essential to its transition to book form. My greatest debts are to my parents, Peggy and Victor Head, for their unfailing support and encouragement, and to Tricia, without whom this work could not have been undertaken.

CHAPTER I

The short story: theories and definitions

The rise of the modern short story in the 1880s and 1890s indicates that the written story enjoyed a period of significant development – arguably the birth of a new kind of short story – which was concurrent with the emergence of literary modernism.[1] This concurrence is more than circumstantial: there are various connections between the formal properties and capacities of the short story and the new ways of representing the social world displayed in modernist fiction. This survey seeks to investigate the nature of the relationship between modernism and the short story, an area, strangely neglected by critics, which has important resonances both in terms of literary history, and in defining the role of fiction-making in the twentieth century: the short story encapsulates the essence of literary modernism, and has an enduring ability to capture the episodic nature of twentieth-century experience.

I am proposing a connection between the generic capacities of the short story and the way in which writers have depicted their social world, a connection which stems from a special kind of literary experience relevant to readers, as well as to writers, of short stories. L. P. Hartley, discussing the status of the short story in the 1960s, noted how readers were apt to 'devour them singly on a news[s]heet', but would be disinclined to read them in collections. The reason for this was (and is) the 'unusual concentration' the genre demands, a concentration which permits no respite in a *series* of short stories because '"starting and stopping" exhausts the reader's attention just as starting and stopping uses up the petrol in a car'.[2] Hartley's yardstick was the comparatively favourable fate of the novel, and this

same comparison – novel versus short story – has proved pervasive in short story criticism, as we shall see. The main point
here, however, is Hartley's emphasis on a unique kind of
attention demanded by the short story. Susan Lohafer writes
that short stories 'put us *through* something – reality warp is the
shorthand for it', and this may be the best shorthand definition
we can come up with, indicating as it does two key elements of
the short story: its intensity and its exaggerated artifice.[3]

The remainder of this opening chapter examines short story
theory and indicates how the critical field has been dominated
by a simplified 'single effect' doctrine, derived from Edgar
Allan Poe, which invites a reunifying approach to familiar short
story characteristics such as ellipsis, ambiguity and resonance.
A different methodology is then outlined which acknowledges
and interprets the *disunifying* effects of ellipsis and ambiguity,
indicating how this kind of disruption establishes a connection
between text and context. This methodology is particularly
helpful in approaching the modernist short story because there
is a stress on literary artifice in the short story which intensifies
the modernist preoccupation with formal innovation. The
approach indicates how form and context work together, how
experimentation is the linchpin of modernism and of the social
perspectives it offers. This premise and its theoretical foundation
are tested in the body of the book, which comprises five author-
specific chapters – on James Joyce, Virginia Woolf, Katherine
Mansfield, Wyndham Lewis and Malcolm Lowry – in which
close readings of major modernist stories are made.

Any attempt to define a literary form has to mediate between
conflicting requirements. The impulse to provide a terse,
aphoristic description, based on empirical formal characteristics, must be tempered by an historical understanding: literary
forms are continually evolving, even when they rely heavily on
conventional gesture and device. Thus a *single* definition of the
short story is both inaccurate and inappropriate: the diachronic
perspective should always qualify the synchronic observation.
The valid, historical definition of a literary form, therefore,
examines *prevailing tendencies* rather than essential qualities, and

the current work, taken as a whole, is an extended attempt to define the modernist short story by accounting for the adaptation, in a particular era, of certain perceived generic qualities. Before beginning this extended analysis, however, it is necessary to consider the prevailing tendencies of the short story as an emerging modern form, and in this field of genre criticism extant scholarship is both a help and a hindrance.

Various attempts have been made to establish a taxonomy of modern prose forms, and a major problem with much of this work is its failure to account fully for the mutable, evolving nature of genre.[4] Susan Lohafer's book on the short story, though an important work in the field, is representative of this failure, based as it is on an avowed 'interest' which 'is not historical but generically aesthetic'.[5] However, much short story criticism engages with the form as an emergent, modern one (conceived in the nineteenth century) and so the qualities described can quite properly be appropriated as historically specific tendencies.[6] Moreover, this criticism also decribes a tradition which was the immediate inheritance of the modernists, a tradition which they questioned and subverted. Short story criticism, then, locates itself historically (often inadvertently) because it deals with a young form. The following survey of short story theory is designed to locate certain tendencies which were often modified and adapted by the modernists. Inevitably, such a survey is not in accord with the monolithic tendency of some of the critical work examined.

The most obvious problem facing the short story critic concerns narrative length, and this problem is usually tackled by a quantitive distinction between novel and story. This approach is epitomized in an important essay by Mary Pratt, who proceeds from the premise that 'shortness cannot be an intrinsic property of anything, but occurs only relative to something else'. Pratt takes the novel as the yardstick which 'has through and through conditioned both the development of the short story and the critical treatment of the short story', and, in doing so, she replicates the bias she analyses: she allows her *own* critical approach to be governed by the novel which supplies her with a neat, but reductive, binary opposition. This results in a very distorted definition of story, a conviction that a 'hierarchical relation' obtains between novel and story. It is the use of this extrinsic 'hierarchical relation' to account for 'the *practice* of the short story' as being somehow 'conditioned by its relation to the novel, as the smaller and lesser genre' that is particularly dubious.[7]

The assumption that short story length is relative only to the novel is plainly inadequate, and applies, again, to a hidebound critical purview more than it does to fictional practice. A story offers a *short* experience in comparison with many things – watching a film, for instance – and the novel is only one point of comparison, however important. Any comparison based purely on quantity serves only to reinforce an unreasoning 'bigger-is-better' value judgement, and to obscure the main issue: the length question must be secondary to a consideration of *technique*. It is only when quantity and technique are examined together, as mutually dependent factors, that quantity acquires any significance. So, although E. M. Forster's assertion that 'any fictitious prose work over 50,000 words' constitutes a novel has provided a rough basis for distinguishing novels from short fictions,[8] we must still concur with Norman Friedman that a measure based purely on a word-count 'is a misleading one because it centres on symptoms rather than causes'.[9] Anthony Burgess suggests a (more suitable) holistic approach when he claims that in the Sherlock Holmes stories of Conan Doyle we witness 'the story doing a kind of novelistic job and doing it briefly'.[10] Elizabeth Bowen makes a similar point about the stories of Henry James and Thomas Hardy: 'their shortness is not positive; it is nonextension. They are great architects' fancies, little buildings on an august plan'.[11] The charge here rests on an over-intricacy of plot, a problem which identifies a fundamental structural divergence. Short story critics generally agree that in the novel 'the dramatic events...are linked together by the principle of causality', as in the Holmes stories, or in the stylized folk-talkes of Hardy. A little-known collection of short fiction by G. B. Stern, entitled *Long Story Short*, constitutes a practical investigation of the implications of length and technique in the story. The most significant feature about the pieces in this volume is their complexity of plot. They are far more involved and convoluted than is usual, a fact indicated in the collection's title: these plots have been artificially compressed – they are long stories rendered short. The prime example is 'The Uncharted Year', a 7,000-word fiction with a fantastically complicated plot, but which contains nothing else: the experiment results in a thin surface narrative – pure anecdote – with a trite moral tacked on at the end, in an attempt to give the piece a depth its structure cannot support.[12]

There is general critical consensus that the genuine short story severely restricts its scope for plot or action, and concentrates rather on reiteration through pattern. The short story, according to this view, involves only '*one dramatic event*', with other subordinate events which 'facilitate the understanding of the main event'.[13] Hierarchical comparisons between novel and story have also proved inviting over this issue of action and its scale. Mary Pratt has summarized this comparative exercise in which 'to some extent, the moment of truth stands as a model for the short story the way the life stands as a model for the novel'. The 'hierarchical relation' between the two genres, in the critical literature, results in a tendency to view the restricted action of the story as feeble novelistic imitation:

The identification of the short story form with moment of truth plot was to some degree prescribed by the prior association between the novel form and the life. The lurking associations are these: if the short story is not a 'full-length' narrative it cannot narrate a full-length life: it can narrate a fragment or excerpt of a life. And if from that fragment one can deduce things about the whole life, then the more novel-like, the more complete, the story is.[14]

The 'lurking associations' here are those of a critical prejudice which favours the novel as the fictional norm, a view of the novel which is obviously vulnerable: the identification between novel and full-length life is clearly inadequate, especially in relation to the modernist novel. It is sometimes claimed that the unit of time in modernist fiction is the day, whereas in nineteenth-century fiction it is the year.[15] One can compare *Mrs Dalloway* with *Under the Greenwood Tree*, *Ulysses* with *Emma*. Naturally this is not a hard-and-fast rule, but it does indicate a general shift in the treatment of time. It is interesting to note that *Mrs Dalloway* and *Ulysses* were both originally conceived as short stories. Even in their final forms both novels hinge on single significant events – Clarissa Dalloway's party, the meeting of Bloom and Stephen – the episodes around which these books are structured. In their suggestion, through limited action, of the full-length life, *Ulysses* and *Mrs Dalloway* are representative of a tendency common in modernist literature, and a tendency particularly well suited to the short story. The question of length is relevant here, but in a way which actually reverses the formula identified by Pratt. Many readers, for instance, may find the extended, piecemeal evocation of character in early twentieth-century fiction tedious. Virginia Woolf's novel *Jacob's Room* would be an extreme example of this formless technique that may be better suited to short fiction. The modernist story, in other words, may be seen to contain the distilled essence of the modernist novel, at least as far as it is usually perceived.

A conventional distinction between novel and story – the whole life, or the crucial year, against the single episode – might, then, also apply to the most obvious differences between the nineteenth-century novel and modernist fiction in general (and the modernist story in particular). This evolving opposition reinforces the notion of genre as contextually variable, but it also indicates a major fault with the simple novel/story opposition: the modernist story, far from being 'smaller and lesser' in any technical sense, actually exemplifies the strategies of modernist fiction.

The taxonomy of prose forms is complicated by the introduction of a third term – novella – which occupies a midground between novel and story.[16] Although the term itself is problematic, the theory which accompanies it is helpful in basing distinctions on matters other than length. Judith Leibowitz, in her *Narrative Purpose in the Novella*, is concerned with 'the functions served by techniques in specific contexts', and establishes a scale of technical function for the three prose forms: she claims that the narrative task of the novel is 'elaboration', while that of the short story is 'limitation'. Narrative purpose in the novella, characterized as 'compression', combines the two in such a way as to give a 'double effect of intensity and expansion'.[17] This apparent contradiction in terms centres on the novella's dependence on a 'theme-complex', the development of interrelated motifs which suggest an outward expansion of thematic concern, even while a limited focus is maintained. A parallel device is 'repetitive structure' which also suggests thematic expansion through a redevelopment of ideas and situations.[18] Such techniques, according to Leibowitz, enable Thomas Mann (for example) to imply (without stating and without shifting focus) that the personal dissolution of Aschenbach in *Death in Venice* is indicative of the downward path of all civilization.[19] Leibowitz's distinction between short story and novella may be unworkable: the use of theme-complex and repetitive structure are relevant, to some extent, to the shortest fiction examined in this survey. Yet this foregrounding of technique – the cultivation of expression through form – accurately locates the central tendency of modernist short fiction.[20]

This coincidence between the modernist preoccupation with form and the capacity of the story is significant, and is only one of several such correspondences. The modernists' compression of time and dependence on symbolism are the two most obvious parallels: the short form often implies the typicality of a specific episode, while narrative limitation demands oblique expression through image and symbol.

Beyond these obvious parallels, the artifice of the story, particularly amenable to the artistic self-consciousness of the modernists, has further implications for the presentation of material: reception and analysis proceed from a grasp of pattern, of juxtaposition and simultaneity. Michael Chapman makes this point through comparison, as one might expect, with a notional novelistic convention:

Discussion of the novel usually proceeds most fruitfully by way of a detailed consideration of surface structure (which is syntagmatic and governed by temporal and causal relations); shorter fiction with greater immediacy signals deep structure (paradigmatic and based upon elements...which are not in themselves narrative).[21]

The artifice of the short story facilitates another modernist preoccupation: the analysis of personality, especially a consideration of the fragmented, dehumanized self. The self-conscious nature of the story 'alerts us to the fact that ... characters ... are within the text part of the design that bears and moves them',[22] a meta-fictional capacity resulting from 'the artificiality of the genre [which] makes authorial distancing a prerequisite of success', and this involves 'contrivances which mark the author's detachment from his [or her] characters'.[23] An inevitable corollary of these factors is a generic tendency towards paradox and ambiguity, another modernist hallmark: authorial detachment and the resulting emphasis on artifice and structural patterning (paradigmatic elements) give rise to an uncertain surface structure.

These capacities of modernist short fiction conform to the accepted characteristics of modernist literature in general: the limited action and an associated ambiguity and preoccupation with personality; and the self-conscious foregrounding of form and the concomitant reliance on pattern – paradigmatic devices – to express that which is absent from the surface, or syntagmatic level of the narrative. It is in the interpretation of these elements, however, that the real problems of short story criticism present themselves. There has been a general tendency to unify these elements, to view them as constitutive of an implicit formal unity not explicitly emphasized in the narrative. The modernist project, however, is far more radical than this would suggest, and actually gives rise to highly unstable work in which many elements are problematized. The notion of a single, exemplary action, for instance, is often taken as a structural centre, the validity of which is implicitly questioned. Indeed, most familiar tenets of short story criticism correspond to devices which the modernists deployed in an ambiguous way. A more detailed look at short story theory, and its monolithic tendency, will illuminate this problem of perception.

When one begins to read in and around the field of short story criticism two things soon become obvious. The first thing is that the theory is patchy and repetitive, with no strong sense of enlargement and development. This has to do mainly with the dominance of the short story's bigger sibling the novel; dominant, at least, in the minds of literary critics who have established a cumulative poetics for the novel out of all proportion to that achieved for the neglected short story. The second realization is that, by virtue of the repetition, a single aesthetic *does* appear to emerge: a consensus by default, in effect. This consensus involves reiterations or adaptations of Poe's short story theory, affirmations, with differing degrees of enthusiasm, of Poe's stress on the importance of 'unity of effect or impression'. This 'single' and 'preconceived effect' doctrine, in its purest form, states that 'in the whole composition there should be no word written, of which the tendency, direct or indirect, is not to the one preestablished design'.[24]

If this tradition of story surveys beginning with Poe is due partly to a lack of critical concentration and development, it is also due partly to the power and suggestive half-truth of Poe's theory. Structural aspects of the short story have provided a great deal of evidence in support of different unity theories, and Poe's work is an important landmark here. His well-known dictum that the story, unlike the novel, can be 'read at one sitting' is seminal. Of course, the dictum eschews such contextual variables as hard chairs and tender posteriors, but it does locate a comparative 'totality' which the novel lacks. This sense of aesthetic wholeness leads Poe into an analogy with the visual arts: 'by such means, with such care and skill, a picture is at length painted which leaves in the mind of him who contemplates it with a kindred art, a sense of the fullest satisfaction'.[25] Valerie Shaw, building on this observation, makes the claim that 'at every stage of its development the short story reveals affinities with the style of painting dominating the period in question'. Shaw's 'parallel between the modern short story and Impressionist art' is an astute one, as it accurately locates a 'share[d] acute consciousness of form', but the limitations of the analogy (of which Shaw seems partially aware) curtail its critical usefulness.[26] After all, literature remains, primarily, a temporal medium and painting a spatial one. Consequently, Shaw's assertion that 'the story can offer a picture' does not really square with her stated interest in 'the differences between words and visual images' as well as the similarities.[27] The analogy risks obscuring the basic distinction between the metaphorical story 'picture' and the literal spatial image on a painter's canvas.[28] The same problem complicates an analogy between photography and story writing, an area into which Shaw extends her discussion.[29] The comparison is irreducibly metaphorical, since it provides no theoretical basis for associating the different media, and the notion of a written 'picture' is obfuscating because its metaphorical aspect is partially hidden. There *is* a sense in which a short story has a unity which is not so evident in a novel, but this unity has to do primarily with linguistic reception and assimilation. Any spatial pattern is grasped by accumulation, or with hindsight, and, as such, is a kind of illusion generated progressively as the text is produced through reading. In short, the perception of story unity, in a spatial sense, is at odds with the inherent temporality of reading and writing.[30]

Visual metaphors abound in short story theory, a fact which underlines the 'spatial' aspect of the genre, but which also obscures the illusory nature of this aspect. In contrast to 'linear' stories, some critics have discerned 'circular' or 'spiral' story types. Avrom Fleishman discusses the circular stories of Virginia Woolf, stories which return to the point at which they start (and which include 'The Lady in the Looking-Glass' and 'Moments of Being').[31] Johannes Hedberg adds to this the refinement of the 'spirally' constructed story, a type which 'winds gradually to the centre'; Joyce's 'The Dead' is adduced as an example.[32] These spatial metaphors imply a structural unity and also some kind of thematic unity, but there is an unwarranted methodological tidiness in such criticism. Woolf's stories 'The Lady in the Looking-Glass' and 'Moments of Being' both rehearse Woolfian ideas about the fragility of understanding and the intangible complexity of personality. Joyce's 'The Dead' examines the fragmentation of experience and personal identity in a different way, but creates an effect of uncertainty much as the Woolf stories do. These elements of uncertainty derive from a crossover between story and theme, a disjunction between the story pattern or form and the experience (with its external referents) that is not reducible to the form. The conclusion of Woolf's 'Moments of Being' deliberately makes this point when the characterization of Julia Craye, established in the reverie of her pupil Fanny Wilmot, is effectively exploded; and this is a representative example of a tendency often found at a deeper level: the modernist circular, or spiral story, is usually an exploration of disunity rather than of the simple unity that the visual metaphor suggests.

The perceived difficulty with the cyclic and spiral story concepts may not be confined to the question of modernist uncertainty: it may point to an inappropriate way of thinking about the short story. An underlying problem with the supposed unity of the circular story is indicated in an essay by Rüdiger Imhof on minimal fiction. Imhof examines the ultimate circular story, John Barth's 'Frame Tale' which consists of the two lines 'ONCE UPON A TIME/THERE WAS A STORY THAT BEGAN' printed vertically, back to back, on either side of a single sheet. The piece is presented as if for cutting out and fastening to create a Möbius strip which reads, endlessly, 'ONCE UPON A TIME THERE WAS A STORY THAT BEGAN ONCE UPON A TIME…'. 'Frame Tale', as Imhof points out, is 'viciously circular', 'self-referential' and, by virtue of the paradox it represents, it has an 'unmistakable ambiguity'.[33] Whether or not one agrees with Imhof's dubious claim that these factors make 'Frame Tale' literature need not concern us here. The important point is that all perceived circular stories must contain an element of self-referentiality (they 'revolve' around their own points of reference), and that, even when confined to this reflexive dynamic, they can contain elements of paradox and ambiguity, but an ambiguity which is without a context. In the case of 'Frame Tale' this ambiguity stems from the inherently paradoxical nature of the Möbius strip, but this uncertainty may be an inevitable consequence of the circular-story concept: the story which can only explicitly describe its own universe must appear foreign (and hence inaccessibly ambiguous) to those readers (all readers) whose understanding is fashioned by a different system. But no writing occurs in a vacuum: it is always grounded in its social and intellectual context, and the circular-story concept tends to obscure this connection.

Short story writers since Poe have helped to perpetuate the notion of story unity, often using visual metaphors. John Wain has written that successful story writing is a 'knack', 'something almost physical, the movement of the wrists'. Consequently the writing is 'like a cook turning out a blancmange', since 'with a short story, it turns out right, or it doesn't turn out right'.[34] Again, the metaphorical sleight of hand threatens to elide important differences: the 'turning out' of a story is in no technical sense comparable to the 'turning out' of a blancmange, and the comparison amounts to little more than a verbal conceit. This idea of artistic success being dependent upon physical perfection is apparently echoed by other story writers. Katherine Anne Porter has commented that, 'if I didn't know the ending of a story, I wouldn't begin',[35] while Katherine Mansfield felt that 'the *labour*' of writing came 'once one has thought out a story'.[36] In these expressions of the compositional process, that worrying visual metaphor for the story artefact hovers in the wings. It is shoved unceremoniously onstage in A. E. Coppard's formulation, which stresses the importance of 'see[ing] all round and over and under my tale before putting a line of it on paper'.[37] The precise composition of this three-dimensional and scientifically charted object remains unclear. Possibly it is some sort of blancmange.

Theories about story 'shape' also appear in more sophisticated formulations which have their roots in Aristotelian prescriptions about beginnings, middles and ends. Cay Dollerup has summarized various diagrammatic representations – triangles and inverted 'V's – of the tri-part story theory (and its variants), and the interested reader is directed to Dollerup's essay.[38] My interest in this kind of theory centres on the effect it has had on less strictly formalist criticism. Ian Reid, in his brief but valuable book, considers the possibility that 'a deep-rooted aesthetic preference' lies behind the 'tripartite sequence'. It is true that the tripartite sequence is a familiar and effective rhetorical device: one thinks not only of fairy-tales, jokes and anecdotes, but also of the structure of very different cultural texts such as political speeches (the three-part list is a basic oratory ingredient), or academic works (which often follow the thesis-antithesis-synthesis structure of Hegelian dialectic). The tri-part theory has some relevance to those short stories which develop traditional tale motifs, but this relevance should be seen as merely one element among others, rather than as a generic principle. Reid extends and refines his structural discussion, and suggests the notion of 'formal poise' as a basic short story ingredient. In doing so he courts the danger of an over-simplified formal prescription.[39] Elaine Baldeshwiler, in an important essay, teeters on the brink of the same reductionism. D. H. Lawrence's short fiction, she feels, achieves a satisfyingly lyrical effect when he 'permits structure itself to be guided by the shape of feeling'.[40] The idea that the responses of readers, or the emotions of characters, can be anticipated or represented through formal shape can be misleading, and the dangers of this type of theory are manifest in John Gerlach's *Toward the End: Closure and Structure in the American Short Story*: in his introduction Gerlach writes of 'an underlying narrative grid that I think each reader applies to any story and that every writer depends on the reader knowing'.[41] This ready-made narrative grid, with its essential ingredient of closure, lies behind all of Gerlach's subsequent comments, even in relation to the open-ended story because 'the short story is that genre in which anticipation of the ending is always present'.[42] In a sense this is true, because non-closure in fiction generates its effects from a tension with the closure it denies (a matter discussed more fully in my concluding chapter). Yet this tension is complex, invariably governed more by the anti-closural gesture than by an anticipation of closure. Gerlach's book develops the line of argument put forward in a much earlier essay by A. L. Bader, who claims that the modern short story, despite its apparent lack of structure, actually derives its form from a more con-ventional, plot-bound story type. The reading process is then a kind of dot-to-dot exercise in which 'the reader must supply the missing parts of the traditional plot'.[43] A good way, perhaps, of indicating theoretical continuity – in this case the continuity of the unity aesthetic – but this is not a method particularly suited to analysing literary development and innovation.

In her structuralist account of the short story, Susan Lohafer argues that expectations of closure operate at the level of individual sentences, an approach which (despite its suggestive-ness in many ways), is greatly restricted by a delimited, synchronic view of language. She writes of 'a grammar of fiction' which 'starts with the assumption that fiction is a conscious manipulation of the universal processes underlying the very structure of language itself'.[44] Lohafer threatens to reduce language and experience to 'universal' structures and shapes, making manifest a danger which is latent in much short story criticism. Lohafer anticipates Gerlach in arguing that the 'idea of progression-toward-an-end concentrates thought and regulates feeling whether or not the end really comes'.[45] This recurring idea of the story as an end-oriented totality, which makes its presence felt even in absence, is of limited use. As a starting-point for a consideration of formal innovation it can be helpful, but beyond that it can impede critical insight. This absence-as-presence argument seems, ultimately, circular and unproductive.

Visual metaphors for the short story, and the prescriptive narrative frame they often imply, cannot elucidate the form's complexity and (productive) ambiguity. The unity aesthetic which underpins the kind of approach I have been examining also crops up in less formulaic writing on the genre. Clare Hanson, who perceives that 'writers such as Joyce and Katherine Mansfield had rejected the "plotty story" because it seemed to depend too heavily on conventional assumptions about the meaning and value of human experience', can still speak of the 'composed and harmonious whole' in the work of these two writers, and of the 'central symbolic intention' around which modernist short fiction is 'deliberately shaped'.[46] The fallacious notion of central symbolic intention helps bolster the conception of story as visual artefact, especially when the critic is able to locate a single dominant symbol. In the light of the present discussion Kafka's famous objection to having the insect of 'Metamorphosis' depicted by his illustrator takes on a special resonance.[47] Kafka's motivation might be plausibly interpreted as a strategy for protecting a resonant, multivalent fiction from the powerful reductionism of the single image.

To speak of multivalence in the context of modernist fiction is not, however, to suggest that a principle of undecidability is operative. Rather, specific kinds of ambiguity are examined in specific ways. This is a process which Frank Kermode overlooks in *The Genesis of Secrecy* where he reflects on the various interpretations that narrative can support and employs Kafka's parable 'Before the Law' to illustrate a general principle of undecidability in narrative. The Kafka parable is worth considering briefly here since it is, in certain ways, a representative modernist short fiction. It concerns a man who attempts, without success, to gain access to 'the Law', but who is kept out by a doorkeeper. After many years vigil outside this door, before dying, the man discovers that the door, which is now to be shut, was intended only for him.[48] Kermode's point is that the man in the parable, denied access to the Law, is comparable to the reader of any parable (and, by extension, of any narrative): 'the outsider remains outside'. The point is reinforced by an account of the discussion between K and the priest concerning the interpretation of the parable. Kermode points out that K 'is offered a number of priestly glosses, all of which seem somehow trivial or absurd, unsatisfying or unfair, as when the doorkeeper is said to be more deserving of pity than the suppliant, since the suppliant was there of his own free will, as the porter was not'. The fact that the parable itself 'incorporates very dubious interpretations, which help to make the point that the would-be interpreter cannot get inside, cannot even properly dispose of authoritative interpretations that are more or less obviously wrong', is offered as a representative characteristic of parable.[49]

Yet surely this does not fully account for Kafka's deliberate cultivation of ambiguity, or for the parodic nature of his parable: the 'uninterpretable' nature of 'Before the Law', as a statement about the inscrutability of authority, is the whole point; and the method chosen for this statement is a deliberate short-circuiting of lucid didacticism (the quality conventionally associated with parable). Of course, Kermode's argument is that all narrative is inscrutable in this way, but this overlooks Kafka's deliberate subversion of a notional convention. 'Before the Law', in terms of its broad characteristics, is an exemplary modernist story. Its enactment of ambiguity is typical, as is its simultaneous dependence on, and subversion of, convention:

the rejection of parable as message, as a parallel to the inscrutability of authority, is itself presented in the form of a parable.

One way of getting beyond the unity aesthetic is to develop the view that the modernist story represents some kind of new beginning, an out-and-out rejection of generic convention and device, and there is some precedent for pursuing this convenient idea. A critical commonplace in short story theory is the notion that there are, essentially, two types of story, differentiated by their differing dependence on 'plot', or external action. This is a development and refinement of the novel/story dichotomy discussed above: generally, plot is here seen as part of a formal pattern, but even in this capacity it is not held to be a fundamental factor in some stories. The plotted story, of which Maupassant is seen as a figurehead, is set against the less well structured, often psychological story; the 'slice-of-life' Chekhovian tradition. It is to this tradition that the stories of the modernists (those of Joyce, Woolf and Mansfield in particular) are usually said to belong.

Suzanne Ferguson defines these two types as simple (the anecdote or tale) and complex (the episode). Simple stories concern 'a single character in a single, simple action', while in the complex episode 'the forming elements are thus marshalled towards the ordered revelation of character or, in some cases, the development of symbol, rather than toward plot'.[50] Eileen Baldeshwiler has supplied alternative terms for this binary opposition: she distinguishes between the conventional, plot-based story ('epical') and the 'lyrical' story, often open-ended, which focuses upon 'internal changes, moods, and feelings'.[51] These succinct terms seem to deal very neatly with the perceived dichotomy.

The two trends – epical and lyrical – are seen by Baldeshwiler as seminal to an historical survey of the short story. Indeed, she begins her article by asserting that 'when the history of the modern short story is written it will have to take account' of these 'two related developments'.[52] As if in response to this assertion Clare Hanson has structured her history of the short form, *Short Stories and Short Fictions: 1880–1980*, to set the two trends in opposition. She has even posited a new terminology to distinguish between short *stories* – the conventional, epical, plot-based type – and short *fictions* in which plot is subordinate to internal psychological drama, a category that roughly equates with Baldeshwiler's lyrical story, and Ferguson's complex episode. Hanson's chapter on the modernist era locates Joyce, Woolf, and Mansfield within the latter camp, as writers of short fictions rather than stories.[53] The tidiness of this taxonomy is appealing, but when one examines its implications, problems present themselves. To begin with, the term 'short fiction' carries a burden of signification which is not easily cast off: short fiction is frequently used as an imprecise, all-purpose term which subsumes 'sketch', 'story' and 'novella' – any fiction which is not a novel, effectively. The problem with trying to recoup such a generalized term as a specific critical tool is self-evident, and this terminological quibble suggests a larger problem of descriptive accuracy, especially in relation to Hanson's treatment of the modernists. It is true that plot is de-emphasized in the stories of Joyce, Mansfield and Woolf, and this distinguishes their work from the more carefully plotted short fictions of, for example, Henry James and Joseph Conrad. But this de-emphasis is not a rejection: on the contrary, the adaptation of well-plotted story types is an important feature in the stories of Joyce, Mansfield, and Woolf, in whose works a consciousness of conventional story forms provides structure and referential landmarks, even where such conventions are subject to revisionist or ironical treatment. In other words, the dichotomy is apparent rather than real, an overstatement of a shift in emphasis. An accurate analysis of the modernist story must be more flexible than this; it must focus on the innovation achieved through adaptation, rather than on uniqueness as some kind of self-contained entity.

A key aspect of the unity aesthetic is the idea that the short story concentrates on a single character, and the artistic possibilities of this focus are often seen as limited in a particular way. Whereas the novel has the scope to *develop* characterization, the story is usually deemed to have space only to *show*, to illuminate a certain aspect of character (and/or situation) in a single moment of insight. Mark Schorer's aphoristic statement – 'the short story is an art of moral revelation, the novel an art of moral evolution' – forcefully represents this tenet of belief.[54] Elizabeth Bowen concurs with this view: 'I do not feel that the short story can be, or should be, used for the analysis or development of character. The full, full-length portrait is fitter work for the novelist'.[55] There is an element of obvious truth, of *truism* almost, in these statements, yet they also contain an undercurrent of simplification and distortion. The suggestion is that characterization in the novel can attain a complexity unavailable to the short story, and while this is obviously true in some sense, its implied corollary – the assumption that the short story *reveals* its characterization, suddenly and intensely – is uncritically reductive. Approaches to the short story have expended great effort in explicating the nature of the inner character, revealed in key moments, often through the poetic use of symbol and image. The critical literature, in effect, has established an impression of short story characterization as a puzzle, the solution to which can be found by the application of a kind of generic cipher. This is the critical heritage which has given rise to those text-books, in which famous stories are given the once-over with regard to theme-plot-character. These books are often designed as training grounds for a formulaic study of the novel, and represent a deeply entrenched attitude to the study of literature. The pedagogic and cultural implications of this kind of 'puzzle-solving', with its underlying will to order, reduce and assimilate, are disturbing, especially when it is foregrounded as the key to a literary genre.[56]

Characterization is, admittedly, seminal in the modernist story, where the *emphasis* falls on internal rather than external action. This body of short fiction, therefore, has provided much material for the character-revelation school of reading, an approach underpinned by Joyce's 'epiphany' concept, the 'sudden spiritual manifestation'[57] which is usually seen as the key to characterization:

The emphasis of modernist short fiction was on a single moment of intense or significant experience. It was not generally thought desirable to break down experience into smaller units still, for example units of language: such a breakdown could theoretically proceed infinitely, leading to a complete degradation of meaning and value. So the 'epiphany' or 'blazing moment' came to form the structural core of modernist short fiction (and...of many modernist novels). This stress on the fleeting moment is consistent with the prevailingly relativist philosophy inherited by modernist writers.[58]

Clare Hanson here locates an important difficulty in character-revelation readings of modernist stories, a tension founded on the contradiction of interpreting 'a discrete moment or unit of experience' in a particular way, and yet linking such an interpretation to the problematized 'external personality' which, for the modernists, is 'an ever-changing, infinitely adjustable "envelope" surrounding the real self'. The problem is further exacerbated, as Hanson perceives, by 'the "indirect free" style of narration in which the voice of the narrator is modulated so that it appears to merge with that of a character of the fiction'.[59] This, apparently, is an advance on the 'moral revelation' approach to the significant moment, since, if the narrative itself is problematized, there is no authoritative *voice* to point a moral. Hanson, however, overlooks the possibility that this might be the whole point, and pursues a more conventional way of solving the problem of uncertainty. Her account of Katherine Mansfield's art indicates the kind of 'solution' she finds. Overemphasizing Mansfield's Symbolist inheritance, Hanson actually buttresses the reductive character-revelation approach: 'the strength of Katherine Mansfield's Symbolist technique can be fully appreciated only through close readings. "The Escape" (1920) is, like her other fictions, a total image, a carefully composed expressive appearance in which each naturalistic detail also functions symbolically, contributing to the expression of a mood or a state of mind.' This kind of analysis, in which 'the idea of a concrete image can be extended...to mean the entire composition of a fiction and not just a single motif,' facilitates a moral vantage point for deciphering character. Hanson enables herself to conclude that the husband in 'The Escape' 'comes to full consciousness of his position, of the exhaustion of his spirit and the impasse reached with his wife', and her purpose in doing so is to present this neatly unpacked epiphany as exemplary: 'such a moment of vision is the quintessence of modernist short fiction'. The

husband's vision is complicated by a simultaneous perception of
'the beauty of the external world and of art', but the reading is
far from complex in that it hinges upon a preconceived approach
to symbolic pattern and order.[60]

This, surely, is a distortion of the modernist project, especially
as it is manifested in the short fiction. If narrative authority and
the stability of personality are both problematized, what
grounds are there for this emphasis on authorial order and
control? One might equally interpret the use of symbol as
objective correlative for internal mood as fluid and uncertain;
as *emblematic* of that 'ever-changing' personality. Indeed, *not* to
do so implies more about the reductive habits of critical theory
in general (and short story criticism in particular) than it does
about modernist writing.

Pertinent here is Wayne Booth's argument that even in the
most impersonal novel there is an implied author whose
personal values are expressed in the total form.[61] This indicates
a unity established through the back door, and Hanson seems to
have a similar conviction about the short story. Yet the
cultivated disunity of the modernist story should lead us away
from the search for a unifying authorial presence, and towards
a focus on the historical gaps and conflicts in a text. These gaps
and conflicts, which I take to be the central aspect of evolving
generic form, inevitably result in an uneven textual surface.

Hanson's delimited reading of Mansfield is anticipated by
Valerie Shaw, who rightly points out that 'Mansfield moves so
freely in and out of the minds of all of her characters that they
end up existing on the same level, leaving no way of gauging the
author's attitude to her subject'. The problem, as Shaw
perceives it, is solved by an integrated use of 'figurative'
language – a strategic use of symbol and metaphor – which
enables Mansfield 'to balance sympathy and judgement'. The
aesthetic preference for 'balance', and for the 'judgement' it
affords, lies behind Shaw's conservative view of the epiphany as
an ordering principle: 'most worthwhile short stories do contain
a definite moment at which understanding is attained, sometimes involving a response no deeper than, "So it *was* the butler
who killed Lord Mountjoy", but often turning the reader

inward to reassess his [or her] own moral or ethical stand-point'.[62] If one agrees that a 'worthwhile' story involves some kind of 'moral or ethical' challenge, one might also argue that the significant moment in modernist fiction can, with worthy intent, challenge the concept of momentary understanding itself. Woolf's 'Moments of Being', referred to above, can be seen as structured around a *non*-epiphany which makes just such a challenge. In fact, most of the accepted modernist 'epiphanies' are problematic. The 'significant moment' in *Dubliners* consti-tutes the most surprising example of this, being consistently undercut by unreliable narrative.

The problem facing short story critics is to find a way of escaping their own reductive formulae. Indeed, the critical literature often exhibits the kind of contradiction that can point beyond the formulae. Julio Cortázar, for instance, has con-tributed to the visual artefact aesthetic, but his comments also reveal its limitations. Cortázar's metaphor for story composition is 'modelling a sphere out of clay', and, despite the obvious comparison with Wain's blancmange theory, the idea is developed into a more significant area: 'to put it another way, the feeling of the sphere should somehow be there before the story is ever written, as if the narrator, subject to the form it takes, were implicitly moving it and drawing it to its maximum tension, which is what makes for, precisely, the perfection of the spherical form'. There is an inherent contradiction here between plasticity and physical perfection, not perhaps in the process of fashioning clay, but certainly in relation to the short story as a finished product. Cortázar develops the misleading aspect of this analogy in discussing the 'autarchy' of the 'great story', denoted by 'the fact that the story has pulled free of its author like a soap bubble from a bubble-blower'. The con-tradiction, however, is illuminating. Cortázar effectively locates the dynamic of the modern short story which is actually at odds with its *apparent* formal unity, and this dissonance is identified in his resonant statement that 'a story relie[s] on those values that make poetry and jazz what they are: tension, rhythm, inner beat, *the unforeseen within fore-seen parameters*' (emphasis mine).[63]

An apparent conflict between form and content has been

noted by several critics. János Szávai detects 'an internal contradiction' in the short story which derives from its origins in the oral anecdote. As in the spoken tale, argues Szávai, there is an illusion of reality – an authorial effort to present a story as *true* – which is at odds with the higher plane where the story's 'essence' is to be found; 'the actual meaning lies beyond' the 'first stratum of reception'.[64] Another critic writes of '"slice-of-life" stories' (the Chekhovian tradition), and considers how they 'reflect the confusing and complex formlessness of life itself', yet their 'structure can still be thought of as the inverted "V"' because 'in their unique view of reality these stories imply a conscious plotting that is not antithetical to the view of plots with beginnings, middles, and ends'.[65]

Despite the formalist emphasis of his book, John Gerlach also displays awareness of an anti-formalist story element. Apropos of Hemingway, he considers the significance of stories which are structurally closed, yet thematically open.[66] John Bayley makes several remarks which point towards dissonance as an informing generic factor. He considers 'the short story element' to be 'an unexpressed paradox'. Stated less paradoxically, Bayley's belief here is that 'one of the most vital effects of the short story' is 'the impression that there is always something more to come'.[67] Bayley continues to refine this imprecise, but suggestive aesthetic:

Fully to succeed the short story must forgo its self-conscious emphasis on concentration, and appear both leisurely and enmeshed in the speculative, as any other genre may be. It must seem both formally to preclude, and secretly to accept, speculation on matters excluded by itself... The incompatibility between its art and its mystery must become its own justification.[68]

The frequency with which these formulations appear attests to the importance of paradox to the short story, yet the question of the *significance* and *function* of paradox remains unaddressed by these critics. The major stumbling-block is the contradiction perceived between form and content, a perception which results from a preconceived notion of form. A more helpful approach would construe the new form as content itself, innovation as statement, and as a contradiction only of the old notion of form. It is a question of 'grasping form no longer as the symbolic mould into which content is poured, but as the "form of the content": which is to say, grasping form as the structure of a ceaseless self-production, and so not as "structure" but as "structuration"'.[69] The problem hinges on finding a critical approach and a language which is rigorous enough to theorize the evolving, hidden side of a text. Such a language has generally been missing from short story criticism, and, since the elements of ambiguity and paradox cannot be precisely dealt with without such a language, critics have taken refuge in the nebulous concept of 'mystery'. Bayley believes that the short story must suggest 'that its mystery cannot be yielded up',[70] and this idea of 'mystery' has been mentioned by several critics, usually as a *fundamental* generic factor. Eudora Welty has written that

the first thing we see about a story is its mystery. And in the best stories, we return at the last to see mystery again. Every good story has mystery – not the puzzle kind, but the mystery of allurement. As we understand the story better, it is likely that the mystery does not necessarily decrease; rather it simply grows more beautiful.[71]

Another example is found in Ian Reid's book, which concludes with a chapter on 'Essential Qualities?', the query indicating the uncertainty of the concept. The chapter ends with a quote from William James concerning his brother Henry's tales and the 'feeling' they arouse 'of baffled curiosity as to the mystery of the beginning and end of their being'.[72]

These theories of mystery and uncertainty might appear to represent the polar opposite of the unity aesthetic; but the idea of narrative mystery has not proved to be at all incompatible with the 'decoding' approach which redeems the ambiguous story from uncertainty by imposing symbolic order upon it. Clare Hanson summarizes this view in writing that 'the ellipses in the works of the modernists generally occur...when the author...sacrifices narrative continuity to symbolic order'.[73] But even if the mystery element is perceived as apparent rather than real – as the result of the rejection of epical narrative convention – there remains a resonant dissonance between order and disorder which needs to be addressed. The dot-to-dot exercise re-establishes order at the expense of devaluing, and hence *misrepresenting*, the element of disorder.

An example of symbolic effect will help to clarify this problem of misrepresentation. Extant readings of Katherine Mansfield's story 'Bliss' indicate the problems that arise when a 'symbolic order' is sought in modernist writing. The story traces the happiness of its protagonist, Bertha Young, during a day which culminates in a dinner party at which she is the hostess. Her feeling of elation, which she cannot define, becomes focused into an imagined bond with a dinner guest, Pearl Fulton, a beautiful young woman who is 'a "find" of Bertha's'.[74] Her buoyant feelings, caused largely by her attraction to Pearl, she channels into a newly found sexual desire for her husband Harry. Her bubble of euphoria is burst when she sees Harry and Pearl in each other's arms as the guests are leaving.

Bertha's 'epiphany' involves a dawning (but incomplete) awareness of her own latent homosexuality, a development conveyed by the symbolic associations of the pear tree in the story. Initially, the tree is assessed by Bertha as a symbol of her own life, and then, as she and Pearl stand admiring it together, she imagines it unites them. Finally, having discovered Harry and Pearl embracing, she turns to the tree apparently expecting to find it somehow changed in accordance with her new mood, only to find it 'as lovely as ever'.[75] Walter Anderson is fully justified in arguing that the polarity of the love triangle here is homosexual rather than heterosexual: it is not that Pearl and Bertha are in competition for Harry, but rather that Harry and Bertha are rivals for Pearl. Accordingly, Anderson interprets the pear tree as a symbol of Bertha's sexuality, its tallness representing her (unrecognized) homosexual aspirations and its rich blossoms expressing her desire to be sexually used.[76] That these aspirations remain unfulfilled is conveyed by the sight of the tree 'as lovely as ever' at the story's close.

The story's symbolism has provoked much debate, a fact which suggests that it may be less determinate than the symbol-hunting critical approach has allowed.[77] Anderson's reading, I feel, is accurate as far as it goes. Indeed, an explicit association is made between Bertha and the tree when 'she seemed to see on her eyelids the lovely pear tree with its wide open blossoms as a symbol of her own life'.[78] There is, however, a fluidity in the tree's symbolic purport; in addition to its function as emblem of Bertha's sexuality, there is also a sense in which the tree and that which it embodies is distanced from her. This is made manifest when Bertha, having witnessed the embrace, rushes to look at the pear tree, her happiness destroyed:

> Bertha simply ran over to the long windows.
> 'Oh, what is going to happen now?' she cried.
> But the pear tree was as lovely as ever and as full of flower and as still.[79]

Bertha here has cause to revise her earlier evaluation of the tree as a symbol of her own life: it is now thoroughly out of tune with her feelings. These different functions of the tree are reinforced by the pun on 'pear', which can also be heard as 'pair', suggestive of Bertha's personal identification with the tree, and also of her (later) notion that it somehow unites her with Pearl. 'Pear' can also be heard as 'pare', suggestive of the peeling away of Bertha's delusion, a process which presumably begins when she feels the tree to be divorced from her situation as the story ends. In creating this distance between character and symbol Mansfield skilfully widens her symbolic scope: the pear tree is now both emblematic of Bertha's sexuality *and* representative of the blossoming, fecundating processes of nature from which she is excluded. This exclusion highlights her predicament as frustrated homosexual and as unwilling participant in a heterosexual system. The symbol is at once Bertha and yet not-Bertha, a formal contradiction which summarizes Bertha's personality contradiction and non-identity. (This disruption of symbolic order is consonant with the modernists' fragmented presentation of personality.) Such a complex use of symbolism is commonly detected in poetry, but is rarely observed in discussions of short fiction.

This example demonstrates how disorder and contradiction can be productive. In concentrating on symbolic pattern, however, the reading, as it stands, is geared to exposing the limitations of the symbol-hunt: to some extent it discredits, by following, the same restricted methodology. This is not to say that symbolism is irrelevant in reading the story, but that its role is complicated and enriched by other factors, particularly the use of discourse and fictional frame.

The premise of this chapter has been that the literary effects generated in modernist stories derive from a tension between formal convention and formal disruption, and that this paradoxical dual essence has been recognized, but not adequately theorized in existing short story theory. A more coherent approach, and one which removes the apparent paradox, can be achieved through an application of the Althusserian concept of 'relative autonomy'. Basically, this involves seeing the disruptive literary gesture as an instance of relative autonomy; as something which is simultaneously conditioned by, yet critical of its ideological context, a context which can be equated with literary conventions and whatever world-view they encompass. This element of criticism need not always be an overt aspect of the text, and may be the product of a contemporary reinterpretation; for the modernists, however, the disclosure of ideological context is often an integral part of their formal experimentation.

The value of this approach can be illustrated by a brief consideration of a well-known text as an example, for instance, Hardy's novel *Jude the Obscure*: if we consider the economic exigencies of magazine publication to have had an important influence on the novel's *structure* – its episodic and incident-full nature – we are still left with a great deal more to say about its effects, what it can be made to show.[80] The point here is that although the convention of episodic writing often imposes a powerful force of trivialization, Hardy was yet able to engage with the serious contemporary issues of sexual morality and education, and in a challenging way: formal convention is disrupted to provide the structure for a new kind of content. Hardy, though obliged to cram the book with happenings, does not allow his readers to become involved simply with the plot; rather, he spoils and disrupts a straightforward identification with the novel's causal progression. A key example of this follows the death of the children, when Jude and Sue, in the midst of their grief, pause to discuss the *Agamemnon*, from which Jude finds himself quoting. As John Goode perceptively remarks, 'not only does Jude produce an apt quotation which shows his knowledge more than it illuminates the situation, but Sue suddenly looks out of her understandable hysteria and both awards him an accolade and tells the reader how to assess his quotation'. We are called upon to question the value of Jude's knowledge and, by extension, the worth of the type of education he values. This is typical of a novel, which 'again and again... breaks out of its frame' in 'mak[ing] an intervention in highly controversial issues of the day'.[81]

Certain problems arise in trying to define and theorize this relative autonomy, or partial distantiation, and the principal difficulty should be briefly mentioned. Althusser has been charged with political capitulation for his theoretical stance in this area; and this charge hinges on the amorphous category of the aesthetic, and on the way in which the concept of relative autonomy has been linked with the aesthetic quality of art. If the element of autonomous vision is equated with the aesthetic (as some form of universal category), then one can easily see how Althusser could be 'charged with reinscribing the categories of bourgeois aesthetics within Marxism'.[82] The issue can be viewed more positively, however.

A crucial document here is 'A Letter on Art in Reply to André Daspre', in which Althusser outlines the concept of relative autonomy in art: '*I do not rank real art among the ideologies*, although art does have a quite particular and specific relationship with ideology.' The duality of this relationship hinges on the fact that 'what art makes us *see*, and therefore gives to us in the form of "*seeing*", "*perceiving*" and "*feeling*"... is the *ideology* from which it is born, in which it bathes, from which it detaches itself as art, and to which it *alludes*'.[83] Later in the letter, Althusser, discussing the language of art as a '"spontaneous" language', points out that 'every "spontaneous" language is an *ideological* language, the vehicle of an ideology, here the ideology of art and of the activity productive of aesthetic effects. Like all knowledge, the knowledge of art presupposes a preliminary *rupture* with the language of *ideological spontaneity* and the constitution of a body of scientific concepts to replace it'.[84] Here, there are two things in particular to note. The first thing is that 'the knowledge of art' is distinguished from the 'language of *ideological spontaneity*', the art language itself. This mid-ground of knowledge implies a critical position, a political interpretation *externally* applied. The second (connected) point is that aesthetics and ideology are presented as linked in some way. The 'aesthetic effect', in essence, is relatively autonomous, but is simultaneously delimited by the ideological factors bearing upon it. The 'knowledge of art' is accorded a privileged status, but this is dependent upon an external political understanding of ideology. One should be wary of putting too much weight on so slight a document as the 'Letter on Art', but it is highly valuable as a preliminary signpost to the politicizing of the aesthetic as a variable, contextually dependent category.

The dual essence of art – its simultaneous contextual dependence and contextual critique – is only viable if the context in question can be made available (at least partially) through the text. History, that is to say, has to exist as an extra-textual reality which locates and defines literary production. This may amount to no more than an imperfect reconstruction by the critic, based on a personal period-knowledge, but it is this element of referentiality which redeems the knowledge of art from the 'subject-less discourse of conceptual science' and gives it a context.[85]

If the category of relative autonomy (and its application) is accepted, together with the possibility of reconstructing history as absent cause, then one can follow a critical methodology which corresponds to the Althusserian '*symptomatic*' reading. This is the reading which 'divulges the undivulged event in the text it reads, and in the same movement relates it to *a different text*, present as a necessary absence in the first'.[86] This type of interpretation, in Fredric Jameson's formulation, is characterized as 'the rewriting of the literary text in such a way that the latter may itself be seen as the rewriting or restructuration of a prior historical or ideological *subtext*, it being always understood that that "subtext" is not immediately present as such, not some common-sense external reality, nor even the conventional narratives of history manuals, but rather must itself always be (re)constructed after the fact'.[87] The question remains of where to look for 'the undivulged event', the revealing 'ideological subtext'. Jameson, again, suggests an answer:

> In the case of Althusserian literary criticism proper... the appropriate object of study emerges only when the appearance of formal unification is unmasked as a failure or an ideological mirage. The authentic function of the cultural text is then staged rather as an *interference* between levels, as a subversion of one level by another; and for Althusser and Pierre Macherey the privileged form of this disunity or dissonance is the objectification of the ideological by the work of aesthetic production.[88]

In citing Macherey Jameson alludes to the former's *Theory of Literary Production*. In a later essay, however, Macherey rejects the category of aesthetics, but, even so, the interpretive formulation outlined in this collaborative essay with Etienne Balibar is apposite in this context:

> The first principle of a materialist analysis would be: literary productions must not be studied from the standpoint of their unity which is illusory and false, but from their material disparity. One must not look for unifying effects but for signs of the contradictions (historically determined) which produced them and which appear as unevenly resolved conflicts in the text.[89]

For an illustration of historically significant dissonance in a short story, let us return briefly to Mansfield's 'Bliss'. As we have seen, Bertha's 'epiphany' in the story involves a dawning awareness of her own latent homosexuality, but this semi-revelation is greatly compromised by the personal confusion and alienation which are simultaneously uncovered. This equivocal 'epiphany' – the laying bare of personal dissolution, which is the point of the story – is also partly determined by a certain contextual, ideological restraint: the cultivation of obscurity in dealing with matters of sexuality was determined as much by social restriction as by aesthetic formula. C. A. Hankin, discussing 'The Modern Soul' (1911) and 'Bain Turcs' (1913), has pointed out this historical determinant:

> In dealing with bisexuality, Katherine Mansfield was entering difficult territory.... she was writing about a subject which in the aftermath of the Wilde trial was considered morally wrong, if not 'forbidden'.... There is an ambiguity, then, in the texture of these two stories which reveals itself in devious plot structures, confusing shifts of point of view, innuendo and a heavy reliance upon symbols.[90]

The subtext of 'Bliss' (1918), which centres on Bertha's sexual confusion and indecision, can be seen as having been repressed, in part, by the same historical conditioning. The sexual plot, impossible to present overtly, is conveyed by a sophisticated symbolism. The divergence of critical opinion over the story's symbolism is an understandable response to the story's indirect method, a method partially inspired by the silencing force of social taboo.

Yet Mansfield is not contained by this silencing force. The focus of her story is on the personal muddle caused by the selfsame taboo: the historical limit, or ideological restraint, corresponds to the story's thematic content. The point is to indicate the psychological confusion caused by the ideology of heterosexual conformity, an ideology which prevents Bertha from understanding and expressing her own bisexuality. The ambiguity of Mansfield's method skilfully replicates the uncertainty of the experience. This is the relative autonomy of the story: its ability to reveal the ideology under which it operates.

The imposition of formal unity on a story like 'Bliss' cannot help but obfuscate this interplay between content and context, since those creative elements which cut across the form must be misrepresented, if not ignored. And if, as in my characterization of modernist writing, dissonance is the *crux* of the creativity, such an approach is obviously inadequate.

Those nebulous story concepts discussed earlier, such as 'implication', and 'mystery', are more adequately accounted for in this approach. It follows, therefore, that the problem of ellipsis or silence in the short story is solved productively not by ignoring it (as the unity aesthetic demands) but of accounting for it, by means of a different aesthetic theory sensitive to history:

> The aesthetic is that which speaks of its historical conditions by remaining silent – inheres in them by distance and denial. The work 'shows' rather than 'states' those conditions in the nature of the productive relations it sets up to the ideological significations which found it.[91]

This notion of 'showing' is diametrically opposed to the conventional idea of story as implication, because here the focus is on the gaps rather than on the supposed links between them.

The unity approach also provides a vacuous theoretical mould for defining the posited autonomy of modernist art, its supposed disembodiment from social context. It is an approach which makes the story – with its emphasis on form and artifice – appear to intensify those modernist characteristics to which Georg Lukács objected: a social impotence deriving from a deliberate technical distancing from 'reality'.[92] The concept of relative autonomy, as I have shown, can be used to illustrate the radical gesture of evolving literary form. The conceptions of story as 'mystery', as the expression of an 'internal contradiction' or of 'the unforeseen within fore-seen parameters', can all be seen as starting-points for a dialectical explanation of short story dissonance: formal rupture is here conceived as one locus of literature's social justification, its ability to question and transform.[93]

The central chapters of this book constitute a practical investigation of the technical issues highlighted in this survey of short story theory. The perceived affinities between modernist disruption and the short story form are demonstrated in separate chapters on five modernist writers: (2) James Joyce, (3) Virginia Woolf, (4) Katherine Mansfield, (5) Wyndham Lewis and (6) Malcolm Lowry. This selection of authors affords a detailed and representative account of the subject; it also incorporates analysis of the major stories of the British modernists, as well as discussion of many stories which have been undeservedly neglected. The concluding chapter, like the introduction, is primarily theoretical: it develops some central issues raised earlier and speculates on the contemporary relevance of the short story. The book is thus structured as a 'sandwich' in which close readings of central texts are enclosed by theoretical discussions. This structure is designed to facilitate a detailed account of the modernist short story which also indicates its formative role in the history and theory of the genre, and which considers its relevance to a contemporary audience.

There is a strong relationship between the opening chapter and the rest of the book, and this indicates two things: first, that the theory of the short story has been largely determined by modernist practice (usually an oversimplified perception of this practice); and, secondly, that the mistaken emphases and assumptions of the genre criticism are reproduced in work on individual authors. Indeed, many of the misleading aspects of short story theory are prevalent in the criticism relating to the authors selected for chapter-length treatment. Work on Joyce's *Dubliners*, for example, has been founded on a simplified aesthetic of unity, and on a 'rebuilding' approach sanctioned by a visual metaphor of Joyce's own, the motif of the 'gnomon', the incomplete geometrical figure mentioned in 'The Sisters'. Perhaps the most misleading aspect in the criticism of *Dubliners* is the stress placed on the linked ideas of entrapment and paralysis, elements which are seen to recur from story to story, creating a governing thematic unity. This focus on common elements implies that the book is more of a novel than a collection of stories, and inevitably obscures the technical effects – and so the generic distinctiveness – of the different pieces. The most enduring tenet of *Dubliners* commentary, however, concerns the supposed illuminating moment or epiphany. The stories in *Dubliners*, often taken to be masterpieces of the moment of sudden revelation in the short story, are here read as problematic narratives, and, consequently, as subversions of the epiphany concept.

The challenge to the unified story concept is continued in the chapter on Woolf, in which the importance of disunity to the genre becomes obvious. Woolf's experiments in the short story are set in the context of her major objectives as a fiction writer. Her stories – here presented as investigations of narrative fallibility – are shown to put into practice the ideas adumbrated by Woolf in two important essays, 'Mr Bennett and Mrs Brown' and 'Modern Fiction', ideas concerning the de-authorization of narrative voice, and the complex portrayal of character.

The question of character and personal identity is central to Mansfield's stories, which are shown to develop a complex and ambiguous method of characterization through complex and ambiguous technical effects. The generic convention of co-herent, single-character presentation is disrupted by Mans-field's investigations into the ambiguity of personality. As in *Dubliners*, the moment of 'epiphany' in Mansfield's stories is a point where different impulses converge and conflict, creating dissonant effects. These points of conflict reveal a complicated view of personality, a stress on impersonal identity, determined by a variety of social forces.

The readings made of stories by Joyce, Woolf and Mansfield all draw on the theoretical framework outlined in this opening chapter: formal dissonance and relative autonomy are shown greatly to illuminate the techniques of these authors. The tensions and dissonances discerned in their work are centred on a simultaneous dependence upon, and extension of, the con-ventional short story form. The resulting disruption is used to express a complex view of the interaction between individual experience and social organization.

Another (associated) theoretical component of the book, common to the chapters on Joyce, Woolf and Mansfield, is drawn from the writings of Mikhail Bakhtin. Bakhtin's concept of dialogics is employed to show how the modernists frequently cultivate a dialogized style – involving a conflict of voices – as an integral part of their disruption and complication of narrative. This understanding of dialogics differs from some applications in which the dialogized text is merely one which contains a variety of coexisting voices. I place an emphasis on the idea of *conflicting* voices, which is a crucial aspect of Bakhtin's writings about narrative. This concept of dialogized narrative provides a further challenge to any simplistic notion of short story unity, and supplies a rigorous way of interpreting the modernists' ambivalent portrayal of character.

Chapters 2, 3 and 4 cover what I take to be the core of the modernist short story, and demonstrate its principal attributes: the cultivation and celebration of complex identity, and the rejection of ideological restrictions of various kinds. These chapters account for the main impetus of literary modernism, and engage with features commonly identified as seminal to the modernist project. It is particularly significant that key modernist features and documents – such as the celebrated essays by Woolf, 'Mr Bennett and Mrs Brown', and 'Modern Fiction' – have a special relevance to short story composition. Joyce, Woolf and Mansfield are essential authors for consideration in a discussion of modernism, and, effectively, they select themselves for inclusion. The other author often identified strongly with British modernist fiction is D. H. Lawrence, and a brief explanation of the exclusion of Lawrence from this survey is, perhaps, called for.

Lawrence stands in a difficult relation to mainstream modernism, and critics continue to debate his relationship to the movement. Where his novels are concerned this issue is certainly problematic, but, as a short story writer, Lawrence's position is far easier to determine. Unlike the extravagant formal experiments of his major novels – witness the exuberant excesses of *Women in Love*, for instance – Lawrence's stories are predominantly conservative in structure and form. There are local exceptions to this, such as the impressionistic ending of 'The Prussian Officer', but the stories usually exhibit a highly disciplined use of the conventional story form, placing great emphasis on careful plotting. Important Lawrence stories such as 'New Eve and Old Adam', 'The Blind Man', 'The Horse Dealer's Daughter', 'The Man Who Died', 'The Man Who Loved Islands' and 'The Woman Who Rode Away' betray a dependence on the traditional materials of short narrative, a dependence indicated by their fabulistic titles. Indeed, as Lawrence matured as a story writer, his work moved increasingly towards fable (away from the realism of his early stories) and this trend underlines how his work in the genre is distinct from the modernist short story proper, with its clear rejection of stable plotting.

Having established the key features of the modernist story in the chapters on Joyce, Woolf and Mansfield, the book then goes on to acknowledge and examine a different, uncompromising tendency of the period, exemplified in the work of Wyndham Lewis. Chapter 5 – which deals with Wyndham Lewis's collection *The Wild Body* – thus contributes to a more comprehensive representation of modernism. Lewis's fiction is of a very different order to that of mainstream modernism, and symptomatic of its darker, elitist side; *The Wild Body* reveals a bleak view of individual personality, yet the presentation is typically modernist – in a technical sense – because it is bound up with Wyndham Lewis's use of the short story form. The stories are examined in terms of the Vorticist movement, as enactments of the Vorticist aesthetic: they deliberately cultivate an art/life dichotomy (following the Vorticist stance of detachment) and they adapt certain conventions regarding short story 'shape' in accordance with the Vorticist concept of dynamic form. These stories provide an alternative test for the analytical approach propounded in previous chapters: they cultivate, yet implicitly reject, a unified story form in their satirical portrayal of circumscribed human behaviour. Yet the rejection – a striking formal dissonance – is a limited gesture which fails to redeem an impression of personal failure and individual isolation.

Lowry's collection of stories *Hear Us O Lord From Heaven Thy Dwelling Place* offers an important contrast with the work of Wyndham Lewis: Lowry's stories also examine individual experience, but the presentation is expansive and positive, and in this sense Lowry extends the central modernist preoccupation with individual identity and its social definition. The argument of this chapter is that although the short story is often seen as inevitably limited to a consideration of human isolation (another development of Poe's 'unity aesthetic'), it can be viewed differently. Lowry's stories, which apparently confirm the reductive isolation-thesis, are read, through an 'expanding circle' motif, as celebrations of broader, societal themes. This structural principle exaggerates the kind of formal disruption detected in previous chapters: in his story 'The Forest Path to the Spring', for instance, Lowry effectively deconstructs the notion of sudden revelation through a dispersed, composite 'epiphany' which consists of three separate episodes. Another way in which the Lowryan story deliberately extends the formal parameters of the genre is through its use of symbolism: Lowry frequently overloads the capacity of the narrative circuit with an excess of symbolic significance, and this deliberate avoidance of a closed story form is at one with his continual attempt to link personal preoccupations with public themes. The chapter also offers a bridge between modernism and postmodernism: the literary self-consciousness of the modernists is pronounced in Lowry and anticipates the overt metafictional style of much postmodern fiction.

The concluding chapter indicates the continuing relevance of the issues discussed earlier, and speculates on the particular importance the short story may have as a means of portraying twentieth-century life, and the experience of modernity. The genre is often described – in an intuitive way – as having the capacity to encapsulate the fleeting and episodic nature of contemporary experience; this final chapter attempts to locate some preliminary landmarks for theorizing such intuitive descriptions. Discussion focuses on fictional closure, apocalypse, and on postmodernism and its social moment. The collection *Einstein's Monsters*, by Martin Amis, is considered (together with an exemplary postmodernist story by Donald Barthelme) to demonstrate how a crisis of social organization is replicated in the cultivated disruption (and sometimes the incoherence) of some representative recent short stories. The basic theoretical foundation of the book – the connection between literary form and social context, emphasized throughout – becomes particularly significant here, in a gesture designed to re-emphasize the *social* relevance of formal innovation. It is this kind of formal innovation – this energy – which gives the stories discussed here their enduring power and importance.

CHAPTER 2

James Joyce: the non-epiphany principle

The stories in *Dubliners* illustrate very well the difficulties outlined in the previous chapter. Critical work on the book has tended to make the same mistaken emphases that pervade general short story theory: a focus on visual metaphor and on simplified symbolic effects are the main elements of a predominant, reunifying reading of *Dubliners*. Much critical effort has been expended on removing the ambiguities caused by ellipsis in Joyce's stories, and on locating key epiphanic moments. These two elements – ellipsis and epiphany – are indeed seminal to an understanding of *Dubliners*, but they are made problematic in Joyce's story technique, and cannot be viewed as pointers to a simple, unified meaning.

Although ambiguity is an integral aspect of *Dubliners*, much of the critical literature on the collection has served to obscure this fact. Of course, the Joyce industry has produced a vast and heterogeneous body of readings of all the major texts, but there is still a conventional reading of *Dubliners* which remains influential, especially for short story critics: a palpable unanimity of opinion has emerged with regard to the book's corporate 'message'.

This orthodox approach views the stories, prior to the composition of 'The Dead', as studies in the spiritual paralysis of a modern city. The final story, it is often argued, 'transforms the nature of the book' through an empathic tone which, though ambivalent, modifies the detached cynicism of the earlier pieces.[1] This view hinges upon interpreting Gabriel Conroy's epiphany at the end of the story as indicating a new-found acceptance of his social and cultural milieu: his previously ambivalent attitude to his homeland is seen to find its resolution in his serene acceptance of his wife's past life and love in the west of Ireland. This development, together with the presentation of Dublin hospitality in the story, is taken as an indication of Joyce's own wish to reconsider and acknowledge his roots less inflexibly than he had done in the earlier stories.[2] In the other pieces, following this conventional view, moral and spiritual enervation is perceived as an omnipresent entity, and one which is given obvious symbolic expression at certain key moments, such as in the description of debased holy artefacts (Father Flynn's broken chalice) and holy practices (the bargaining of Farrington's son, reduced to offering a Hail Mary in exchange for not being beaten). A recurring motif of entrapment, especially evident in 'Eveline', 'The Boarding House', and 'A Little Cloud', is taken as another unifying element which corroborates the paralysis reading of the collection. This reading has obvious advantages and can be clearly supported from the text, up to a point. The major problem arises when it is taken as evidence of a special Joycean aesthetic of unity, because such an overview obscures the disruptive nature of particular technical gestures. A conventionally 'conclusive' reading of 'The Dead' would be particularly vulnerable, since Gabriel's supposed realization of oneness with his world is expressed in a language of continuing romantic self-absorption: the moment seems irreducibly ambiguous since the tone contradicts the apparent semantic meaning. The same kind of disruption operates throughout the book, indicating that the perceived revelation of paralysis is usually more complex than it appears, and also that 'The Dead' is not distinct from the rest of the collection, in terms of its technical effects.

There are various comments by Joyce which are frequently quoted in support of the simple paralysis reading, and these have given this approach a spurious and enduring validation. In 1904 he described his projected volume of stories thus to Constantine Curran: 'I am writing a series of epicleti – ten – for a paper. I call the series "Dubliners" to betray the soul of that hemiplegia or paralysis which many call a city.'[3] Here the concept of the significant moment is yoked together with the notion of paralysis; 'epicleti', Joyce's mistaken plural for epiclesis (the invocation of the Holy Spirit at the point of consecration in the Eucharist – plural *epicleses*), indicates an intended series of significant moments in which 'hemiplegia or paralysis' will be 'betrayed'. The connection is treated more explicitly in Joyce's submission to his brother, Stanislaus:

Don't you think... there is a certain resemblance between the mystery of the Mass and what I am trying to do? I mean that I am trying... to give some kind of intellectual pleasure or spiritual enjoyment by converting the bread of everyday life into something that has a permanent artistic life of its own... for their mental, moral and spiritual uplift. (Final ellipsis original)[4]

There is clearly a point of contact between this kind of analogy and the stories in *Dubliners*, redolent as they are with religious imagery. Joyce's correspondence with the publisher Grant Richards, in which he emphasizes repeatedly the putative 'moral' content of the stories, is often adduced in support of a straightforward paralysis reading. Below are two key extracts from this correspondence in which Joyce attempts to justify his artistic intention in the face of charges of indecency:

My intention was to write a chapter of the moral history of my country and I chose Dublin for the scene because that city seemed to me the centre of paralysis. I have tried to present it to the indifferent public under four of its aspects: childhood, adolescence, maturity and public life. The stories are arranged in this order. I have written it for the most part in a style of scrupulous meanness and with the conviction that he is a very bold man who dares to alter it in the presentment, still more to deform, whatever he has seen and heard.[5]

It is not my fault that the odour of ashpits and old weeds and offal hangs round my stories. I seriously believe that you will retard the course of civilization in Ireland by preventing the Irish people from having one good look at themselves in my nicely polished looking-glass.[6]

Florence Walzl considers the first of these passages to be 'the most significant critical commentary that has ever been made on *Dubliners*', a typical analysis which indicates alignment with the conventional paralysis reading.[7] These passages, however, should be treated with caution. This is not to say that they should be dismissed, nor, indeed, that they are inaccurate; the problem is that Joyce leaves his analysis open to misinterpretation, possibly quite deliberately. After all, Joyce's primary intention was to make the work as attractive as possible to Richards, and to assuage any worries of legal liability, a motive which must surely qualify his statements. The full correspondence, in fact, is marked by wilful misunderstandings on both sides. Richards, his hand forced by his printer's objections to 'indecent' content, fails to sympathize with Joyce's stated artistic concerns, and stresses the necessity of compromise: 'I speak commercially, not artistically', he explains.[8] Joyce, meanwhile, stubbornly refuses to accept the liability of the printer (who could have been prosecuted along with the publisher): 'I cannot permit a printer to write my book for me. In no other civilized country in Europe, I think, is a printer allowed to open his mouth.... A printer is simply a workman hired by the day or by the job for a certain sum.'[9]

One can understand Joyce's impatience with Richards who, reacting to Joyce's refusal to change certain passages in 'Counterparts', remarks: 'After all, remember, it is only words and sentences that have to be altered.'[10] In his reply Joyce expresses a predictable annoyance at Richards' consistent failure to address the issue of artistic nuance:

You say it is a small thing I am asked to do, to efface a word here and there. But do you not see clearly that in a short story above all such effacement may be fatal. You cannot say that the phrases objected to are gratuitous and impossible to print and at the same time approve of the tenor of the book.[11]

Joyce's tone does seem a little self-righteous, however, when one considers how the passages in question *were* altered, and, as Robert Scholes has shown, were altered for the better (this is discussed below). The Joyce–Richards correspondence soon reaches impasse with both parties arguing on different grounds. Richards, for his part, eschews Joyce's point about the precision of words, and attempts to uncover pedantry in Joyce's stance through a reductive argument about the correctness of the word 'bloody': 'it is, as you say, the right word; on the other hand a publisher has to be influenced by other considerations.'[12] Joyce's response was to re-emphasize the notion of 'moral history' and of 'spiritual liberation', his ultimate weapon (becoming blunt through overuse) in this bludgeoning exchange of sophistry.[13]

The strident emphasis on a moral programme implies that the text itself contains clear evidence of an authorial stance of disapprobation, and this implication glosses over the element of narrative ambiguity in the book. Joyce also tacitly suggests that the book continues a nineteenth-century tradition of 'improving' literature. Never fear, he is saying, this work is not indecent – it is not even radically new – see how I am working within the constraints of the established canon, my intentions honourable and morally sound. Simple prudence demands that his summary exhortation of an (unrespected) publisher be considered with caution; these letters quite obviously contain the rhetoric inspired by creative impatience and commercial exigency, not merely an unqualified artistic manifesto.[14]

Joyce's share of this correspondence – which *invites* a simplistic unifying approach to the book – is usually taken at face value. Indeed, it has been cited so often in the past, without qualification, that it has come to be viewed as something of a 'key' to the collection.[15] Joyce's claim for the simple unity of his text also suggests that it is a kind of novel (which it is not) rather than a collection of separate stories requiring individual interpretation: the same stress on unity in the critical literature has distorted the generic issue, resulting in a neglect of specific short story effects. The notion of a moral centre to the book is misleading; it applies only to three or four moments in the same number of stories. While Joyce's insistence on his moralizing, by covert appeal to literary tradition, is disingenuous, the emphasis accorded by critics to the systematic exposure of paralysis in *Dubliners* is attributed in good faith, following the author's lead. Joyce's sophistry, written for the inducement of a single man, has misled dozens of others, better equipped both historically and professionally to see through it. Ironically, it was Grant Richards who refused to be convinced.[16]

While taking issue with this convention I do not reject its insights out of hand: clearly many of the stories do engage with a certain paralysis of inaction and/or indecision. The essential point of contention concerns how this is conveyed and, consequently, how determinate it is. It is particularly important to note that Joyce's calculated defence of the book, if taken at face value, invites the kind of over-simplified interpretation that has governed the theory of the short story. Criticism of *Dubliners* has laid an undue stress on the identification of unifying techniques, and the most significant of these is derived from Joyce's use of the term 'gnomon'. This term appears in the opening paragraph of the opening story, 'The Sisters', when the boy-narrator associates in his mind three strange-sounding words: paralysis, gnomon and simony. Much symbolic significance has been divined in this association. The Euclidean gnomon is defined as what is left of a parallelogram after a smaller parallelogram has been removed from one of its corners.[17] Thus a gnomon is what remains when a part of the whole has been removed, and this image of incompleteness does seem suggestive of paralysis, an association first made, I believe, by Gerhard Friedrich. Discussing the terms 'paralysis' and 'parallelogram' Friedrich considers how

a purposeful imaginative connection between the two words is established by way of their etymology and semantics, for 'paralysis' means literally a loosening or weakening at the side (and hence the crippled and often helpless condition of having partially or totally lost the faculties of sensation and voluntary motion); parallelograms that are non-rectangular may be thought of as loosened at the side; and the Euclidean gnomon has moreover the appearance of an impaired, cutaway parallelogram.[18]

Friedrich, like many critics after him, here discusses 'The Sisters' as representative of the collection as a whole, the literal paralysis of Father Flynn being emblematic of a spiritual paralysis endemic in Joyce's Dublin. This geometric reasoning provokes minor quibbles – perfect rectangles are also parallelograms, for instance – but the important point to note is the unity aesthetic that underpins it: that which is incomplete is also 'impaired, cutaway'. Consequently it must be rebuilt (or imagined as a whole) in order to be understood, and it is this exercise in linguistic geometry that has provided a key to character analysis which Joyceans have found indispensable: Father Flynn (the incomplete priest), Corley (the incomplete gallant) and the rest of the atrophied Dubliners have repeatedly been seen as gnomons. The text of *Dubliners*, then, is often seen to provide its very own visual metaphor for story composition: meaning and characterization can be located by a process of reconstruction, much as a gnomon can be rebuilt as the original parallelogram with the help of a ruler and a pair of compasses. Some commentators of the gnomonic principle in Joyce have even included diagrams of the geometric figure itself, in a tautological gesture designed to re-emphasize their conviction of a discoverable whole codified in the impaired final story.[19]

The word 'gnomon' has the additional meaning of a pointer on a dial – the pillar on a sundial for instance – and this use of the gnomon concept as a pointer highlights the way it has been overused. (Technically the geometric term 'gnomon' is also a kind of pointer since it contains the information necessary for it to be rebuilt.) According to this law a perfect priest (or the need of one) may be defined elliptically by describing an imperfect one. The use of gnomon as character indicator does not end here, however. For Robert Day it applies to character traits and associations which can suggest indirectly the influence of a character. Day argues, for instance, that the presence of Lenehan, in 'Two Gallants' and, particularly, *Ulysses*, can be detected 'if we see even one of the objects or gestures that are his pointers, emblems, or gnomons, and we can be sure that the idea or process he represents is going on'.[20]

The reconstruction approach hinges on a particular view of Joyce's language in *Dubliners*, the view of language as implication, as something with a unity that has been partially, but not irredeemably, disrupted. This, then, is the conventional view of the book: an account of spiritual paralysis made available, following a geometric metaphor, by an ultimately recoverable, unified language. The Joycean gnomon, as employed by critics, is undoubtedly the most discussed visual metaphor in short story criticism, and is clearly related to the visual artefacts discussed in the previous chapter – the tradition of John Wain's blancmange theory and Julio Cortázar's perfect sphere. But, like these metaphors for the story 'commodity', the gnomon concept can be very misleading. The usefulness of the geometric motif is restricted from the beginning, because language does not conform to the absolute laws of geometry. An elliptical language is, by definition, ambiguous, and this ambiguity is explored by Joyce in his stories. Joyce's short story technique is 'gnomonic' in the sense that it explores the different possibilities contained in the hidden side of the narrative. The predominant style in the collection cultivates an ambivalent narrative stance which precludes any simple interpretation, because the ambivalence (and the cumulative uncertainty it causes) is usually an integral part of Joyce's purpose.

The reconstruction approach, rather than examining the implications of what is there (ambiguity and disunity) must concentrate on what is absent, and this can result in ingenious, but tangential, speculation. Hugh Kenner's reading of 'Eveline', for instance, accurately locates the questionable nature of the sailor Frank's intent, but attempting to reinforce this character's moral vacuity, Kenner makes an implausible 'appeal to realities outside literature', starting with the *Irish Homestead* where the story first appeared. On the basis of 'any *Irish Homestead* reader's knowledge that no boat sails from Dublin to Buenos Aires' Kenner concludes that Frank proposes to elope with Eveline to Liverpool, initially, and probably no further, and only for the purpose of a brief sexual conquest. The promised home and marriage in Argentina are exposed as fiction.[21] An interesting way of filling the gaps, but this interpretation does not focus on the narrative itself which enacts the limited consciousness of the title character. To be sure, a lack of judgement regarding Frank is implicit in this narrative, but a clear indication of his motive is absent from the text. Also missing, even by implication, is the 1904 timetable of boats from Dublin's North Wall.

The rebuilding approach has licensed some very inventive readings. Edward Brandabur's psychoanalytic study of *Dubliners* contains some useful insights; psychoanalytic aproaches to the short story, in fact, supply some appropriate frameworks for accounting for the 'repressions' that are frequently to be found in the narrative strategies typical of the genre. But Brandabur's book also offers some extraordinary interpretations of specific details. In relation to 'Two Gallants', Brandabur seeks to explain the characterization of Corley as an emotional vacuum, capable of trading on his ability to influence lower-class girls. The precise nature of his liaison with the girl in the story is not examined, but Brandabur, probing deeper, manages to find symbolic evidence of oral sexual activity. The fact that Lenehan partakes of a plate of peas while Corley is with the slavey is offered as an indication that Corley may simultaneously be stimulating the girl by oral means, or 'eating' her. The point is reinforced by Lenehan's admiration for Corley's manipulation of the slavey – 'that takes the biscuit!' (53)[22] – because '"biscuit" is... a symbol for the female genitals, especially when imagined as an object for oral gratification'.[23] The logic of this symbolic connection seems to rest on a peculiar anthropomorphism (what gratification does a biscuit derive from being eaten?), but the major point, inconsistencies aside, is that Brandabur invents his own subtext to reunify an uncertain text.

Some gnomonic criticism does examine the implications of absence. One example is an article by Joseph C. Voelker which, focusing on disorder, characterizes *Dubliners* as 'a book which derives its power from ambivalence'. Vagrancy and truancy, Voelker perceives, have their positive side in preventing open conflict with authority while duty is evaded. He also understands how the 'ambiguously rich condition' of 'errancy', which is 'central to the *Portrait* and *Ulysses*' has a place also in *Dubliners*, especially with regard to artistic vocation, which, in an embryonic form, is apparent in several characters in the collection. Having established this ambiguous richness in the characterization, however, Voelker does narrow his horizons by indicating a kind of moral growth that this condition can facilitate, a higher kind of unity which still depends on narrative stability: Gabriel Conroy, for instance, has advanced 'to the higher dimensions of vagrancy, where wisdom lies in refusing self confinement and drifting in the unfrightened knowledge of a dark affinity between love and death'.[24]

Phillip Herring's *Joyce's Uncertainty Principle* represents a significant advancement in the field of gnomonic readings in considering the function absence and ambiguity may serve. He considers the historical limits – social taboos – which necessitated the oblique expression of certain topics:

> Why Joyce should wish to employ subterfuge in *Dubliners* rather than targeting his enemies directly as he did in later works is obvious when one contemplates what actually happened to the collection of stories. Irish publishers such as Grant Richards and George Roberts, with whom Joyce negotiated about publication, anticipated censorship and demanded changes in the text; Roberts's printer John Falconer eventually destroyed the proofsheets. All had good reason to fear litigation that could have landed them in prison.[25]

The main objections concerned suggestions of sexual immorality, and the use of bad language, and, as we have seen, Joyce was loath to make any compromises. In fact, he acquired a set of proofs from the edition which John Falconer destroyed, and these became the printer's copy for the book's first publication.[26] Yet Joyce did make some alterations on the basis of Richards' advice, the most important of which affected a passage in 'Counterparts' which Richards' printer had found indecent. Robert Scholes has made a valuable commentary on this revision, giving first the original version:

> 'Farrington said he wouldn't mind having the far one and began to smile at her but when Weathers offered to introduce her he said "No," he was only chaffing because he knew he had not money enough. She continued to cast bold glances at him and changed the position of her legs often and when she was going out she brushed against his chair and said "Pardon!" in a Cockney accent.'

> ... when [Joyce] came to revise the text after losing his argument with Richards he took it upon himself to expunge the offensive legs, discovering that he could do all he wanted to with arms and eyes. The vastly improved (if censored) passage reads as follows in the late Maunsel text:

> 'Farrington's eyes wandered at every moment in the direction of one of the young women. There was something striking in her appearance. An immense scarf of peacock blue muslin was wound round her hat and knotted in a great bow under her chin; and she wore bright yellow

gloves, reaching to the elbow. Farrington gazed admiringly at the plump arm which she moved very often and with much grace; and when after a little time she answered his gaze, he admired still more her large dark brown eyes. The oblique staring expression in them fascinated him. She glanced at him once or twice and, when the party was leaving the room, she brushed against his chair and said *O, pardon*! in a London accent. He watched her leave the room in the hope that she would look back at him but he was disappointed.'

In the revised version we are not told so bluntly what Farrington is thinking, but we are brought much closer to his point of view.... Even the girl's accent seems different when seen from Farrington's perspective rather than the narrator's. Where the narrator and the reader heard Cockney, redolent of slums and sordidness, Farrington hears London, as exotic to him as Araby to the little boy of the earlier story. The reader can form his own opinion of that blue and yellow colour combination, and he can judge the woman by the way she brushes against Farrington, but he is not told that her glances are 'bold.' One is tempted to come to the conclusion, however reluctantly, that if Joyce had taken some of Richards' advice instead of battling him on principle at every point, he might have saved himself a lot of grief and not done *Dubliners* any harm.[27]

We might question Scholes' association of a Cockney accent with sordidness, but he does clearly identify how Joyce used the occasion of an imposed revision to refine the orientation of the writing, to improve his characterization, and to efface explicit judgement. (Ironically, this removed a moral judgement of the kind that Joyce had wanted Richards to approve.) In this instance an external restraint gave rise to a subtle realignment of the point of view, a fusion of the narrator's perspective with the character's. But even when Joyce ignored editorial interference, such interference is evidence of a highly restrictive climate which must have tempered his *initial* treatment of not just sex, but of religion and national politics too. This might suggest that, because social commentary is repressed, a re-unifying approach is required to uncover such commentary, an approach commended by Phillip Herring:

Adopting a gnomonic perspective helps us to see more clearly the nature of Joyce's embittered social commentary, the interplay of presence and absence from the viewpoint of a subversive artist with a social conscience. Readers alerted to the implications of the three key words from the first, 'trained' to read the stories skeptically, could feel more deeply the political impact they contain. In theory the author then need not fear censorship because libelous thoughts are in the reader's mind, not in the text. *Gnomon* therefore has the effect of enlisting a reader as co-creator in the production of meanings that are in harmony with the author's political concerns.[28]

In dealing with contentious matters Joyce may well have been compelled to develop an oblique narrative style, and Herring's emphasis here identifies a hidden agenda which suggests political expediency as a major reason for the gnomonic story style. Herring is actually reunifying the collection in a simplistic way to characterize it, summarily, as Joyce's 'political indictment of his city using a hidden rhetoric of absence. ... "gnomonic" language may contain ellipses, hiatuses in meaning, significant silences, empty and ritualistic dialogue. We note the continual emphasis on emptiness, incompletion, solitude, loneliness, shadow, darkness, and failure, which so affect the lives of Joyce's Dubliners and allow subtle expression of his political views.' These observations are acute in identifying a primary motivation of Joyce's story technique, but they lead to a reductive methodology in which 'the reader must supply the missing pieces for the puzzle to be complete'.[29] The quarrel here is a fundamental one concerning how the hidden agenda is best approached: Herring's puzzle-solving analogy betrays a dependence on an illusory unity rather than on material disparity and conflict. The puzzle analogy, an all-too-frequent formulation in the theory of the short story, obscures the value of the disruptive text. In the previous chapter the concept of relative autonomy was shown to offer a more appropriate way of explaining how the short story makes its social interventions – through the very presence of material disparity, the formal sign of historical determination. It is this approach which is employed, below, in discussions of individual stories from *Dubliners*.

Apart from ellipsis, the other major device in the Joycean story (as it is commonly perceived) is epiphany, the single illuminating moment. The Joycean epiphany, in fact, is the archetypal model of the single-effect doctrine in short story theory since Poe: after the modernist era the epiphany technique has become a central principle in short story composition, as well as a key term in short story criticism. My argument, however, is that the epiphany in Joyce is made problematic, and becomes a nexus of a *variety* of forces rather than a *single* effect. This is a crucial issue: if the Joycean 'epiphany' is a misnomer, then the very notion of a single illuminating moment in the modern short story becomes unconvincing, underpinned by a major misreading.

Despite the long-standing objections of Robert Scholes,[30] epiphany is widely accepted as a term which means '*revelation* or *illumination* in certain literary and technical senses', in the words of Florence Walzl.[31] The conviction is that in the epiphanic moment an essential 'truth' about character and/or situation is revealed in a flash of insight, whether this 'truth' is grasped by character and reader or reader alone. This understanding of the term is a basic premise of paralysis readings of *Dubliners*, which assume that there is a 'truth' concerning moral failure to be revealed. Morris Beja is the principal spokesman for the stability of the epiphany in modernist literature and, where *Dubliners* is concerned, he has written that 'the works in this collection' seem 'written almost to provide an introduction and background to an epiphany'.[32] There is a problem here, however, concerning the grounds for this conviction of the inherent truth of the epiphany. One suspects that the conviction, which can lead to a mechanical and unquestioning reading of epiphany as device, is merely the result of critical convention. This convention has been pertinently challenged by Zack Bowen, in an article entitled 'Joyce and the Epiphany Concept: A New Approach'. Here Bowen poses the seminal question: 'are the epiphanies really revelations of truth or character, or do they merely appear to be truth to the consciousness which experiences them?'. Bowen amplifies the doubt by appeal to actual experience. He observes with acuity and wit: 'I regularly come to truths about myself that the next morning I dismiss in sheer horror, and I do not think that I am in this respect substantially different from other people.'[33]

It does not require a textual intuition, however, to perceive the falsity of many of the epiphanies in *Dubliners*. (For the sake

of convenience I shall follow the tradition of terming these
moments – in which a crisis of some kind is certainly reached –
epiphanies.) One needs only to look at the narrative strategy to
perceive a *lack* of illumination in many of the epiphanies. The
determining factor is the consciousness that is taken to be
experiencing the revelatory moment, and this is considerably
complicated by the destabilizing narrative technique of indirect
free discourse. The conclusion of 'Araby', for instance, has to be
viewed in the light of the story's overall strategy which involves
a complex narrative stance. L. J. Morrissey sees this story as
'the mediation between first- and third-person stories in the
collection', and points out how the perfect third-person opening
gradually gives way to first-person narration.[34] This observation
seems to affirm John Gordon's conviction that 'the first three
stories are first-person dialogues of a familiar literary type: an
older man remembering his younger self'. For Gordon, these
stories represent explicit examples of a principle which operates
throughout the book, a principle which means that 'each of the
stories is a kind of dialogue between two versions of one
consciousness, one sensitive and one reflective'. This schema
enables Gordon to locate two selves in 'Araby', and to aver that
'the moody child is recognizably father to the nostalgic man', a
reading which depends upon seeing the story's narrator as a
more mature (but equally deluded) version of his earlier self.[35]
Gordon's approach identifies the kind of uncertainty that
operates throughout *Dubliners*, where the narrative appears to
merge with the thoughts and feelings of a character, but the
notion of a single, fixed dialogue does not account for the
fluidity of this technique.

　'Araby' is one story that *does* seem, initially, to be reducible
to the kind of dialogue that Gordon proposes, especially in its
conclusion where a self-evaluation is attempted: 'Gazing up into
the darkness I saw myself as a creature driven and derided by
vanity; and my eyes burned with anguish and anger' (36). Here
the tone of mature reflection jars with the scene of adolescent
humiliation. The narrator claims to report what his earlier self
felt, but the attempt to project this objective self-revelation onto
the consciousness of the boy is unconvincing. The boy has just
been intimidated by a salesgirl, and turns away without

purchasing a gift for Mangan's sister, which is the object of his quest. The salesgirl, in effect, brings home to the boy his sexual inadequacy (she rebuffs him to continue flirting with two young men) just as he is on the verge of asserting his sexuality by buying the gift. Whatever understanding he has of his own vanity is, therefore, complicated by further vanity in the form of a recoil from humiliation. The objective self-assessment of the narrating voice belongs, in this 'epiphany', to the mature present which is no longer fully in touch with the past event. Interestingly in 'Araby' the religious motif of revelation confirms the negative reading. The supposed moment of insight occurs in a darkened hall dominated by 'a silence like that which pervades a church *after* a service' (35) (my emphasis): if the 'service' is over, then we can conclude that the moment of genuine epiclesis has been missed. But even here the differing perspectives of the narrator – in youth and maturity – are complicated by the simultaneous presence of an implied authorial accent: the ironic religious allusion reveals a stance beyond the narrator, and this is typical of the complexity of voice that pervades *Dubliners*.

Focusing on the *characterization*, we can say that the narrator of 'Araby' projects a mature piece of self-analysis onto an intense boyhood experience of humiliation, thus falsifying it. Even though this gives rise to a belated understanding, the epiphany as reported is exposed as false. The 'truth' or 'falsity' of the epiphany can be seen as irrelevant, however, if we agree with Morris Beja that

what matters is what a given character *feels* about an epiphany or the revelation it provides. An epiphany need not, after all, be 'objectively' accurate;...an epiphany is in its very conception and description a *subjective* phenomenon. So whether Mr. Duffy and the boy at the end of 'Araby' are 'correct' is much less relevant than how *they* feel about what they have learned.[36]

This argument, of course, presupposes the possibility of identifying, clearly, what a character feels him- or herself to have learned. The simple dialogue theory, which the ending of 'Araby' seems to reinforce, makes such an identification possible. Yet the narrative stance as a whole is more fluid than this, and contains a palpable vacillation between empathy and distance which serves to render even subjective feelings in-determinate. L. J. Morrissey, in the article mentioned, indicates how the opening of the story evolves from third- to first-person narrative, and how the decreasing use of collective pronouns – 'we' and 'our' – accompanies this development. The use of collective pronouns, however, is clearly undisciplined, and this confusing usage is in tune with the youthful, immature character, who initially identifies himself with his family ('our house'), but who soon shifts the collective focus, without indicating the distinction, to describe the activity of himself and his peers ('out shouts', 'our play'). The effect of this lack of stylistic discipline is twofold: in the first place it accurately reproduces the assumptions of a child's mind, untroubled by the need fully to explain its meaning, and secondly, because neither collective (family or peer group) is stipulated or individuated, the isolation of the self-absorbed adolescent – lacking a coherent sense of belonging – is subtly suggested.

The narrative style, then, can suggest both empathy with and distance from character, and sometimes both tendencies are evident at the same time:

One evening I went into the back drawing-room in which the priest had died. It was a dark rainy evening and there was no sound in the house. Through one of the broken panes I heard the rain impinge upon the earth, the fine incessant needles of water playing in the sodden beds. Some distant lamp or lighted window gleamed below me. I was thankful that I could see so little. All my senses seemed to desire to veil themselves and, feeling that I was about to slip from them, I pressed the palms of my hands together until they trembled, murmuring: *O love! O love!* many times. (31)

This account of adolescent infatuation clearly suggests absurdity – the desire for sensory impercipience mirrors the metaphorical blindness of the emotion itself – yet the rhythm and structure of the passage represents an attempt to emulate these boyhood feelings: the description of the passion reaches a crescendo and in the very next paragraph an account is given of the boy's first conversation with the girl, a juxtaposition which emphasizes the importance of the memory, despite its irrationality. This sudden juxtaposition of different scenes, and different times, is an accurate representation of the boy's illogical and self-obsessed yearning: the scene of heightened introversion leads naturally into a recollection of a mundane conversation, wrung for significance by the self-deluding mind.[37]

This fluid form, which allows the narrative both to expose and to identify with character – sometimes simultaneously – clearly makes it impossible to locate a simple 'truth' arising from the 'significant moment'. 'Araby' subverts the story principles of the single impression and the significant moment, as well as the literary convention of the confession/recollection narrative, and, in doing so, it examines, in a radically inconclusive way, different states of consciousness, the inter-action of different timescales, and the nature of identity. The narrative ambiguity of 'Araby' is also apparent in 'The Sisters' and 'An Encounter', both of which are accounts of boyhood episodes, also narrated in the first person in such a way as to reveal both distance and empathy.

Only three of the stories in *Dubliners* are rendered directly in the first person, but the type of narrative ambiguity which characterizes the opening three stories is to be found in several others in which Joyce's indirect free style merges with the consciousness of the central character. In 'A Painful Case' the following description of the protagonist is given:

He lived at a little distance from his body, regarding his own acts with doubtful side-glances. He had an odd autobiographical habit which led him to compose in his mind from time to time a short sentence about himself containing a subject in the third person and a predicate in the past tense. (120)

Here is the most overt suggestion in the book of a relationship between character and third-person narrator, and this under-scores the significance of the first-/third-person confusion at the beginning of 'Araby'. Duffy is in the habit of inditing his own story, a hint which invites us to read this story as Duffy's own, and which is also suggestive of similar structures in the rest of the collection.

This is the predominant mode of *Dubliners*: an enactment of the ambiguity and uncertainty of personality through a disruption of structural and narrative unity. There is, however, a more conventional type of story in the collection which approaches uncertainty, but finally retreats from this radical gesture. The stories 'Clay', 'Counterparts' and 'Two Gallants' all contain narratives which are entwined with the consciousness of the central character, but, in each case, there is a withdrawal in the key moment of epiphany; consequently these three stories contain epiphanies which are beyond the potentially distorting lens of the protagonist, and which conform to the critical convention of the device. This is an important point because it shows that there is some basis in *Dubliners* for the theory of the illuminating moment. These conventional epiphanies – which are the exception rather than the rule – may well have influenced interpretations of the other stories where superficial similarities are apparent.

Joyce's two epiphany types provide a gauge of the narrative experimentation in the collection: the minority conventional epiphany represents a lurking traditionalism which is partly at odds with the indirect free style which frames it and which seems one-dimensional in comparison with the disruptive 'non-epiphany' principle which dominates the book. The double-sided nature of the epiphany in *Dubliners* is outlined in *Stephen Hero*, where Joyce allows Stephen to formulate his epiphany theory:

By an epiphany he meant a sudden spiritual manifestation, whether in the vulgarity of speech or of gesture or in a memorable phase of the mind itself.[38]

The sudden spiritual manifestation is either *external* – observable in speech or gesture – or an *internal* phase of the mind. If we apply some convenient philosophical terms to this distinction we can talk of empiricist epiphanies and relativist epiphanies. Now on the face of it the theory is a philosophical contradiction since the external event can only have the spiritual content that an observing mind ascribes to it, but in the context of Joyce's stories the distinction is extremely helpful; the external type corresponds to those stories in which the moment of revelation is perceived to be beyond the consciousness of the central character. By recourse to empirical details – the coin in 'Two Gallants', the clay in 'Clay' – the narrative reveals, instantaneously, the essence of the character and his or her situation.

This type of revelation is not confined to symbolic objects: in 'Counterparts' the epiphany derives from a different empirical commodity – the pleading of the terrified boy. Because of the extensiveness of Joyce's indirect style, however, we find, even in 'Clay', 'Counterparts' and 'Two Gallants', a narrative which has been written to emulate the consciousness of the central character in each case, but in these three stories a narratorial presence beyond the character is implicated in each epiphany. This presence, which equates to that immanent author which has erroneously been seen as operating overtly throughout the book, renders these epiphanies external and empirical.

The crucial presence of the immanent author is demonstrable through a brief examination of the revelatory moments of 'Clay' and 'Two Gallants'. Here is the relevant passage from 'Clay' in which the blindfolded Maria takes her turn in the Hallow's Eve game:

> They led her up to the table amid laughing and joking and she put her hand out in the air as she was told to do. She moved her hand about here and there in the air and descended on one of the saucers. She felt a soft wet substance with her fingers and was surprised that nobody spoke or took off her bandage. There was a pause for a few seconds; and then a great deal of scuffling and whispering. Somebody said something about the garden, and at last Mrs Donnelly said something very cross to one of the next-door girls and told her to throw it out at once: that was no play. Maria understood that it was wrong that time and so she had to do it over again: and this time she got the prayer-book. (117)

This passage leaves us in no doubt as to what has occurred. Some children have played a cruel trick on a blindfolded old woman, placing a saucer of clay beneath her descending hand. The children are reprimanded by Mrs Donnelly who then supervises a second attempt in the game, which she fixes to ensure that Maria gets the prayer-book. This is what we infer by reading between the lines of a narrative which mirrors the impercipience of the character at the time of the event. The paralipsis, of course, may be interpreted as evidence of a deliberate 'misunderstanding' on the character's part, a self-protective charade of innocence, but Maria does seem oblivious to the cruelty and continues happily to enjoy the party. More significant is the symbolic use of the clay, indicative of death as the next important stage for this ageing, childless spinster: this calculated detail is the product of a literary consciousness. The unnamed substance is skilfully left to chime with the story's title image. Such subtlety and sophistication cannot be attributed to the limited Maria who is blindfolded metaphorically as well as literally. This is an empirical epiphany for the reader, pointed by an immanent authorial presence.

The epiphanic conclusion of 'Two Gallants' moves beyond the consciousness of the central character in a similar way. When Lenehan is described as Corley's 'disciple', the presence of an external consciousness is felt, making the kind of acute, belittling judgement that would be out of character as self-evaluation on Lenehan's part (65). The symbolic gold coin, which summarizes the betrayal of Corley's girl and the hopeless mercenariness of both gallants, represents a profound withdrawal from empathy with character. An external truth is being pointed by the immanent author who is implicated both by the detached tone and by the literariness of the symbol, with its biblical overtones. The ending of 'Counterparts' – in which Farrington's son offers to say a Hail Mary for his father to escape a beating – echoes the simoniacal motif introduced in 'The Sisters', and encapsulates the story's representation of power, hyprocrisy and subjugation.

These empirical epiphanies all lack certain features which are integral to the relativist epiphany. In these examples a withdrawal of empathy occurs in the epiphanic moment, and the mood of the character at the time of the episode does not have a bearing on the nature of the revelation. Most important of all, however, is the lack of surrounding details which combine to discredit or complicate the 'truth' that is revealed; the relativist epiphany is always surrounded by details that undermine its validity.

An instance of an invalidated revelation occurs in 'After the Race', another story which emphasizes the moral failure of a falsified reconstruction. The youthful naiveté of Jimmy Doyle is expressed in his lyrical images which present a one-sided exuberant world-view, *reported* here in the narrative:

Jimmy, whose imagination was kindling, conceived the lively youth of the Frenchman twined elegantly upon the firm framework of the Englishman's manner. A graceful image of his, he thought, and a just one. (48)

It is precisely this lyrical naiveté which infuses the narrative from time to time, revealing the presence of the character himself:

Jimmy set out to translate into days' work that lordly car in which he sat. How smoothly it ran. In what style they had come careering along the country roads! The journey laid a magical finger on the genuine pulse of life and gallantly the machinery of human nerves strove to answer the bounding courses of the swift blue animal. (47)

The action of the piece concerns the partial disabusement of Jimmy's ingenuous sense of excitement at his involvement in the world of international motor racing. The day ends with a drunken card game in which Jimmy, who is being groomed as a potential sponsor, loses heavily. The outcome of the game sobers him a little and brings him to the verge of a realization, though precisely what this realization concerns is not made explicit:

He knew that he would regret in the morning but at present he was glad of the rest, glad of the dark stupor that would cover up his folly. He leaned his elbows on the table and rested his head between his hands, counting the beats of his temples. The cabin door opened and he saw the Hungarian standing in a shaft of grey light;
    – Daybreak, gentlemen! (51)

The game, presumably, has suggested to Doyle that the motivation of Ségouin's friendship may be mercenary and that he will be taken for a ride metaphorically, just as he was, literally, in the race. The notion is hazy, however, and so the epiphany is partial, indistinct. Accordingly the symbolic shaft of daylight that stretches towards him at the end is *grey*, representing a qualified enlightenment. Unlike Maria's symbolic clay, or Corley's gold coin, this symbolic shaft of grey light can legitimately be associated with the consciousness of the central character: the unsophisticated symbolic image is convincing as a product of Doyle's limited perspective. The haziness of the epiphany faithfully represents his ambivalent attitude to his continental friends and the fast lifestyle they enjoy: he is both wary of their motives, yet flattered and exhilarated by being a part of their circle. In this instance the ambiguous narrative emulates an uncertain response.

The question of implied, authorial judgement, however, requires sharper definition. In fact the interplay between narrative uncertainty and authorial presence is a highly complex issue because the balance of these elements varies from story to story. It is this dynamic – a vacillation between uncertainty (usually at the level of narrative discourse) and implied judgement (usually by means of structure) – that is the distinguishing feature of Joyce's modernism in *Dubliners*. The resulting dissonance affords a valuable refinement of Julio Cortázar's formula: the unforeseen element of narrative ambiguity is contained within a foreseen, but receding fictional frame. This sense of tension, or formal dissonance, is the central recurring feature of the modernist short story. The story 'A Little Cloud' demonstrates particularly well how this principle of disruption and (re)structuration operates.

The narrative of 'A Little Cloud' is presented, almost entirely, through the consciousness of Little Chandler and this empathy is tantamount to a disguised first-person narrative. Genette's theory of focalization in narrative is helpful in explaining this effect, as it involves the illuminating distinction between 'mood' and 'voice', the separation of 'the question *who is the character whose point of view orients the narrative perspective?* and the very different question *who is the narrator?* – or, more simply, the question *who sees?* and the question *who speaks?*'. When the narrator is entirely limited by the language and consciousness of the character who sees (the focalizer), then, in Genette's terms, the narrative belongs to the category of 'internal focalization'. Such stability can be proved if the narrative can 'be translated into the first person without obvious semantic incongruity'.[39] Most of 'A Little Cloud', despite an occasional difficulty with tenses, can be adapted in this way. After the opening paragraph of the story, which presents Little Chandler's impercipient and approving assessment of his shallow friend Gallaher, the narrative appears to move, in the second paragraph, to a stance of omniscience. The apparently objective description of the protagonist soon reveals an element of self-portrait, however. When the narrator talks of Chandler's habit of using 'perfume discreetly on his handkerchief' the convergence of character and narrator is apparent: one has to be favourably disposed towards a gratuitous use of scent to regard even the most restrained deployment as 'discreet' (76). But even here different accents coexist: a mocking, narratorial irony is embedded within the character's own voice. This type of multi-accentual discourse accounts for much of the ambiguity in Joyce's stories, and is a characteristic which will occasionally be discussed in the readings which follow. I have chosen to *focus*, however, on the development of character through voice – a necessary selectiveness – without always pausing to emphasize the confusion of voices which is consistently in attendance to qualify the tone.

Characteristic of Joyce's short stories, 'A Little Cloud' moves through a series of events which give rise to an apparently epiphanic moment, the purport of which is complicated by the falsification of the character's point of view. Chandler, in fact, contrives to extract a poetic sensation from what was a mean-spirited act prompted by social and domestic frustration.

The story's action hinges upon the meeting between Chandler, a pretentious, untalented man with literary aspirations, and his old friend Gallaher, now a successful journalist. The anticipation of the meeting elicits a piece of blinkered self-evaluation from Chandler, prompted by his imminent encounter with the world of letters (personified for him by Gallaher). Chandler exhibits a naive enthusiasm for his own imagined poetic talents:

As he crossed Grattan Bridge he looked down the river towards the lower quays and pitied the poor stunted houses. They seemed to him a band of tramps, huddled together along the river-banks, their old coats covered with dust and soot, stupefied by the panorama of sunset and waiting for the first chill of night to bid them arise, shake themselves and begone. He wondered whether he could write a poem to express his idea. Perhaps Gallaher might be able to get it into some London paper for him. Could he write something original? He was not

sure what idea he wished to express but the thought that a poetic
moment had touched him took life within him like an infant hope. (79)

This preliminary non-epiphany provides a measure of
Chandler's lack of poetic vision and his self-deception. The
single, uninspired and juvenile image of the houses as tramps is
taken as evidence of a literary vocation, yet the conceit exposes
a vacuous, asocial perspective. Chandler romantically imagines
a row of tramps stupefied by a beautiful sunset, before being
galvanized into action by the chill of night: two contradictory
states, one of poetic contemplation, the other of destitution, are
presented in juxtaposition without any apparent understanding
of the moral implications. Chandler's 'poetic' vision settles on
superficial images without establishing a depth of coherence,
and the 'poetic moment', in its immaturity, fittingly gives rise
to an 'infant hope', the hope being infantile as well as inchoate.
Chandler's self-assessment, of course, stresses the opposite of
this: it is asserted that 'his temperament might be said to be just
at the point of maturity' (80).

The conversation between Chandler and Gallaher, which
exacerbates Chandler's welling feeling of dissatisfaction, centres
on their contrasting domestic situations. Gallaher speaks
suggestively of life in Paris and London, and his experiences
evoke feelings of jealousy and frustration in the safely married
Chandler. The narrative, however, avoids mention of domestic
frustration here, and instead supplies professional rivalry,
inspired by Chandler's imagined literary potential, as the
reason for the jealousy:

He felt acutely the contrast between his own life and his friend's, and
it seemed to him unjust. Gallaher was his inferior in birth and
education. He was sure that he could do something better than his
friend had ever done, or could ever do, something higher than mere
tawdry journalism if he only got the chance. What was it that stood in
his way? His unfortunate timidity! He wished to vindicate himself in
some way, to assert his manhood. (88)

The dominance of Chandler's point of view results in a new
construction being put on his feelings of frustration. His rejection
of his timidity and his roused manhood suggest a desire for
sexual assertion, but the narrator dissembles, offering literary

aspiration as the bogus reason. Chandler's mood has changed, however, from the moment when he conceived the 'poetic' image on Grattan Bridge. At that point he considered Gallaher a powerful contact from the literary world who might put his poem in 'some London paper', but now he displays snobbishness, contempt and arrogance, all of which are presented as the justifiable emotions of a thwarted talent. Yet the change of mood has been prompted by a conversation which has had nothing to do with literature. The dialogue has brought to the surface implied details of Gallaher's licentious existence in London and Paris (possibly a fiction), and the starkly contrasting domesticity of Chandler: the newly found contempt for Gallaher's literary ability is entirely illogical, being merely a displacement of Chandler's jealousy and frustration. The sexual motive for these feelings becomes glaringly apparent when Chandler, having returned home, looks at a photograph of his wife:

He looked coldly into the eyes of the photograph and they answered coldly. Certainly they were pretty and the face itself was pretty. But he found something mean in it. Why was it so unconscious and lady-like? The composure of the eyes irritated him. They repelled him and defied him: there was no passion in them, no rapture. He thought of what Gallaher had said about rich Jewesses. Those dark Oriental eyes, he thought, how full they are of passion, of voluptuous longing!... Why had he married the eyes in the photograph? (91; original ellipsis)

No analysis is required to bring out the elements of domestic dissatisfaction and sexual fantasy in these reflections, even though Chandler's point of view serves to poeticize the emotion by suffusing the narrative with ambiguous words such as 'rapture' and 'passion', which might apply equally to a desire for the romanticized qualities of the literary life as to erotic daydreams. His feelings of frustration explode into anger when his crying child distracts him from his reading of Byron. (Significantly, Chandler has taken refuge in poetry in an attempt to sublimate his feelings into an artistic outlet, though the immaturity of the poem he reads, written by the teenage Byron, provides its own implicit critique.[40]) In this context – with Chandler continuing his attempts to sublimate domestic frustration into artistic energy – the intrusion of the crying child is an emblem of stifling domesticity. The furious Chandler shouts into the infant's face thus causing a louder outburst, this time of sheer terror, and the mother arrives to console the baby, leaving Chandler to experience his 'epiphany':

Little Chandler felt his cheeks suffused with shame and he stood back out of the lamplight. He listened while the paroxysm of the child's sobbing grew less and less; and tears of remorse started to his eyes. (94)

This remorse is too easily come by, and appears to be a falsification of what has occurred. A sense of his own petty futility, tinged with self-pity, would be a plausible emotion, but genuine remorse is not. The episode seems staged, with Chandler standing back out of the lamplight, and the language belongs to his own 'poetic' turn of phrase, the cheeks being delicately described as 'suffused with shame', a description chosen for its alliteration, without regard for the weariness of its cadence which is inappropriate for a scene of highly charged emotion. The language echoes the earlier descriptive efforts that can be attributed to Chandler, indicating his attraction to the surface qualities of words and his lack of poetic depth and integrity. A viable interpretation of this episode, therefore, is that it is constructed by Chandler: the epiphany is thus a falsification, designed to suggest that a magnanimous spirit of remorse allows him to display contrition for the hurt he has caused, despite the great burden of artistic restriction he has to bear. By this reading, Chandler is implying something heroic about himself, and attempts to frame the moment with the kind of poetry he wishes his life could represent: the fabricated epiphany is a defence, succour for a frustrated life, generated by a myth of lost artistic potential.

Although Chandler's point of view dominates the narrative, there are still other perspectives which complicate the discourse: the story is, after all, actually written in the third person even though it closely resembles a first-person narrative, and the presence of a narratorial opinion, independent of character, can occasionally be detected. This can give rise to some complex effects, as in this passage:

The golden sunset was waning and the air had grown sharp. A horde of grimy children populated the street. They stood or ran in the roadway or crawled up the steps before the gaping doors or squatted like mice upon the thresholds. Little Chandler gave them no thought. (77)

The superficial and basic descriptive work is recognizably Chandler's, particularly the cute, juvenile simile 'squatting like mice' which betrays impercipience in the face of social deprivation. This idea of observing without really seeing is implied in the omniscient comment 'Little Chandler gave them no thought': it can be argued that, at a functional level, Chandler is thinking about the children, because his perspective governs their description; so 'thinking' here must be seen to carry the connotation of 'concern' or 'understanding', and, hence, introduces a value beyond the character's point of view, which is adversely judged. The clearest example of this withdrawn perspective occurs at the end of the story when Chandler's wife Annie runs in hearing her crying child, and is described simply, and impersonally, as 'a young woman' (93); the purpose here seems to be to effect a straightforward contrast with Chandler's emotive description of his wife as passionless, defiant, and irritatingly composed, a view which now more clearly reveals the central character's own disaffection.

These, however, are the only clear-cut instances of a withdrawn point of view, although in the bar scene Chandler is judged by a more complex interplay of perspective involving the view of Gallaher: 'Little Chandler smiled, looked confusedly at his glass and bit his lower lip with three childishly white front teeth' (86). In the context of this scene, in which Gallaher's conversation displays condescension, and almost ridicule of Chandler, this representation of him as childish and confused involves Gallaher's opinion. Similarly, when we learn that Gallaher had taken 'refuge' in clouds of cigar smoke, we can sense his own belittling judgement of his companion's tedious personality, and a desire to escape (85).

However, despite the occasional complication of the narrative perspective, the point of view is primarily Chandler's, and this principle can be said to extend to the structure of the story itself which, superficially, reinforces the construction he puts on the action. The story is divided into three sections which, together, comprise a significant episode framed by a 'before' and an 'after' (a narrative convention which is as old as story-telling itself).[41] This tri-part structure incorporates the elements necessary to a learning or initiation plot which progresses from delusion or immaturity through disabusement/revelation to enlightenment.[42] The first section, in which Little Chandler anticipates the meeting with Gallaher, expresses his superficial assessment of his friend: 'Gallaher had got on. You could tell that at once by his travelled air, his well-cut tweed suit, and fearless accent. Few fellows had talents like his and fewer still could remain unspoiled by such success. Gallaher's heart was in the right place and he had deserved to win' (76). The error of this assessment is implicitly exposed in the second section where the meeting takes place: Gallaher, patronizing Chandler throughout, is undeserving, self-motivated, and definitely spoiled by his worldly success. Chandler, accordingly, reassesses his friend as unworthy and, in the final scene, this realization leads to an angry expression of supposedly professional frustration.

If the structure, on one level, reinforces Chandler's version, it also undercuts it at the same time. For Little Chandler, as we have seen, there is no genuine disabusement: his mood certainly changes, but he is progressing into the deeper delusion of sexual jealousy misrepresented as thwarted talent. The final scene is thus a cruel *parody* of enlightenment and decisive action, in which the pathetic Chandler vents his frustration on his son. The falsity and staginess of that final revelatory moment is reinforced by the structure which suggests that the key revelation should already have occurred in the previous scene. At the same time the story's shape – one of implied learning – notionally supports Chandler's self-portrait: Chandler does change his opinion about Gallaher in an evaluation of comparative talents, but this is a smokescreen since it is the worldly and not the literary Gallaher that Chandler is measuring himself against. The structure, then, exposes *and* reinforces the self-delusion it nominally dissolves; and this ambivalent, dissonant use of a narrative convention – the initiation plot pursued, yet parodied through a structural irony – supplies a key to the story's characterization and its final effect. This interpretation is based on an assessment of the problematic narrative stance, an ambiguity which is exaggerated by the undermining of the conventional structure. The disruption of both elements (narrative line and story structure) emulates Chandler's own personal confusion; and in this way – by embracing the disunity of the story as a whole – an identifiable point to the story emerges. Significantly, it is the sophisticated, disruptive use of a basic, *unified* short story type – the initiation story – which generates the story's effects.

The formal conflicts of the story, which replicate Chandler's personality conflicts, bear a dual relation to its ideological context. This dual relation, or relative autonomy, is the factor which was shown, in the previous chapter, to determine the effects of Mansfield's 'Bliss'. Like 'Bliss', 'A Little Cloud' is partially restricted by the ideologies which it criticizes, primarily the ideology of marital contentment and stability: Chandler's confusion stems from his inability to fit into, or break out of, this social system. An overt challenge to this system would have been unacceptable, as the fuss over morality in *Dubliners* indicates, and it is through Joyce's subversion of literary convention that the consequences of this ideology are exposed. Chandler's attitude is further complicated by his blinkered adherence to another ideology, that of the inherent greatness of literary creativity: it is this which prevents him from addressing or even identifying the domestic basis of his personal crisis. Again, the ideology is exposed through formal disruption, in this case the jarring effect of reading, and then re-evaluating, the poetic failure of Chandler's style. Finally, then, 'A Little Cloud' does reveal paralysing social forces, but it does so through a complex and disruptive composition which the simplified paralysis reading cannot account for.

This interpretation of 'A Little Cloud' indicates that a full representation of the effects produced depends upon an initial understanding of the narrative point of view: the narrative structure, though important, reinforces the effects created by the orientation of the narrative perspective. This dynamic – an emphasis on point of view, and the receding importance of structure and event – is a seminal feature of Joyce's stories, although critics have not given this emphasis sufficient attention. Point of view, for instance, is crucial to an understanding of 'Eveline', yet the better-known analyses of the story have concentrated on its action. A glance at two representative surveys reprinted in 'casebooks' on *Dubliners*, one British, the other American, illustrates this point. Martin Dolch divines a straightforward thematic opposition in 'Eveline' which he represents diagrammatically. In his chart, 'DEATH' and 'LIFE' are placed on either side. According to this schema 'LIFE' is characterized by an 'ESCAPE' abroad and a concomitant 'HAPPINESS in fertile fulfilment', while the 'DEATH' that Eveline opts for involves 'ENTRAPMENT' in Dublin and 'DUTY in sterile family ties'. Phillip Herring reproduces this chart, with an unquestioning approval, in his *Joyce's Uncertainty Principle*.[43] Clive Hart, in the British casebook (published in the same year as the first), sees precisely the same conflict between paralysis and action, in which paralysis is the victor.[44] This representative view is still in need of refutation: such is the power of the literary casebook, to enshrine articles in positions of enduring credibility merely through accessibility.

The shared approach of Hart and Dolch, as I have intimated, is flawed by its avoidance of narrative texture, because 'Eveline' seems to be centred on a romanticized epiphany. It is a short piece, the narrative of which is identified, mainly, with the discourse of the central character. (The problematic final scene is the principal exception.) The bulk of the story consists of Eveline's reverie as she ponders on her plan to run away with the sailor Frank, and on the life she will leave behind. The ties as well as the burdens of her existence exert pressure on her, so that when she deserts Frank at the quayside, we can interpret her decision in terms of her 'promise to her [now dead] mother...to keep the home together as long as she could' (41). The denial of her own romantic life is thus presented as an act of self-sacrifice, and this is how Eveline would view it. If the final scene is read as Eveline's recollection – as a self-portrayal of passivity and helplessness – then we can discern an expression of regret, a suggestion by the character that her family life in Dublin imprisoned her and thwarted her happiness.

As in my earlier analyses in this chapter I am advocating a method geared to detecting the coexistence of a character's voice and narratorial voice, an approach which falls under the umbrella of 'dialogics'. Dialogics – the style of narrative analysis derived from the theoretical writings of Mikhail Bakhtin – is founded on a conception of language not as a single, shared system, but rather as a complex mixture of different variations:

The word, directed towards its object, enters a dialogically agitated and tension-filled environment of alien words, value judgements and accents, weaves in and out of complex interrelationships, merges with some, recoils from others, intersects with yet a third group: and all this may crucially shape discourse, may leave a trace in all its semantic layers, may complicate its expression and influence its entire stylistic profile.[45]

That is to say that there are a number of versions of a language – vernacular, official, literary, for instance – and that these different versions interact because they are in conflict with one another; consequently, any utterance takes its meaning from its relationship to various other versions of the language, which are implicitly present, and with which the utterance is, effectively, in dialogue.

Dialogics can thus be defined as the analysis of how different versions of a language interact in the generation of meaning. Yet this interaction is also conflict because, for Bakhtin, there is a tendency in any culture to establish, or attempt to establish, a single, official language, and this tendency is inevitably undermined as social conditions change and the language adapts:

Every concrete utterance of a speaking subject serves as a point where centrifugal as well as centripetal forces are brought to bear. The processes of centralization and decentralization, of unification and disunification, intersect in the utterance.[46]

Each utterance, each manifestation of discourse, is subject to a process of struggle in which (centripetal) forces of stability, of a unitary language, are undermined by entering into dialogue with disunifying (centrifugal) forces. The conflict, therefore, amounts to a debunking of the official, unitary language achieved by the unofficial voices. An example of this might be a local BBC newsreader slipping into the vernacular of his or her region to deliver a humorous signing-off remark, as local newsreaders are wont to do. The official language – in this case a regional version of BBC English – would thus be undermined by the vernacular which momentarily displaces it. As far as literature is concerned, it is narrative fiction that most interests Bakhtin, because it is in narrative fiction that this debunking of official languages is most evident.

In narrative analysis this has a direct application to the complexity of narrative voice, to detecting the presence of a character's point of view bound up with what is, on the face of it, omniscient narrative. In other words, the approach helps us locate a dialogue between a narratorial voice and a character's voice: that is, we can detect *dialogized* narrative. The effect of such a dialogized narrative is to undermine any position of omniscient judgement, just as official languages, for Bakhtin, are continually debunked by conflicting versions.

There is a crucial connection here with the concept of relative autonomy, the dual essence of art which locates a conflict between ideological restriction and subversion: the dialogized text displays an analogous dual essence in which (for example) omniscient narrative authority coexists with, and yet is undermined by, other voices in the text. A similar dual essence also obtains in more complex dialogic readings; subsequent interpretations of individual stories will show, particularly, how characterization can be established through conflicting voices, voices employed precisely to define certain ideological struggles.

Dialogic conflict is a major feature of the modernist short story, and has a particular relevance to Joyce's characterization through voice. 'Eveline' is a notable dialogic text in which a position of stable narrative authority is undermined. If this is the case, then the interpretations of the story alluded to above must be inadequate: if the narrative itself is infused with the character's words, and the character's perspective, then the straightforward thematic opposition between 'life' and 'death', 'happiness' and 'entrapment', must be too simplistic, since there can be no single judgemental voice to indicate this.

An indication of Eveline's point of view is given early in the narrative, in an account of her childhood:

> One time there used to be a field there in which they used to play every evening with other people's children. Then a man from Belfast bought the field and built houses in it – not like their little brown houses but bright brick houses with shining roofs. (37)

There is an uncertainty in the account – they played with 'other people's children', while the field was bought by 'a man from Belfast' – and this lack of specificity suggests that this is Eveline's own hazy recollection of childhood experience, an assessment which is reinforced by the child-like description of the houses: 'not like their little brown houses but bright brick houses with shining roofs'.

If this complicity between narrator and character persists, we can read the story's outcome as the presentation, by an older Eveline, of a revelatory moment of herself as a dehumanized, atrophied captive of Dublin. The question that then arises is: what, exactly, constitutes the happiness Eveline imagines she has tragically rejected? The shadowy Frank, rather than being the calculating figure that Hugh Kenner suggests, appears to be merely somebody that Eveline scarcely knew.[47] With hindsight, however, she has dreamily built him up into a symbol of imagined romantic possibilities, an ideal figure. Eveline's relationship with Frank is presented in a paragraph of twelve short sentences, the brevity of which underlines their status as strangers. Yet the sentences appear in an urgent list which suggests an eagerness to create, by process of accretion, an impression of intimacy. Some of the facts that Eveline sees fit to report about Frank are plainly banal:

> He was awfully fond of music and sang a little.... He used to call her Poppens out of fun.... He had tales of distant countries. He had started as a deck boy at a pound a month on a ship of the Allan Line going out to Canada. He told her the names of the ships he had been on and the names of the different services. (40)

These vague, inconsequential details have the air of someone trying to remember a slight acquaintance, and this effectively negates the suggestion of intimacy. As so often in *Dubliners* the narrative discourse, in complicity with character, strives to assert that which is implicitly refuted.

When one perceives the doubt surrounding the romantic option, the epiphany of Eveline as helpless animal, captive in Dublin, seems melodramatic. Possibly the epiphany represents the emotions of an older, sadder Eveline who dwells on the loss of romantic possibilities, projecting onto the episode a significance that it did not have at the time. If one reads 'Clay' as a continuation of 'Eveline', as some critics have done, the older Eveline as narrator can be seen as a version of the sad spinster figure Maria.[48] Yet the impercipience of Eveline is more complicated than this suggests, and there may be a significant paralipsis.

This sense of melodrama can be defined using another aspect of the dialogic approach, the location of other cultural texts and voices speaking through individual characters. Here we can detect the discourse of pulp romance fiction filtered through Eveline's consciousness. The lovers' parting is presented, in the final scene, through the exaggerated language of romantic fiction, and this other discourse is implicit throughout the story, even though it only now appears overtly. Eveline is presented here as the desired, semi-swooning heroine: 'All the seas of the world tumbled about her heart. He was drawing her into them: he would drown her. She gripped with both hands at the iron railing' (42).

This other dialogizing of the text contributes significantly to our understanding of the characterization, because it indicates a strategy of defence. It is clearly important that it is Eveline's decision not to go with Frank, and, given the superficiality of their relationship, this does suggest a laudable instinct of self-preservation, and a level-headedness which is at odds with the romanticized epiphany. Yet to acknowledge the unreality of the elopement would be to approach a dreadful self-knowledge: without the *possibility* of an alternative, Eveline would have to face the fact that her life is one of unredeemed drudgery, and this vision of nullity may be too much for her. The romantic option can therefore be seen as a strategy of self-preservation, a wilful act of self-delusion.

This reading implies a negation of plot in the sense that the possibility of action is exposed as fabrication. Eveline casts herself as Cinderella without any tangible justification for doing so. The fairy-tale motif, however, underpins Eveline's internal confusion, and the allusion to this traditional tale structure clearly contributes to the story's effect. Indeed, several critics have used this story to discuss narrative grammar, assuming that its dependence on conventional narrative structures is seminal. Jennie Skerl has made an extended attempt to apply Vladimir Propp's narrative grammar of the folk-tale to the story and, although she acknowledges 'a manipulation of the narrative grammar far more complex than in any folktale', she nevertheless finds a 'detailed structural similarity between Joyce's "Eveline" and the fairy tales analyzed by Propp', and concludes that they belong 'to the same genre'. This argument assumes that 'Eveline' is based on a 'narrative grammar made up of functions, character roles, spheres of action, and sequential syntax'.[49] Some of Propp's 'functions' are certainly evident in 'Eveline', and help to define the protagonist's situation: in particular the functions involving an 'interdiction', the 'villain', and 'lack' or 'desire' have an obvious relevance to (respectively) Eveline's mother's deathbed request, Eveline's hard life, and her yearning for happiness.[50] Yet Propp's grammar is potentially misleading since it cannot properly distinguish between actual functions and imaginary ones, and so Skerl accords Frank the structural role of 'donor', the character who facilitates the liquidation of lack and the defeat of villainy, even though, as we have seen, this is a role beyond his capabilities. Such a structural analysis clearly hinders the distinction between internal and external drama upon which the story depends; one can, of course, redefine certain functions to account for this distinction, but, since, this redefinition would depend upon a prior interpretation, it would appear to have a minimal value. The conventional plot-based, or epical narrative style described in Propp's model is a background presence in

'Eveline', though it is, effectively, undermined in a typically
modernist gesture of equivocal disruption.

According to the reading offered here, 'Eveline' withdraws
from the narrative convention to which it alludes, and concentrates on internal characterization. Consequently, it is a
methodology based on point of view, rather than narrative
structure, which has been favoured to locate most effectively the
story's effects. These effects can be fairly complex where a
variety of voices is discernible, as in the following passage which
consists, primarily, of the reported speech of Eveline's father:

> The trouble was to get any money from her father. He said she used to
> squander the money, that she had no head, that he wasn't going to
> give her his hard-earned money to throw about the streets, and much
> more, for he was usually fairly bad of a Saturday night. (39)

The second sentence here begins with the reported discourse of
Eveline's father, but, arguably, a different voice concludes the
sentence with 'he was usually fairly bad of a Saturday night'.
This different accent might be said to represent the voice of the
suffering domestic female, who alludes to the drunken abuse of
the male head of the household, but in a vague, euphemistic
way. The condition of being 'fairly bad' suggests a recurring
illness, a socially acceptable complaint, and this concealment
betrays a voice which represents domestic stability and subjugation. This, possibly, is the voice of the dead mother, and the
society she represents, speaking through Eveline. The apparent
juxtaposition of these two voices – the abusive male and the
subjugated female – provides a succinct and telling commentary on Eveline's situation: the two voices merge in a narrative
which is identified, mainly, with her point of view, and this
mergence demonstrates how she must continue to embrace and
unite the attitudes of the two voices in order to accept her
situation, and maintain the status quo.

Of course, the business of defining shifts in tone is uncertain,
to say the least, but even if the precise definition and allocation
of different voices is problematic, the very existence of a tension
between different accents is significant. My reading here shows
how the coexistence of different voices can reveal an indictment
of a particular social context: in this interpretation the story

implicitly condemns the ideology of Irish domestic affairs – a genuine strategy of containment – which represses those who subscribe to it. For Eveline there is no effective voice which can undermine this particular official language. The discourse of romance fiction represents the only challenge she can muster, and this alternative supplies its own ideological restriction, in the form of self-deception. Once more, ideological containment (a complex paralysis) is revealed through a dual formal dissonance: the dismantling of plot reflects the impossibility of action for Eveline, and the dialogization of the narrative pits the official, unitary language of domestic conformity against an alternative (but finally impotent) language of escapism.

'A Painful Case' presents a still more problematic example of a complex narrative perspective. A first reading indicates another narrative of (primarily) consistent internal focalization, with Duffy as the focalizer; the narrative of this story is infused with self-consciousness and an identification between Duffy and the narrator is easily made. The description of Duffy's eyes which 'gave the impression of a man ever alert to greet a redeeming instinct in others but often disappointed', suggests a piece of self-analysis inspired by wishful thinking; only Duffy can know that he is 'often disappointed', and only he would make the implausible claim that evidence of such disappointment constitutes a feature of his physiognomy (120). His lack of emotion, which the story reveals and which the flatness of the narrative reflects, belies the fanciful claim. Soon after this occurs the account of Duffy's 'odd autobiographical habit' of composing sentences about himself, to which reference has been made above, and which invites the equation between character and narrator.

Duffy has been viewed, convincingly, as a dualist unable to reconcile the 'separatist' and 'sympathetic' aspects of the human psyche.[51] Having isolated himself from humanity, he yet finds himself drawn into a platonic affair with Mrs Sinico. He is 'exalted' by their evenings together, which are characterized by Duffy espousing 'the soul's incurable loneliness'. Unaware of the contradiction implicit in his need to be heard on such a subject, Duffy represses his urge for contact with Mrs Sinico, and recoils from her 'passionate' touch (124). Four years after the termination of the friendship Duffy reads a newspaper account of Mrs Sinico's death, which also intimates the mental and emotional deterioration she has suffered. If the story is taken at face value, Duffy can be said to enjoy an epiphany, prompted by this news, which involves a partial understanding of his personal failure: 'Why had he withheld life from her? Why had he sentenced her to death?' (130). He recognizes his affinity with her: 'Now that she was gone he understood how lonely her life must have been, sitting night after night alone in that room. His life would be lonely too until he, too, died' (130). The culmination of this epiphany stresses Duffy's sense of his own isolation.

The narrative seems to suggest a belated moral development on Duffy's part, an understanding, too late, of the need to embrace the sympathetic as well as the separatist aspect of the psyche. But this simple interpretation of the epiphany is complicated by the dialogic nature of the narrative. Suzanne Hyman's essay on the story identifies 'a sort of linguistic ping-pong' at one point where 'the mode of expression shifts back and forth from Duffy to Mrs Sinico'. When, for instance, the narrative informs us that 'Mr Duffy had many opportunities of enjoying the lady's society' we hear a voice other than Duffy's, a voice of romance and propriety characterized by Hyman as having a 'lady-like, cake-frosting diction'.[52] At this point the narrative incorporates the points of view of both Duffy and Mrs Sinico and, in doing so, indicates the motivation of both. The careful, emotionless and self-protective Duffy is implicated in the scrupulous and precise descriptions, as in the lengthy, almost pedantic opening paragraph; Mrs Sinico's preoccupation with propriety and romance, on the other hand, indicates loneliness qualified by a consciousness of social form and etiquette, and this suggests that she may be motivated as much by social ambition as by emotional need: 'Neither he nor she had had any such adventure before and neither was conscious of any incongruity' (122). (Duffy, we note, is highly conscious of incongruity: he 'had a distaste for underhand ways and, finding that they were compelled to met stealthily, he forced her to ask him to her house' (122).)

Given that the characters' discourses reveal equivocal motivation no simple resolution or moment of revelation is possible in this story. The simplest interpretation of the story is one which takes at face value Duffy's acceptance of responsibility for Mrs Sinico's collapse, and his apparent retreat into introversion while she reaches for the bottle: 'the alliance ended, he will revert to his sterile former life, while Mrs Sinico will turn to alcohol'.[53] There is, however, much more going on in the story than this. The indication of self-interest in Mrs Sinico's attachment to Duffy suggests that his rejection of her may not have been as devastating as he imagines, and that some other factor may have contributed to her collapse. This possibility seems confirmed by her husband's testimony, at the inquest, that it is only 'about two years ago' that she became 'rather intemperate in her habits' (128), yet her death occurs four years after her break-up with Duffy (124). The intervening two years give plenty of scope for a more significant encounter, and a deeper disillusionment. This must remain conjecture, but the very scope for this conjecture discredits Duffy's assumption that it is all his doing. There is a strong suggestion of an egotistical myopia which undercuts his late 'understanding'. There is also a clear indication that Duffy, too, turns to alcohol. His mood before his 'epiphany' is typically introverted and self-congratulatory as he assesses the decision to cut off his connection with Mrs Sinico: 'He had no difficulty now in approving of the course he had taken' (129). His mood, however, begins to soften after he has taken a couple of glasses of hot punch in a public house. The empathic response, and hence the epiphany, is alcohol-induced, and, consequently we must acknowledge an element of maudlin self-pity in the reflections about being 'lonely... until he, too, died' (130). The fact that Duffy has not progressed beyond his pedantic aphoristic habit – twice he announces himself 'outcast from life's feast' – is a further indication of stasis rather than progression (130–1).

This interpretation is supported by a certain vacillation in the narrative between distance and empathy which affords an occasional judgemental withdrawal. In Duffy's self-description, for instance, there is an odd detail – the description of his 'unamiable mouth' – which indicates a momentary disjunction between character and narrator (120). Usually, however, this kind of pointed observation is effected in a seamless way, in a manner which conforms to Vološinov/Bakhtin's account of quasi-direct discourse. In such discourse one does not have to distinguish between character and narrator because (reading 'narrator' for 'author') '*both* author *and* character [speak] at the same time' in 'a single linguistic construction within which the accents of two differently oriented voices are maintained'.[54] This is a matter of different intonations occurring simultaneously and in a highly complex way, a simultaneity that occurs throughout *Dubliners*. A clear example occurs in this story where Duffy's room is described as 'free from pictures' (119); the 'freedom' here connotes the clinical neatness of Duffy, as well as a scornful implication of philistinism in Duffy's character. A more overt instance is found as Duffy considers the death of Mrs Sinico and asks himself: 'Was it possible he had deceived himself so utterly about her?' (129). The rhetorical question is a genuine one for the deluded Duffy, but it carries an obvious ironic undertone.

This reading of the story depends not on the action itself, but on the version given of it. The *story*, as such, is exposed as unreliable, open to question, and it is this uncertainty – the debunking of plot – that is the essence of the characterization. Indeed, the whole episode has a spuriousness which seems to derive from Duffy's egotistical self-deception, an emotion which reasserts itself at the end in a flood of self-pity, thereby negating his attempts to empathize with Mrs Sinico. He remains self-obsessed, 'the hermetically-sealed man', 'the walking embodiment of the Cartesian split'.[55]

Duffy's incomplete emotional profile reveals formative social influences of a distorted and damaging nature. Phillip Herring's account of Ireland's historical emphasis on 'segregation of the sexes' and the 'psychological distance' this creates is relevant here, and it is this context which is implicitly revealed through Duffy's confused and contradictory narrative.[56]

'A Painful Case' epitomizes Joyce's method in *Dubliners*: the stories are enactments of ambiguous experience, though this ambiguity does not connote, for me, a principle of *undecidability*. On the contrary, the uncertainties can be shown to locate complex states of personality fashioned by *particular* contextual forces. In terms of characterization, the stories investigate a complexity of consciousness and motivation and, consequently, bear little resemblance to the notional unified story with its single effect: the denial of a simple, single effect, in formal terms, is usually an integral part of the stories' functions. Yet the stories are partially dependent upon those unifying conventions which they transcend. Consequently, the stories lead towards a supposedly crucial event, creating expectations of an easily identifiable revelation, a single effect, which are dispelled in the complex epiphanies. Joyce's ironic use of structure and plot is one source of this (partially) disruptive tendency, which is extended through the development of a dialogized narrative style. It is these complex dissonances which reveal paralysis – primarily the restrictive ideology of Irish domestic affairs – a paralysis which is not a simple state of character, but rather a hidden network of social forces working on character. The conventional paralysis reading of *Dubliners* constitutes a mistaken diagnosis and concentrates on symptoms rather than causes, on a single state of being (such as Eveline's inaction) rather than on the productive contradictions (Eveline's internal dialectic between stasis and escapism) and the underlying causes of these complex states.

These readings of a selection from *Dubliners* indicate the usefulness of the interpretive formulation discussed in the opening chapter, and epitomized in Balibar and Macherey's exhortation 'not [to] look for unifying effects but for signs of the contradictions (historically determined) which produced them and which appear as unevenly resolved conflicts in the text'.[57] One can say further that these unevenly resolved conflicts – particularly dialogic interference and structural disruption – are an essential part of the characterization, and so can be discussed as *conscious* aspects of Joyce's method, rather than as accidental, symptomatic features to be detected with the privilege of historical hindsight. In short, the critical approach which seeks to explain disunity has a strong affinity with Joyce's problematizing of individual identity, conducted through a disruption of the short story form.

This connection between theoretical method and the modernist development of the genre is, perhaps, even more marked in Virginia Woolf where, again, a concentration on literary form goes hand in hand with the development of character. But this formal element is *intensified* in Woolf: her most significant stories are really *experiments* in genre, investigations into the appropriateness of the short story form as a vehicle for her presentations of personality. This body of fiction, with its overtly experimental use of the genre, presents a more obvious (and in some ways more challenging) test of the theoretical connections I have been tracing.

CHAPTER 3

Virginia Woolf: experiments in genre

In the opening chapter a recurring distinction between two types of story was discussed, a distinction epitomized in Eileen Baldeshwiler's article 'The Lyric Short Story'. Baldeshwiler perceives a clear division between the conventional, plot-based story ('epical') and the 'lyrical' story, often open-ended, which focuses upon 'internal changes, moods, and feelings'.[1] The value and ultimate limitation of this binary approach can be clearly demonstrated through an analysis of the Woolfian short story. For the student of modernism it is Baldeshwiler's historicizing of the lyrical story's development that is most significant: the 'lyricism' she discerns in Katherine Mansfield and Virginia Woolf is accurately defined as an integral part of their innovative use of the short story form. Yet it is in this area that Baldeshwiler overstates her case, claiming that Woolf 'definitively abandoned the conventional short story to choose new subjects, new themes, new structures, and new language'.[2] The implicit parallel between modernist experimentation and the development of the genre is helpful, but the notion of a definitive abandonment of a literary heritage is plainly wrong: from what follows below it will be clear that Woolf never did finally abandon the conventional short story, and that her experiments in the genre depend upon the adaptation, often the subversion, of existing forms and conventions. This, then, is a fair summary of the Woolfian story, continually reacting against, revolving around, conventional story types, yet never finally abandoning the touchstone of its literary heritage.

This notion of a literary heritage and a 'conventional' short story is problematic, however, because the modernist short story cannot be seen simply to replace an older well-plotted type of story. The conventional, epical story flourishes concurrently with modernist developments in the genre, particularly in the works of Kipling, H. H. Munro ('Saki') and Somerset Maugham, who, as Clare Hanson points out, continue 'a renewal of traditional story forms' stimulated by the stories of Stevenson and the early Kipling.[3] Consequently, Woolf's debate with the conventional story is an integral part of her challenge to the fictional practices of her contemporaries.

The tension between convention and innovation can be seen in terms of the epical–lyrical split in Woolf's major stories, in which investigations of the 'plotless' story are made within well-structured frameworks: in 'Moments of Being', 'An Unwritten Novel' and 'The Lady in the Looking-Glass' Woolf conducts a dialogue between the epical and lyrical principles. These stories are really metafictions and, consequently, Woolf's theme in each case is an investigation into what she can achieve in the genre. These stories, however, are straightforward in their treatment of point of view: a single consciousness dominates each narrative, and a clear evaluative distance is maintained. A more radical direction is suggested in 'The Evening Party', 'Kew Gardens' and 'A Haunted House', stories with a destabilized narrative voice, but at the same time Woolf employs detailed formal controls to give shape to these fictions and to point her meaning. The experiment in formlessness reaches an extreme in the prose poems 'Monday or Tuesday' and 'Blue and Green', fictions which have no point of contact with convention. This scale of innovation in the short fiction provides a framework for analysing the various uses Woolf made of the genre, but it does not indicate any kind of chronological progression. If Woolf can be seen as working things out in her stories, there is no indication of her arriving at any obvious conclusion, or developing in a single direction: it is often a surprise to readers, familiar with the novels, to discover Woolf publishing conventional plot-bound stories like 'The Duchess and the Jeweller' and 'Lappin and Lapinova' as late as 1938 and 1939.

The goal of Woolf's experimentation in the short story can be set in the context of her objectives at large, and these are broadly outlined in her two essays 'Mr Bennett and Mrs Brown'

(1924) and 'Modern Fiction' (1919).[4] These essays, which are frequently employed by critics attempting to establish a Woolfian manifesto for fictional composition, have a particular relevance to the stories, some of which put into practice the innovatory ideas adumbrated in the essays. We saw, in the case of Joyce, a problematic relationship between the fiction and the author's comments upon it, but the example of Woolf eschews this issue because there is sometimes no clear distinction between her fictional work and her essays. Indeed, it is often difficult to determine whether some of her brief works and sketches should be termed essays or stories. The works discussed in this chapter were all published, or prepared for publication, as fiction, but are greatly illuminiated by the essays cited.[5]

The terminology employed by Woolf in these essays can be imprecise and so some extrapolation and interpretation is necessary. First, I should stress that I read the two essays as outlining the same goal, though in different terms. In 'Modern Fiction' Woolf appeals for a fictional form capable of rendering what 'life' is like. This 'life' is determined by the impressions received by 'an ordinary mind on an ordinary day', and is described as 'a luminous halo, a semi-transparent envelope surrounding us from the beginning of consciousness to the end'.[6] Equally elusive is Mrs Brown, explicitly discussed (in the other essay) as the representative of 'human nature' and as 'the spirit' of 'life itself'.[7] The goal, in both cases, is to render faithfully the amorphous and heterogeneous phenomenon of human consciousness, whether in the guise of 'life', 'character' or 'human nature'.

My analysis posits a scale within the stories of developing sophistication, a (non-chronological) scale which reflects Woolf's quest for a narrative texture that might encompass her notion of amorphous 'life'. The two essays mentioned relate to the different ends of the scale which progresses in sophistication from the 'Mr Bennett and Mrs Brown' stories to the explicitly impressionistic fictions in which Woolf seeks to create a narrative consciousness which itself embodies the 'uncircumscribed spirit' mentioned in the 'Modern Fiction' essay.[8]

The 'Mr Bennett and Mrs Brown' stories include 'An Unwritten Novel', 'Moments of Being' and 'The Lady in the

Looking-Glass', all of which represent a quest for 'Mrs Brown' according to the principles laid down in the essay, in which, as we have seen, Woolf calls for a fictional form capable of adequately representing 'human nature' and the 'spirit of life itself'. This is the familiar Woolfian quest for genuine inner characterization and the project is located in the chronology of English literary history: Woolf laments the 'external' approach to characterization made by the Edwardian novelists (Wells, Bennett, Galsworthy), and suggests that the Georgian writers to date (among whom she numbers Lawrence, Joyce and Eliot) have been concerned with breaking and destroying stale conventions, a necessary ground-clearing activity which has nevertheless so preoccupied the Georgians as to prevent them from evolving new ways of approaching 'real' characterization, and, she feels:

This state of things is, I think, inevitable whenever from hoar old age or callow youth the convention ceases to be a means of communication between writer and reader, and becomes instead an obstacle and an impediment. At the present moment we are suffering, not from decay, but from having no code of manners which writers and readers accept as a prelude to the more exciting intercourse of friendship.[9]

The two central strands of the essay – the call for genuine inner characterization and the critique of existing conventions which hamper this development – provide the best possible introduction to the group of stories written from the same motives, for not only do they enact the quest outlined in the essay, but their formal operation depends upon literary conventions: in seeking the new, Woolf's art in these pieces depends upon the old (even though the old is systematically subverted).

The most straightforward story in this group of four, and the least radical, is 'Moments of Being: "Slater's Pins Have No Points"' (1926). The story concerns the imagined construction by Fanny Wilmot of the personal background and history of her music tutor, Miss Craye, and the implied discrediting of this construction at the story's end. Basing her imaginary account on occasional remarks and hearsay, Fanny Wilmot attempts to outline a personal history to explain why Miss Craye never married. Fanny imagines a proposal scene (involving a fictional 'moment... of revelation' (218)) in which Miss Craye, sundered by personal conflict, interrupts her suitor at the crucial moment. The story's ending, which suggests that Miss Craye may be homosexual, renders the preceding narrative conjecture invalid. The final moment of reversal also represents an apparent instant of revelation with regard to Miss Craye's 'true' character.

It is easy to read this story as a simple demonstration of the 'unknowability' of the inner person, but, if read with 'Mr Bennett and Mrs Brown' in mind, the story seems more a demonstration of the inadequacy of a particular literary style, of the unknowability of a character if approached with inadequate fictional tools. Fanny's imagined Miss Craye is a construction based on things she has heard about her from Miss Kingston, an impression built up from external data. In the essay Woolf criticizes the Edwardians for precisely this approach to characterization, faulting Arnold Bennett especially for 'trying to hypnotize us into the belief that, because he has made a house, there must be a person living there'.[10]

The projection of the ideas in the essay into the story is well achieved. The location of the limited Edwardian-style narrative invention within the person of Fanny Wilmot is a fine stratagem. What could have become transparent theoretical metafiction is concealed beneath a convincing naturalistic surface in which an inquisitive young student ponders the personal life of her elderly spinster-teacher; the esotericism of the author in quest of a style obtains at a concealed level. This reading of the story renders it a rehearsal of how *not* to delineate character, a process which depends upon the fictional conventions it would transcend. It is also important to note that the revelatory moment is not an epiphany in the sense that the genuine Miss Craye is unveiled in a flash. The suggestion of homosexuality which negates the characterization does not, in itself, provide an alternative history of Miss Craye: that would require another short story. The moment of reversal simply indicates that Fanny's history, and therefore the narrative approach she embodies, is probably based upon a false premise.[11] The disjunction here is between

Fanny's imagined Miss Craye – the passive female who, unsuccessfully wooed, is consigned to spinsterhood – and the real,
assertive Miss Craye who kisses Fanny (220). The ideology of
female passivity – Fanny's fiction of Miss Craye and her suitor
– is rejected in the dissonant moment, a rejection which,
significantly, coincides with the rejection of the narrative
formula: the story implicitly links the repressive sexual convention with the restrictive narrative style.[12] The story's rebuttal
of a stable characterization involves a subversive formal
dissonance: the disruption of literary form coincides with the
exposure of ideological restraint.

Woolf had already taken her quest for 'Mrs Brown' to a more
advanced level in 'An Unwritten Novel' (1920), the story
which most closely resembles the essay. ('Mr Bennett and Mrs
Brown' clearly alludes to this story in the scenario it envisages.)
The first-person narrator of this piece constructs the imaginary
background of a fellow traveller in a train carriage, and again
the story is 'about' the narrative consciousness that does the
constructing. As in 'Moments of Being' the invented history is
apparently discredited when the supposedly suffering, forsaken
and oppressed spinster Minnie Marsh is met at the train station
by a young man she refers to as her son (with whom she leaves,
talking animatedly). Woolf's focus here is very different,
however, and the narrator of the piece clearly does not embody
the same limitations which restrict Fanny Wilmot. This
narrative, though invented, has a value of its own, having been
prompted by a direct surveillance of the character in the train
carriage. This apparently nice distinction is actually crucial, as
the following passage from the essay indicates:

Mr Bennett has never once looked at Mrs Brown in her corner. There
she sits in the corner of the carriage – the carriage which is travelling,
not from Richmond to Waterloo, but from one age of English
literature to the next, for Mrs Brown is eternal, Mrs Brown is human
nature.[13]

The attempt to capture human nature in fiction, symbolized by
Mrs Brown in the essay and the problematic characters in these
short stories, depends for success upon a close examination of

Mrs Brown herself. In 'An Unwritten Novel' the narrator is deeply affected by the emotional presence which 'Minnie Marsh' exudes from her corner of the carriage:

The Times was no protection against such sorrow as hers. But other human beings forbade intercourse. The best thing to do against life was to fold the paper so that it made a perfect square, crisp, thick, impervious even to life. This done, I glanced up quickly, armed with a shield of my own. She pierced through my shield; she gazed into my eyes as if searching any sediment of courage at the depths of them and damping it to clay. (112–13)

Woolf here uses *The Times* as an obvious symbol of factual and ordered descriptive writing – ('births, deaths, marriages, Court Circular, the habits of birds, Leonardo da Vinci, the Sandhills murder, high wages and the cost of living – oh, take what you like…it's all in *The Times*!' (112)) – which comprises an obstacle between the writer and human nature. The scene quoted above is thus an enactment of the authorial consciousness relinquishing conventional habits in the irresistible presence of genuine human nature. The narrator, finding her shield superfluous and with her 'eyes upon life' (113), creates a fictional account of 'Minnie Marsh'. The moment of reversal, in which the fictional account is apparently discredited, forces the narrator to assess the value of the imagined story. The narrator is shocked into a momentary loss of faith in the value of her fiction: 'Well, my World's done for! What do I stand on? What do I know? That's not Minnie. There never was Moggridge. Who am I? Life's bare as bone' (121). This loss of faith lasts for only a paragraph, however, and the sight of the departing mother and son elicits further fictional creation in the same vein as the rest of the story:

Mysterious figures! Mother and son. Who are you? Why do you walk down the street? Where tonight will you sleep, and then, tomorrow? Oh, how it whirls and surges – floats me afresh! I start after them. People drive this way and that. The white light splutters and pours. Plate-glass windows. Carnations; crysanthemums. Ivy in dark gardens. Milk carts at the door. Wherever I go, mysterious figures, I see you, turning the corner, mothers and sons; you, you, you. I hasten, I follow. This, I fancy, must be the sea. Grey is the landscape; dim as

ashes; the water murmurs and moves. If I fall on my knees, if I go
through the ritual, the ancient antics, it's you, unknown figures, you
I adore; if I open my arms, it's you I embrace, you I draw to me –
adorable world! (121)

This reassertion of the narrative consciousness at the story's
close indicates the value of a characterization based on an
encounter with the subject, even if the external facts do not
appear to work in concert. The fiction which is responsive to the
human subject, in other words, has a value which is not
dependent upon a transparently realistic portrayal of the real-
life context to which it refers.

As in 'Moments of Being' Woolf ensures that the metafictional aspect is contained beneath a story surface which
operates on its own terms, though again the assured manipulation of fictional form is an inherent aspect of the artistic
quest. This scenario of fellow train travellers offers an archetypal
story situation in which personal histories may unfold: restrictive social mores usually have a bearing on the action, most
obviously as a source of tension, but also as a catalyst. The
treatment can be humorous (as in Saki's 'The Mouse' in which
Theodoric Voler suffers great anguish at having to strip in front
of his female travelling companion, to retrieve an irksome
rodent, only to discover that the lady is blind); the situation also
offers scope for more fundamental subjects, as in Maupassant's
'Idyll' where a starving young man relieves his own suffering,
and that of the overweight, lactating peasant woman who
shares his carriage, by drinking her excess milk. In 'An
Unwritten Novel' restrictive mores provide a naturalistic
narrative situation, which develops in a more symbolic direction: the ubiquitous trappings of train compartments – the
newspaper as shield, the discomfiting eye contact, the aura of
another passenger – are Woolfian symbols with a sound naturalistic basis. The reversal, when it comes, provides the
traditional story crisis-point which is subsequently dismissed.

'An Unwritten Novel' is about the potential value of fictional
narrative, a value which may reside above and beyond its real-
life stimuli. This idea is treated more concretely in the third
story belonging to this group, 'The Lady in the Looking-Glass:
A Reflection' (1929). The piece concerns the narrator's attempt

to uncover the character of Isabella Tyson, the 'lady' of the story's title. Her true nature eludes the narrator until a close-up image of Isabella in her looking-glass is seen, an image which exposes her as 'perfectly empty' (225) and which, apparently, cuts through the mystery surrounding her. The story alludes to Tennyson's 'The Lady of Shalott' in which the Lady is 'cursed' when she looks beyond the 'shadows of the world' in her mirror and sees reality for the first time. Woolf uses the motif of the mirror in a similar investigation into the tension between reality and withdrawal, though for her, typically, this investigation is overtly metafictional.

The power of the looking-glass, for Woolf, is clearly a metaphor for artistic creation, the pursuit of the real Isabella Tyson being another quest for Mrs Brown. The special focusing capacity of the looking-glass, and its implications, are investigated in the opening paragraphs: the narrator, sitting in Isabella's drawing-room, finds the room 'full of... nocturnal creatures' (221), and feels that 'the room had its passions and rages and envies and sorrows coming over it and clouding it, like a human being. Nothing stayed the same for two seconds together' (221). The narrator's unmediated perceptions of the world form a complete contrast with the world reflected in the looking-glass:

But, outside, the looking-glass reflected the hall table, the sunflowers, the garden path so accurately and so fixedly that they seemed held there in their reality unescapably. It was a strange contrast – all changing here, all stillness there. One could not help looking from one to the other. (221)

These contrasting states provide a distinction between the raw materials of life and the way in which they are transformed in the creative act, the same distinction which informs 'An Unwritten Novel', but which is here treated more concretely in the sense that it is supplied with a visual metaphor. The recurrence of the visual metaphor in short story theory, and in *Dubliners*, has been noted in previous chapters. Woolf's use of the looking-glass has affinities with Joyce's gnomon in the sense that it relates to the nature of characterization, rather than, specifically, to the overall 'shape' of a story. By extension, however, the reflection (like the Joycean gnomon) can be taken as a metaphor for the story as a whole, since it deals exclusively with a single character, a single 'picture'; and, on the face of it, this visual metaphor seems to represent the kind of evidence that might be amassed in support of the unity aesthetic, the concept of the story as coherent artefact. But, like the problematic techniques of characterization in *Dubliners*, Woolf's use of the looking-glass is, finally, disruptive, a point that emerges clearly from the story's equivocal ending.

As with the other 'Mr Bennett and Mrs Brown' stories the structure of 'The Lady in the Looking-Glass' closely follows the revelatory ending convention, and again the actual content of the revelation is subordinate to the mode of discovery: the narrative consciousness represents the perceiving *potential* of the literary artist. The symbolism is complicated by the looking-glass as metaphor for the artistic *process*. The metaphorical logic of the story is straightforward: the narrator (narrative consciousness) experiences difficulty in attempting to impose a meaningful structure on amorphous reality or on the character of Isabella without the mediation of the looking-glass (representing a rigid artistic process). The convergence of narrative consciousness and a fixed compositional principle occurs at the story's conclusion as Isabella walks up the garden path, her reflection in the glass becoming larger and more meaningful as she approaches the house until, standing by the mirror, a genuine characterization is possible:

All the time she became larger and larger in the looking-glass, more and more completely the person into whose mind one had been trying to penetrate. One verified her by degrees – fitted the qualities one had discovered into this visible body.... At last there she was, in the hall. She stopped dead. She stood by the table. She stood perfectly still. At once the looking-glass began to pour over her a light that seemed to fix her; that seemed like some acid to bite off the unessential and superficial and to leave only the truth. (225)

The story's conclusion, however, is ambiguous, and this ambiguity stresses Woolf's preoccupation with, and uncertainty about, the mediatory role of fiction. The discovery that Isabella, the 'woman herself', is 'perfectly empty' (225), is a reminder that the writer is always apt to fail to achieve genuine characterization in the process of composition and be left with a void. The visual metaphor of the looking-glass becomes unreliable: Woolf, investigating the complexity of the mediatory role of fiction, implicitly rejects a simple notion of art as reflection. The equivocal nature of this ending hints also at Woolf's own uncertainty and vacillation with regard to the nature of 'life'. In her diaries she wrote: 'Now is life very solid, or very shifting? I am haunted by the two contradictions.'[14]

A later story, 'The Shooting Party' (1932), stands on the periphery of this group. This is another piece in which a fellow train traveller inspires a narrator to supply a personal history and background. In this case the narrative dislocates itself from the original scene and becomes a surreal satirical portrayal of squires and hunting, of male aggression and oppression and of the women emotionally disfigured by this world. It reads as a powerfully recalled nightmare with a validity of its own. The narrative invention is what counts here as the original stimulus becomes forgotten.

All of these stories show Woolf writing, ostensibly, in a traditional short story vein, but subverting the plot-based story to her own considerations on artistic composition. This subversion of generic types is at one with 'the sound of breaking and falling, crashing and destruction' which Woolf discerned in the writing of some of her contemporaries.[15] Each story enacts the problem highlighted in 'Mr Bennett and Mrs Brown', an enactment which depends upon certain expectations, on the part of the reader, derived from conventional story types which are subsequently undercut. Thus in 'An Unwritten Novel' one has to recognize the convention of plot reversal before understanding Woolf's point that there is actually no necessary reversal. In 'The Lady in the Looking-Glass' artistic perception and creation are symbolized and finally merged in a story which depends upon the same plot convention where the narrative works towards an apparently significant, but finally problematic, culminating event. The formal disruption apparent in this group of stories reveals an obvious historical determinant: the restrictive ideology of those literary conventions which Woolf attacks explicitly in 'Mr Bennett and Mrs Brown'.

Woolf's dependence upon generic structures and conventions

is a constant feature of her short stories, although in the more experimental pieces the gesture to disruption becomes more prominent. These are the stories I link with the 'Modern Fiction' essay – 'Kew Gardens', 'A Haunted House', 'Monday or Tuesday' and 'Blue and Green' – where, in a quest for the 'uncircumscribed spirit' of life, the narrative persona itself is affected by the dissolution and merging of identity. Woolf's equivocation, and development of narrative fallibility, carried on discursively in the other group, here infests the very syntax. This gives rise to a splintered and complex reading experience, and this is very much the point of the art.

A story which stands on the periphery of this more innovative group is 'The Evening Party' (1918), a piece which provides a bridge between the discursive and the actual explorations of narrative fallibility. 'The Evening Party' is really about its narrator's encounter with the 'uncircumscribed spirit' of life, and the disruption of the encounter caused by the discourses of the party. The narrator arrives at the party with a companion capable of providing rewarding communication. The ideality of this companion suggests that it might be a persona imagined by the narrator, a self-projection facilitating an exploratory dialogue which actual conversation in the story seems to prohibit. Repeatedly the exploration by the narrator of impressions received is interrupted by other guests at the party whose collective conversation betrays a restricted outlook.

The opening paragraph establishes a questing narrative voice, a narrator who makes bold macrocosmic–microcosmic connections. The extraordinary opening description entails a withdrawn description of the planet itself – 'there, rising in a mound against the sky with trees upon it, is the earth' – but this universal vision soon focuses on the minute detail of 'the bark of the apple tree [where] the moths quiver drawing sugar through the long black thread of the proboscis'. Having been transported, as it were, to a particular place (and with a consciousness of this particular in a universal scheme) the narrator now seeks out the party: 'Where are we? Which house can be the house of the party?' (96). The moth image, as a focus of narrative attention, is an important, and recurring feature in Woolf's work: it is an all-embracing symbol of creativity, a symbol which 'induces not only the subjective cycle of creation but its object, the work of art', and which 'is a way of suggesting the very motion of creativity, the stirring of ideas as they rise into consciousness'.[16] The story, then, locates itself in the particular through the moth motif, a detail which indicates an analysis of the process of creation. This focusing is enhanced by wave imagery, a poetic device which is also representative, for Woolf, of the ebb and flow of the perceiving mind: 'The flowing silvery clouds look down upon Atlantic waves. The wind blows soft round the corner of the street, lifting my cloak, holding it gently in the air and then letting it sink and droop as the sea now swells and brims over the rocks and again withdraws. – The street is almost empty' (96). The opening of the story, in effect, is a frame which establishes the narrative point of view: the impression of a frame is reinforced at the end by a narrative withdrawal and the recurring resonant wave motif (101).

Yet this frame-tale structure is subtly undermined. As Woolf dramatizes her preoccupation with creativity, the narrator, as an embodiment of the creating, perceiving mind, encounters other points of view: the story's own episodic nature forms a kind of wave pattern in which heightened narrative reflection is repeatedly disrupted by contact with distracting mundane voices. The structure is thus an ebb and flow of poetic flight punctuated by diurnal reality, and in this way the narrative frame is extended into the rest of the story, and is presented in contact with other voices. The narrator and her companion are initially withdrawn from the action of the party and merely observe:

'Come into the corner and let us talk.'
'Wonderful! Wonderful human beings! Spiritual and wonderful!'
'But they don't exist. Don't you see the pond through the Professor's head? Don't you see the swan swimming through Mary's skirt?'
'I can fancy little burning roses dotted about them.'
'The little burning roses are only like the fireflies we've seen together in Florence, sprinkled in the wisteria, floating atoms of fire, burning as they float – burning, not thinking.'
'Burning not thinking. And so all the books at the back of us. Here's Shelley – here's Blake. Cast them up into the air and see their poems descend like golden parachutes twinkling and turning and letting fall their rain of star-shaped blossoms.'

'Shall I quote you Shelley? "Away! the moor is dark beneath the moon – "'

'Wait, wait! Don't condense our fine atmoshphere into drops of rain spattering the pavement. Let us still breathe in the fire dust.'

'Fireflies among the wisteria.' (97)

This celebration of instantaneous, impressionistic perception is summarized by the image of 'fireflies among the wisteria'. Nadine Gordimer has argued, using the same image, that such instantaneous illumination is the essence of value in the short story form, its ability to express 'the quality of human life, where contact is... like the flash of fireflies, in and out, now here, now there, in darkness. Short-story writers see by the light of the flash; theirs is the art of the only thing one can be sure of – the present moment.'[17] It is precisely this type of certitude, however, that the story challenges. The narrator and her companion reject the interpolation of a different discourse – the poetry of Shelley – realizing that it will alter their 'atmosphere', 'condensing' it 'into drops of rain'. Yet the looming professor forces a dialogue with an alternative voice, an authoritative one bound up with the appreciation of canonical literature, a voice foreshadowed by the quotation from Shelley, and now adopted (with more than a hint of parody) by the narrator who informs the professor of a profound interest in 'the question of Shelley's commas'. The professor, a desembodied voice, like all the story's characters, blusters disjointedly as he sets himself to respond to this 'matter of some importance' (97). The ensuing conversation enacts a conflict between Woolfian literary dissatisfaction and canonical conformity:

'These classics – Shelley, Keats; Browne; Gibbon; is there a page that you can quote entire, a paragraph perfect, a sentence even that one can't see amended by the pen of God or man?'

'S-s-s-sh, Madam. Your objection has weight but lacks sobriety. Moreover your choice of names – In what chamber of the spirit can you consort Shelley with Gibbon?' (97–8)

This discussion of perfection is directed by other voices at the party: the colloquists are disillusioned by 'the conversation of these ladies, earnest and benevolent, with exalted views upon the destiny of the negro who is at this moment toiling beneath the lash to procure rubber for some of our friends engaged in agreeable conversation here' (98). A political reality taints the discussion of aesthetic perfection, because the enjoyment of this perfection demands the exclusion of such realities. This, at least, is the partitionist's view, voiced by the professor: the narrator wants to investigate the alternative, a perspective of inclusion, a perfection which would not be embarrassed by social injustice. The professor withdraws leaving the narrator and her companion to discuss his loss of vision, a loss which is prognostic of their own:

'The professor is already gone? Poor old man!'
'But at his age how could he still possess what we at ours are already losing. I mean –'
'Yes?'
'Don't you remember in early childhood, when, in play or talk, as one stepped across the puddle or reached the window on the landing, some imperceptible shock froze the universe to a solid ball of crystal which one held for a moment – I have some mystical belief that all time past and future too, the tears and powdered ashes of generations clotted to a ball; then we were absolute and entire; nothing then was excluded; that was certainty – happiness. But later these crystal globes dissolve as one holds them: some one talks of negroes. See what comes of trying to say what one means! Nonsense!' (98–9)

A state of inclusive receptivity is here envisaged, a state which represents an innocence that has been corrupted. In the 'fallen' state perceptions are subject to division and fragmentation and the 'crystal globes' of a posited total consciousness 'dissolve'. The talk of negroes ('negro' is a categorical term which fragments the human totality) is evidence of this fallen state.

There is a strong parallel here with Fredric Jameson's notion of 'primitive communism', a state of thinking in which human society is seen as a totality. The fall from this state of grace, for Jameson, is occasioned by the social organization of capitalism, the effects of commodity reification, and the concomitant reduction of human beings to the level of material commodity.[18] 'The Evening Party' offers no overt political analysis, but, covertly, it makes the same analysis in alluding to slavery and exploitation as an index of a modern fragmented consciousness, a disjointedness also implicated in the professor's hierarchial literary canon. The ideological limitation of a particular approach to literary language is thus related to broader issues of ideological control. The story's own subversive gesture is the disruption of a stable and delimited literary discourse, and this delimitation is encapsulated in the views and voice of the professor.

For Woolf, it is the fragmentation caused by hierarchical categorization which prevents her from approaching the 'luminous halo' of life, and which confines literature to be merely 'the record of our discontent', as the narrator of 'The Evening Party' puts it (99). It is important to note that this 'fragmentation' results in apparent unity, such as the hermetically sealed language of the professor. The alternative state, of inclusiveness, will need to disrupt such unitary, authoritative language and, paradoxically, must appear more fragmented. This project is here taken a stage further than in the 'Mr Bennett and Mrs Brown' stories. The problem is again dramatized in the sense that a conventional representation of literary value (the trite party talk which is a parody of reactionary canonical beliefs) is juxtaposed with a challenging, alternative representation of value, but in this story Woolf explores a style of writing which *embodies* that alternative. Having suffered enough of the party's discourses the narrator rushes into the night in pursuit of her already departed companion. They are reunited and the story ends where it started with their impressionistic assessment of the evening atmosphere:

'Don't stay talking. Let's be off. Through the garden; your hand in mine.'
'Away. The moon is dark upon the moor. Away, we'll breast them, those waves of darkness crested by the trees, rising for ever, lonely and dark. The lights rise and fall; the water's thin as air; the moon's behind it. D'you sink? D'you rise? D'you see the islands? Alone with me.' (101)

The familiar Woolfian motif of sea imagery, used to represent the registering of stimuli upon consciousness, is here evident in the analogy of impressions ebbing and flowing. The narrative receptivity to the rise and fall of impressions, read as an investigation of the creative literary act, casts an implicitly ironic shadow (by virtue of its non-judgemental nature) on the contrasting, hierarchical literary judgements of the canon-bound professor ('In what chamber of the spirit can you consort Shelley with Gibbon?' (98).)

There is another 'wave' pattern in the story, a 'peak' and 'trough' rhythm which reflects the encounter between the voice of the narrator and the discourses of the party. This dialogue (rather than the dialogue between the narrator and her arguably imaginary companion) constitutes the main productive conflict of the story. It is productive, not in terms of the outcome (a failure of exchange and a subsequent retreat), but in the sense that this dialogue generates the main satirical event: a counterpoint of poetic flight and bathetic descent.

The dialogic nature of 'The Evening Party', then, is twofold: the overt narratorial dialogue creates the appropriate texture for the more oppositional dialogue concerning literary language and value. The juxtaposition, even the fusion, of disparate voices (most brilliantly achieved in *The Waves*) is one of Woolf's major contributions to the development of modern fiction. In the short story, however, this deliberate dialogizing of narrative discourse highlights a fundamental generic obstacle.

The conflict of voices in 'The Evening Party' represents an attempt to examine discourse as an interactive, unstable phenomenon. In effect, Woolf is conducting an examination into how a unitary language might be decentred by the discourses which surround it, a view of language usually associated with Bakhtin. In the previous chapter an account was given of Bakhtin's concept of language, as always involving the conflict between unifying, centripetal forces, and disruptive, centrifugal forces. 'The Evening Party' dramatizes the resistance of a unitary language to a discourse which undermines it, but, in another sense, the story is definitely dialogized. This element of disunity concerns structure and form, elements that can also be examined in the light of Bakhtin's ideas.

For Bakhtin, the novel is the primary multi-voiced, or

'heterglot' cultural phenomenon: 'Diversity of voices and heteroglossia enter the novel and organize themselves within it into a structured artistic system. This constitutes the distinguishing feature of the novel as a genre.'[19]

If this is an inherent generic feature then a deliberate utilization of diverse voices by the novelist, such as Woolf effects in *The Waves*, might be said to be a technique operating in concert with the available formal possibilities. Bakhtin, however, makes no comment on the short story and so one has to be wary when appropriating his ideas in this context. He does, however, make a vital distinction between poetic and novelistic discourse which may be helpful here. The short story has repeatedly been described by critics as a form which is more 'poetic' than the novel, a form which (following Poe's 'unity of effect' doctrine) is seen to be most effective when it ties its elements together to convey a single impression. In 'Discourse in the Novel' Bakhtin contrasts the novel with poetry in terms that suggest where the short story – *as it is usually defined* – might lie in his schema: he talks of 'the unity and hermetic quality of the surface of poetic style, and of the unitary language that this style posits'.[20] Where the discourse of the novel is dialogic, poetic discourse is monologic.

This distinction has affinities with a perceived dichotomy between short story and novel. Whether or not poetic language is inherently 'unitary' Bakhtin is surely right to point out that there are certain formal properties of high poetic style, such as metre and rhyme, which tend to impose converging effects and which, therefore, help to create a 'tension-filled unity of language'.[21] There are analogous formal properties of the short story – the frame story, the single action, the simple plot reversal – which are familiar devices in the well-plotted, unified story, and which tend to invite a monologic governing narrative discourse, conscious of the controlling structure and so more clearly directed than the discourse of the novel.

Woolf's pursuit of a dialogic short story narrative thus suggests a conflict between structure and style, a conflict defined above as a simultaneous rejection and utilization of convention. In 'The Evening Party' this conflict is manifest in the frame-story structure which introduces, and comments upon, the intervening action, and the dialogized discourse of the frame which dissipates its conventional authority. (Although the narrator and her companion seem to share one voice, they still engage in dialogue – in the exploration of ideas rather than in simple statement.) In its own uncertainty the frame-dialogue offers the paradoxical conclusion that conclusiveness is inapposite: the frame is fully utilized yet it is extended, brought into contact with its subject, and so its distance is eroded, its unitary authority undermined.

Despite the dissolution of the fictional frame, 'The Evening Party' fails to create an integration of voices, but it does stage a collision of centripetal and centrifugal forces, an instance of dialogized heteroglossia. The story's subject – the search for a narrative voice capable of approaching a putative unfragmented human totality – is thus characterized by an exploration of that area where 'discourse lives,... on the boundary between its own context and another, alien, context'.[22]

An interesting point of contact between Woolf and Bakhtin is Dostoevsky, a writer who was influential for both. In various reviews of Constance Garnett's translations of Dostoevsky, Woolf attempts to define her conviction of the importance of 'this great genius', usually focusing on his innovation.[23] In 1917 she writes that 'one finishes any book by Dostoevsky with the feeling that... the range is so vast that some new conception of the novelist's art remains with us in the end'.[24] Woolf is more fulsome in her praise of Dostoevsky's novels that of his stories, but her comments on the shorter fiction are revealing. In a 1917 review of *The Eternal Husband and Other Stories* she writes approvingly of Dostoevsky's ability to capture mental processes:

From the crowd of objects pressing upon our attention we select now this one, now that one, weaving them inconsequently into our thought; the associations of a word perhaps make another loop in the line, from which we spring back again to a different section of our main thought, and the whole process seems both inevitable and perfectly lucid. But if we try to construct our mental processes later, we find that the links between one thought and another are submerged. The chain is sunk out of sight and only the leading points emerge to mark the course.

Alone among writers Dostoevsky has the power of reconstructing these most swift and complicated states of mind, of re-thinking the whole train of thought in all its speed, now as it flashes into light, now as it lapses into darkness; for he is able to follow not only the vivid streak of achieved thought but to suggest the dim and populous underworld of the mind's consciousness where desires and impulses are moving blindly beneath the sod.[25]

'Intuition' is Woolf's definition of this capacity, which is, however, inconsistent and can result in a fiction like 'The Double' which, for all its 'brilliancy and astonishing ingenuity', is nevertheless a 'kind of elaborate failure'.[26] A way of defining the 'intuition' that Woolf detected in Dostoevsky – his capacity to render 'complicated states of mind' – is suggested in Bakhtin's *Problems of Dostoevsky's Poetics*. Bakhtin's comments on 'The Double', based on the conviction that the narrative consists of 'the hero's dialogues with himself', are particularly interesting: he considers the fiction to be an 'interior dialogue' in which the hero Golyadkin's 'inner conflict is dramatized' by the actual appearance of a double.[27] The double, for Bakhtin, is an objectification of the hero's need to conduct 'comforting dialogues with himself', a tendency which, before the double appears, Golyadkin uses to 'compensate for the inadequate recognition he receives' from his 'other' self.[28] The story's dialogic principle extends to the 'transferral of words from one mouth to another, where the content remains the same although the tone and ultimate meaning are changed'. This 'fundamental device of Dostoevsky's' involves 'the sound of parody or ridicule' generated by self-recognition. More important, perhaps, is Bakhtin's location of Dostoevsky's implicit dialogue with his literary heritage, a dialogue which takes the form of numerous 'parodic and semiparodic allusions to various works of Gogol' which 'are directly interwoven with a mimicry of Golyadkin'. This parody amounts to a rejection of a 'conventionalized discourse' with a 'monologic orientation';[29] as we have seen, a similar purpose is fulfilled by Woolf's narrator in 'The Evening Party', especially when she adopts the parodied discourse of conventional literary appreciation. The connection cannot be pushed too far, but there is an obvious affinity between

Dostoevsky's development of 'inner conflict', and Woolf's use of dialogic opposition. It may be significant that 'The Evening Party' was drafted in the year following Woolf's review of *The Eternal Husband*, the collection which contains 'The Double'.[30]

To find a style capable of approaching the inclusiveness called for in 'The Evening Party' is Woolf's unrealizable, Utopian dream, but in 'Kew Gardens' (1917–18), Woolf's most carefully crafted short story, she comes as close as she can to achieving such a style. 'Kew Gardens' is, formally, a unified, highly structured (enclosed) piece of writing, yet this structure is deployed to reinforce, *thematically*, the contrary, all-embracing impetus of the prose itself.

The notion of inclusiveness hinges upon a symbolic presentation of humanity as a single entity, and as an entity which is merged with the natural environment. The arrangement of the piece indicates this thematic concern: four different couples walk past a particular flowerbed, the description of which is interspersed with the human drama. There are four passages of natural description to balance the appearance of the four couples, and the human (H) and natural (N) elements are symmetrically arranged (N-H-N-H-H-N-H-N). Each of the couples represents a different type of relationship, and again the sequence is palindromic, mixed couples appearing first and last: a married couple appears first, followed by two male friends then two female friends, while a young man and woman bring up the rear. The diversity indicates the intention to represent as broad a social sweep as possible in the space available.

All this careful structuring and juxtaposition is submerged in a complex and interwoven narrative. Smooth transitions from the natural to the human world are effected by some descriptive point of contact or comparison. Thus the appearance of the married couple, which interrupts the initial flowerbed scene, is merged with the action of the garden, their 'irregular movement' being 'not unlike that of the white and blue butterflies who crossed the turf in zig-zag flights from bed to bed' (90). The story contains many descriptive details like this: one of the elderly ladies stands swaying while watching some flowers, in sympathy with their movement (93); Simon remembers having

imagined the movement of a dragonfly in the garden to have
determined his erstwhile lover's response to his proposal (90–1);
as Simon and his family group recede, the light and shade plays
upon them just as it was seen to fall on pebbles and creatures in
the flowerbed (90, 91). This descriptive linking is pervasive and,
finally, the natural world envelops the human, all of the
characters having 'both substance and colour dissolved in the
green-blue atmosphere' (95). The broader significance of this
design becomes apparent at the story's conclusion in which the
combined voices in the garden, human and natural, reach out
and merge with the sound of the surrounding city. This
interconnection of the garden with its urban environment is
anticipated by two descriptive touches; these are the mention of
a thrush behaving 'like a mechanical bird' and an aeroplane's
drone being considered 'the voice of the summer sky' (95), a
reversal which conjoins the natural and the mechanical, and
which anticipates the final thematic development:

Voices, yes, voices, wordless voices, breaking the silence suddenly with
such depth of contentment, such passion of desire, or, in the voices of
children, such freshness of surprise; breaking the silence? But there
was no silence; all the time the motor omnibuses were turning their
wheels and changing their gear; like a vast nest of Chinese boxes all of
wrought steel turning ceaselessly one within another the city mur-
mured; on the top of which the voices cried aloud and the petals of
myriads of flowers flashed their colours into the air. (95)

On a thematic level, this is the unified world-view that the
poetic inner logic of the story has been working insistently
towards. This is the outer layer of the system of chinese boxes:
just as the action in the flowerbed was the microcosm of the
macrocosm of the human drama, so is this poetic integration
recontained within the human social context at large, symbolized here by the murmuring city.

The story's thematic concern with a merged human totality
is pursued through its narrative styles which embrace the
different points of view of the various characters. There is a
third-person narrator, who orchestrates the action, but there is
no sense of an unequivocal authoritative centre, because of the
variety of voices: interior monologue and direct speech are

juxtaposed, and sometimes integrated within the third-person narrative.

In addition to this implicit questioning and problematizing of narrative authority, the effect of words on the characters in the story is made problematic, as are the circumstances of their own discourses. For Eleanor and Simon the presence of the garden itself inspires their recollections, while for the old man in the male couple, a flower provokes colloquy:

> After looking at [the flower] for a moment in some confusion the old man bent his ear to it and seemed to answer a voice speaking from it, for he began talking about the forests of Uruguay which he had visited hundreds of years ago in company with the most beautiful young woman in Europe. (92–3)

Even if one assumes that the old man is ranting (an irrelevant question in any case) the important point is that a vital recollection of youth and happiness has been elicited. The verity and semantic logic of this 'answer' (or indeed of the flower's 'voice') are subordinate to the mood that is communicated. As with the reveries of Eleanor and Simon the discourse is inextricably bound up with the atmosphere of the garden. In the case of the elderly women, semantics are explicitly rejected as the sole determinant of the power of utterance:

> The ponderous woman looked through the pattern of falling words at the flowers standing cool, firm and upright in the earth, with a curious expression.... So the heavy woman came to a standstill opposite the oval-shaped flower-bed, and ceased even to pretend to listen to what the other woman was saying. She stood there letting the words fall over her, swaying the top part of her body slowly backwards and forwards, looking at the flowers. (93)

Words here are shown to have a palpable, even hypnotic effect above and beyond their role as signifiers in a linguistic system. The effect of the words is linked with the movement of the flowers. On the following page a similar linkage occurs:

> The couple stood still on the edge of the flower-bed, and together pressed the end of her parasol deep down into the soft earth. The action and the fact that his hand rested on the top of hers expressed their feelings in a strange way, as these short insignificant words also expressed something, words with short wings for their heavy body of

meaning, inadequate to carry them far and thus alighting awkwardly
upon the very common objects that surrounded them and were to
their inexperienced touch so massive: but who knows (so they thought
as they pressed the parasol into the earth) what precipices aren't
concealed in them, or what slopes of ice don't shine in the sun on the
other side? (94)

This 'inadequacy' of words may be a metaphorical commentary on the undirectable nature of language and the
interference involved in its reception. Again, Woolf seems to be
investigating the properties of discourse in a similar way to the
Bakhtin circle: according to Vološinov/Bakhtin, 'the evaluative
reception of another's utterance' is determined by the receptor's
'inner speech', and this is inevitably idiosyncratic since all of the
receptor's personal experiences and 'so-called apperceptive
background' are 'encoded in his [or her] inner speech'. In
broad terms, 'this active inner-speech reception proceeds in two
directions: first the received utterance is framed within a
context of factual commentary... second, a reply is prepared.
Both the preparation of the reply (*internal retort*) and the *factual
commentary* are organically fused in the unity of active reception'.[31] Reception is determined by the interference and
distortion of inner speech, and it seems that an understanding of
this kind of interference lies behind the reflections in the story on
the 'unknowability' of words: 'who knows... what precipices
aren't concealed in them, or what slopes of ice don't shine in the
sun on the other side?'.

The descriptive correspondence between the human and the
natural is continued in the image of the winged words, the
movement of which suggests that of insects and which recalls
Simon's imagined identification of the flight of the dragonfly
with the movement of his erstwhile lover's thoughts and
responses. Here the theme of unity through the amalgamation
of the human and natural worlds is allied to the investigation of
language ('words with short wings'), and this implies an
understanding of the inclusive complexity of discourse, and its
social location. There is an affinity here with Bakhtin's assertion
that 'the authentic environment of an utterance, the environment in which it lives and takes shape, is dialogized heteroglossia'.[32]

In the passage quoted (from p. 94) there is an ambiguity which plays a significant part in this thematic connection: it is not clear whether the final 'them' refers to the 'insignificant words' or to the 'common objects'. Since, however, the poetic design of the story as a whole has been geared to stressing the identity of the human and the natural, of the different 'voices' in the garden, the ambiguity needs no resolution: both words and natural objects are encompassed in the single pronoun.

In the final paragraph the story's thematic strands are clearly intertwined. The merging of the human and the natural is overlaid on the blending of discourses, until all sounds – conversational, mechanical, natural – become 'voices' in the garden. In this respect one can attach a garden-of-Eden symbolism to 'Kew Gardens'. If the story is read as an attempt to create a dialogized 'prelapsarian' discourse of inclusiveness (the theme treated in 'The Evening Party'), then the garden's ability to merge diverse voices would seem to symbolize such a discourse. Further, since the garden's urban locale is insisted upon by the mechanical voices and the concluding chinese-box motif, then the notion that the sought-after discourse must represent social heteroglossia – a matrix of social forces, and a kind of human totality – is reinforced by the garden's situation in the centre of the murmuring city.

Woolf's disembodied and multi-voiced narrative style is especially apparent in her prose poems, though even here formal conventions have a significant role to play. The very brief piece 'Monday or Tuesday' (1920–1), consisting of six short paragraphs, is another consideration of consciousness in relation to literary composition, and Woolf again employs a story frame to structure her meaning.

The title 'Monday or Tuesday' is a phrase which also appears in the passage in 'Modern Fiction' concerning 'an ordinary mind on an ordinary day'.[33] The title tacitly announces the intention to dismiss a rigid structuring of experience: the labels attached to diurnal units of time are, by suggestion, irrelevant, since either Monday or Tuesday (or any other name) will apply equally well as a label.

The heron in the story has been described as representative of narrative consciousness, a judgement which obscures an important distinction.[34] The heron, 'lazy and indifferent' (137), glides over the heterogeneous world much as Woolf described 'an ordinary mind on an ordinary day' receiving 'a myriad impressions'.[35] The heron, then, would seem to be a symbol of such an ordinary perceiving mind, but one must be careful here to distinguish between ordinary consciousness and narrative consciousness, which is neither lazy nor indifferent in Woolf even if, in its quest for truth, the narrative consciousness must attempt to recreate the 'myriad impressions' that would have been amassed by the mind in a passive state.

This distinction between, and ultimate convergence of, questing narrative consciousness and passive receiving mind is what the structure of 'Monday or Tuesday' insists upon. The symbolic heron is employed as a framing device which envelops the intervening four paragraphs of urgent description. Impressions are reported feverishly by a consciousness 'desiring truth' (137), and different sounds and discourses are contained in parentheses, including mechanical city sounds, a clock striking, and snippets of conversation: 'this foggy weather – Sugar? No, thank you – The commonwealth of the future' (137). The concluding paragraph steps us out of the tone of urgent quest to the plane of the symbolic heron, the plane of heterogeneous totality which recontains the preceding narrative: 'lazy and indifferent the heron returns; the sky veils her stars; then bares them' (137). The story's 'truth' is that truth is multifarious and amorphous, affording glimpses of something which soon dissolve.

Again, the conflict of monologic and heteroglot discourses determines the effect of the piece. The frame device of the symbolic heron, which recontains the multi-voiced narrative (just as the heron passes over the world of mental stimuli), provides a yardstick against which the intervening discourse can be measured. This stable point of reference, which offers a unified meaning, represents, structurally, a univocal position and indicates a covert appeal to monologic discourse by the organizing artist. The cadence of 'Monday or Tuesday', perceptively described here by Avrom Fleishman, reflects this disruption and reassertion of the univocal 'chord': 'the finale of

"Monday or Tuesday" comes not merely with the rever-
beration of a previously heard chord but by the reestablishment
of a prior condition; the dynamic equilibrium broken at the
beginning sets in again as language dies away at the close'.[36]

'Monday or Tuesday' clearly has much in common with
'The Evening Party' and 'Kew Gardens'. Since, once more,
the thematic concern is with the conflict of discourses, the
rehearsal of this conflict in terms of narrative texture clashing
with formal controls results in a well-designed piece in which
theme can be read in terms of formal disunity.

Obviously, the kind of 'compromise' I am delineating here is
inevitable: the expression of a single meaning (even the message
that meaning is indefinable is univocal) demands a form within
which to work. Perhaps the attempt to capture in prose the
'luminous halo' of consciousness must involve 'a series of gig-
lamps' of some kind.[37] Woolf's major novels depend upon a
concealed organizing structure: the chiming of the clock which
provides a central reference and point of internal/external
crossover in *Mrs Dalloway*, the strategic references, in *Jacob's
Room*, to Jacob's belongings which enable us to approach his
character and, of course, the symbolic lighthouse in *To the
Lighthouse*, are prime examples of this.

My point is not to emphasize this truism, but to highlight the
special significance and positive utilization of formal controls in
the short stories. Here Woolf makes use of existing convention to
a degree unmatched in the rest of her work. Indeed, the whole
point of the most successful stories depends upon the formal
effect which is crucial to the modernist short story, the special
generic dissonance between fictional convention and its subversion. When Woolf abandons this approach in an attempt to
leave tradition behind the result is less successful. This is the case
with another prose poem, 'Blue and Green' (1921), which is an
imagistic sequence of impressions without formal coherence or
obvious external reference. In this case, freedom from convention has been won at the cost of intelligibility.

Where her short stories are productive, Woolf is always
challenging and developing the capacities of the fictional form.
Her fundamental compositional principle is to adapt fictional

convention in the process of examining the need to transcend it. This principle is exemplified in 'The Mark on the Wall' (1917–21), perhaps the quintessential Woolf short story.

The narrative consists of the reporting of the narrator's stream-of-consciousness, continually brought back to the time and place of the story's opening by the nagging question of what the mark on the wall might be. This constant centre of the story constitutes a reference to a conventional short story organization. The formal convention is the anecdotal one of a puzzle announced at the outset and resolved at the conclusion. Oscar Wilde toys with this convention in his story 'The Sphinx Without a Secret' in which the secretive behaviour of a widow, suggesting an affair, is exposed as the vacuous behaviour of 'a woman with a mania for mystery'; the notion of mystery in characterization is overthrown in a simple narrative.[38] The same riddle or puzzle convention provides the basis of 'The Mark on the Wall', but the subversion is far more complex since it is effected through the narrative stance. The puzzle becomes subordinate to the narrator's reflections, and the discovery that the mark is a snail is added, almost as an afterthought. Although there are times when one's thoughts do seem to revolve around a central focus in this way, the actual *structure* of the story is also a fabrication which allows the analysis of the perceiving mind: an ambivalent use is made of the puzzle structure which is implicitly questioned even while utilized. The story provides an appropriate means of evaluating the reductive, puzzle-solving approach to the short story, discussed in the opening chapter: such an approach plainly lacks the sophistication necessary to deal with such a story which examines the very superficiality of its own puzzle.

The story treats its central problem in a discursive manner. The narrator virtually pronounces the impossibility of presenting a train of thought unfettered by constraining structures:

Here is Nature once more at her old game of self-preservation. This train of thought, she perceives, is threatening mere waste of energy, even some collision with reality, for who will ever be able to lift a finger against Whitaker's Table of Precedency? The Archbishop of Canterbury is followed by the Lord High Chancellor; The Lord High

Chancellor is followed by the Archbishop of York. Everybody follows somebody, such is the philosophy of Whitaker; and the great thing is to know who follows whom. Whitaker knows, and let that, so Nature counsels, comfort you, instead of enraging you; and if you can't be comforted, if you must shatter this hour of peace, think of the mark on the wall. (88)

At this point the story proffers its own piece of succinct exegesis (a prize example of self-reflexive modernism). The narrator's 'train of thought', the story's focus, in threatening 'some collision with reality' (the perpetual Woolfian goal), is contravening a 'natural' law of order, of hierarchical structure represented by Whitaker's Table of Precedency. The story explicitly makes this transgression a feminist issue: it is stated that the kind of thinking which establishes Whitaker's Table represents 'the masculine point of view which governs our lives' (86). This concept of a predetermined structure which governs reality is analogous to the approach of the Edwardian novelists, as criticized in 'Mr Bennett and Mrs Brown': faced with reality personified (Mrs Brown), 'Mr. Wells, in his passion to make her what she ought to be, would [not] waste a thought upon her as she is', while 'Mr. Galsworthy would only see in Mrs. Brown a pot broken on the wheel and thrown into the corner'.[39] Bennett, by recourse to circumstantial evidence (such as the class of carriage) would appeal to hierarchical preconceptions in order to place his character socially:

He would observe, at length, how this was the non-stop train from Windsor which calls at Richmond for the convenience of middle-class residents, who can afford to go to the theatre...And so he would gradually sidle sedately towards Mrs. Brown, and would remark how she had been left a little copyhold, not freehold, property at Datchet.[40]

Wells, Galsworthy and Bennett, according to Woolf, all order their fictional worlds according to personal predetermined patterns which imbrue behaviour and appearances with a particular, immutable set of meanings. Their world-view involves a given hierarchical structure and the application of this structure to the raw data of experience sets up another hierarchy in which the world is subordinate to the novel.

This sheds a significant light on Woolf's own quest and has a special resonance in relation to 'The Mark on the Wall'. The story enacts the limitations of hierarchical fictional convention by tethering the narrative consciousness to a single point of oscillation. The anecdotal story convention is subverted (the resolution of the puzzle dismissed as insignificant), but the convention gives the story its structure. As the narrator covertly concludes, the way to express dissatisfaction with the rigidity of traditional form may be to effect a compromise: 'if you can't be comforted, if you must shatter this hour of peace, think of the mark on the wall' (88). The story, like all of Woolf's successful stories, is forced to look at the mark on the wall, its formal centre, on which its meaning depends. Yet the story's design, which, ostensibly, has a unifying and converging effect, paradoxically ensures that the narrator's discourse is dialogized in the sense that each pattern of reflection is disrupted and replaced by a new one: the narrative is prevented from following a single path.

'The Mark on the Wall' exemplifies Woolf's work in the short story, work which has a seminal relevance to her main goals as a writer. In each of the stories I have examined, effects are generated by a formal disruption deriving from a tension between a conventional, ordered narrative style, and an all-embracing, multi-accentual alternative. These attempts to create a heteroglot text, which are determined by their partial break with conventional narrative order, are characteristically modernist. Woolf's short stories, however, often have an incomplete, investigative 'workshop' quality. In this respect, her stories form an interesting contrast with the work of Mansfield, a writer who conducts similar formal experiments. Mansfield's stories – like Woolf's – create their effects through a disruptive dual essence, or partial break with the established materials of fiction. But Mansfield displays a greater control, and her major innovations in the genre, far from being experimental, display an accomplishment unsurpassed by other modernist writers.

CHAPTER 4

Katherine Mansfield: the impersonal short story

Katherine Mansfield's modernism, like that of Joyce or Woolf, stems from an ambivalent attitude to the nature of personality; and this ambivalence is reflected in the structure and language of her stories. In her journal she once described her philosophy as 'the defeat of the personal', a phrase which has a particular relevance to her investigations into identity and personality.[1] The conflation between the problematic view of character and an ambiguous short story technique has already been demonstrated in relation to 'Bliss', in which an equivocal 'epiphany' emphasizes Bertha Young's personal confusion. The reading of this story made in the opening chapter suggests a dawning awareness on the protagonist's part of her latent homosexuality, a subtext partly suppressed by the social taboo it simultaneously criticizes. The suppression of sexuality results in confusion for Bertha and an imitative ambiguity in the story's form, and this makes it appear indeterminate, admitting the possibility of other readings. One such is that made by Saralyn Daly, who feels that Bertha, 'a treacherously fallible narrator', has her suspicions of the affair between Pearl Fulton and her husband, yet refuses to acknowledge it, and engages in an extended attempt at self-deception. Her sense of intimacy with Pearl can therefore be seen as a fanciful self-projection designed by Bertha 'to persuade herself that she feels "just what" the woman who is loved by her husband does'.[2] It may be that this does not fully account for Bertha's feeling of intimacy with Pearl, but the viability of the reading further complicates the portrayal of Bertha, who is confused in her sexuality and, consequently, hazy in her understanding of the actions and motives of others.

The example indicates the importance in Mansfield's work of disrupting simple patterns: the resulting ambiguity often reveals the point of her art. Very often the significant moment in Mansfield, like many of the epiphanies in *Dubliners*, is a point where different impulses converge and conflict. There is usually no simple 'solution' to the ambiguities of the characterization, but rather a denial of a solution. This is particularly clear in 'Miss Brill', a more straightforward story which is sometimes seen as flawed precisely because its conclusion suggests, but finally eschews, an epiphany of self-awareness. Miss Brill, a lonely spinster, enjoys her only human contact walking in a park on Sundays, observing the crowds, and imagining herself to be involved in some kind of drama: 'They were all on the stage.... Even she had a part and came every Sunday' (376).[3] Emblematic of Miss Brill's self-delusion and isolation is her sentimental, anthropomorphic attachment to her fur, which she treats almost like a pet: 'Little rogue biting its tail just by her left ear. She could have taken it off and laid it on her lap and stroked it' (374). The fur becomes the crucial instrument at the story's crisis point where Miss Brill, eavesdropping on a courting couple, is offered the brutal truth about herself:

Miss Brill prepared to listen.
'No, not now,' said the girl. 'Not here, I can't.'
'But why? Because of that stupid old thing at the end there?' asked the boy. 'Why does she come here at all – who wants her? Why doesn't she keep her silly old mug at home?'
'It's her fu-fur which is so funny,' giggled the girl. 'It's exactly like a fried whiting.' (377)

The story ends as Miss Brill returns home, in an apparent daze:

To-day she passed the baker's by, climbed the stairs, went into the little dark room – her room like a cupboard – and sat down on the red eiderdown. She sat there for a long time. The box that the fur came out of was on the bed. She unclasped the necklet quickly; quickly, without looking, laid it inside. But when she put the lid on she thought she heard something crying. (377)

This ending is sometimes objected to on the grounds of its sentimentality which obscures the revelation that has been offered to Miss Brill in the park.[4] The narrative point of view, however, is consistently that of Miss Brill, and so any sentimentality can be seen as part of the characterization rather than indicative of an authorial lapse. Mansfield herself was satisfied that the narrative was entirely appropriate to the protagonist's perspective:

In *Miss Brill* I choose not only the length of every sentence, but even the sound of every sentence. I choose the rise and fall of every paragraph to fit her, and to fit her on that day at that very moment. After I'd written it I read it aloud – numbers of times – just as one would *play over* a musical composition – trying to get it nearer and nearer to the expression of Miss Brill – until it fitted her.[5]

Since Miss Brill is the single focalizer, the closing anthropomorphic perception – the imagined crying of the fur – is clearly another example of the character's self-delusion, which persists, but in a state of crisis: a revelation of self-awareness has been offered, and now Miss Brill struggles to efface this insight. The conclusion comprises a compex, ambivalent 'epiphany' which emulates the character's own internal conflict between awareness and delusion, and this confusion is the essence of Miss Brill's condition. The story convention of the single point or discovery is here modified, made less determinate, as befits the characterization.

The complex moment in Mansfield often has important structural implications, especially in relation to peripeteia or reversal; an example of this is the suppressed reversal of 'Miss Brill': we have seen how Miss Brill's entrenched perspective denies the progression that her experience offers. A more startling use of reversal occurs in 'Millie' (1913).

The point of view of the character Millie is expressed through a vacillating, but consistently formulaic discourse. The story begins with Millie waving goodbye to her husband Sid who rides off on horseback 'with four of the boys to help hunt down the young fellow who'd murdered Mr Williamson' (134). Millie is left to reflect on the killing of the local farmer and to reiterate, uncritically, her husband's words:

My word! when they caught that young man! Well – you couldn't be sorry for a young fellow like that. As Sid said, if he wasn't strung up where would they all be? A man like that doesn't stop at one go. There was blood all over the barn. (134)

Millie repeats Sid's rhetorical question which implies the social necessity of eye-for-an-eye retribution, an extreme opinion which begs the question, if the youth *is* strung up where would they – the people doing the stringing – be? What is planned is a mob execution, conducted as if to satisfy the requirements of a civilized penal process, but which really will represent the consummation of the primordial 'hunt'. Millie's discourse reveals something of this irrational attempt at justification: the fact that 'there was blood all over the barn', as there might well be after a shooting, whether a murder or an accident, is used to imply the inevitable proliferation of the young man's violence, if unchecked.

The point of the story revolves around the repressed maternal capacity of the stern, childless Millie, whose cast of mind seems infused with masculine aggression. A different sort of response almost reveals itself when she assesses her wedding photograph. Having just expressed disapproval of a print on the bedroom wall entitled 'Garden Party at Windsor Castle' she extends her ostensibly objective visual appraisal to the photograph of herself and Sid on their wedding day: 'Nice picture that – if you *do* like' (134). This colloquially formulaic assertion of irrefutable value conceals the partisan perceptions of the nostalgic wife who subsequently reflects on the passing of time and her failure to conceive a child.

The scene is set for Millie's discovery of, and maternal solicitude over, Harrison, the fugitive her menfolk are hunting. The change of heart, however, is rendered in equally formulaic language: 'They won't ketch 'im. Not if I can 'elp it. Men is all beasts. I don't care wot 'e's done, or wot 'e 'asn't done. See 'im through, Millie Evans. 'E's nothink but a sick kid' (136–7). One set of prepackaged opinions have been exchanged for another, equally assertive and polarized. Millie now allows her altruistic response to be overlaid with notions of sexual stereotyping, especially ideas of female duty. This notion of duty inspires the self-exhortation: 'See 'im through, Millie Evans.' The superficiality of Millie's responses, inspired by stereotypical social pressures and indicated by a strident, irrational discourse, makes her final volte-face predictable. The sight of her menfolk chasing Harrison excites her and draws her back into the masculine world of sanctioned violence: 'A-ah! Arter 'im, Sid! A-a-a-h! ketch 'im, Willie. Go it! Go it! A-ah, Sid! Shoot 'im down. Shoot 'im!' (137). A formal dissonance is discernible here where the traditional story reversal is short-circuited, and, in the process of this disruption, the story reveals the damaging ideology of polarized sexual roles. As in several of Joyce's stories, both 'Miss Brill' and 'Millie' derive their effects from a dissonance between a notional story structure of reversal or progression, and a delimited narrative perspective which indicates confusion or stasis.

A key aspect of the modernist short story is the presentation of character through narrative voice, and this is a seminal feature of Mansfield's technique. This kind of presentation, although straightforward in the two stories examined so far, is far more involved in longer pieces where the narrative combines the voices of a number of characters. Mansfield's quest to present inner consciousness directly through voice can be traced to her early stories, and the outline history of this quest is worth considering. An early story which explores different narrative possibilities is 'A Birthday' (1911) which combines thought sequences reported in the third person, and other sequences given directly in the first person. This method betrays a lack of sophistication in its clumsy use of quotation marks to demarcate direct thoughts. In other early stories like 'New Dresses' (1912) and 'The Swing of the Pendulum' (1911) Mansfield fumbles, not altogether unsuccessfully, with similar techniques, though again thought sequences are separated by quotation marks. 'Ole Underwood' (1913) represents an advance in the stories written before 1914 in presenting consciousness integrated with narrative and not awkwardly highlighted by speech marks.

'Ole Underwood' explores the pathological obsession of its eponymous protagonist. After a twenty-year prison sentence for murder – a crime of passion – Ole Underwood comes out 'cracked'. The story traces a sequence of psychological triggers that leave him on the brink of repeating his crime. Tension is created by a dual narrative which places us at times 'in' the character's head, and which at other times keeps us distanced.

This vacillation is necessary so that we can perceive the inner processes as they develop, while maintaining a sense of their abnormality. The punctuation which separates thought sequences from narrative in other stories is here dispensed with. The nature of the mind in question makes this smoothness of texture possible: no coherent thought processes are required – no precise verbal expression – merely words which reflect an unbalanced response to outer stimuli. Thus Ole Underwood is made distraught by the pounding of his heart, roused as he is to violent repsonse:

> Something inside Ole Underwood's breast beat like a hammer. One two – one two – never stopping, never changing. He couldn't do anything. It wasn't loud. No, it didn't make a noise – only a thud. One, two – one, two – like someone beating on an iron in a prison – someone in a secret place – bang – bang – bang – trying to get free. Do what he would, fumble at his coat, throw his arms about, spit, swear, he couldn't stop the noise. Stop! Stop! Stop! Stop! (131)

The manic appeal for cessation is clearly located within the old man's head. Here, the subject lends itself to a smoother presentation of the psyche; Mansfield had not, in fact, overcome her predilection for 'quoted' thoughts. The later story 'Something Childish but Very Natural' (1914), to take an example, contains snatches of these. Eventually, however, the punctuation marks disappear altogether. In stories like 'Psychology' (1919) and 'The Daughters of the Late Colonel' (1920) no disruption of narrative occurs for the rendering of direct thought. Throughout her *œuvre* one finds thought sequences juxtaposed with narrative, a fact which betrays Mansfield's continuing interest in rendering inner processes.

These investigations in the use of voice result in two sophisticated pieces – 'Je ne Parle pas Français' (1918) and the unfinished piece 'A Married Man's Story' (1921) – in which Mansfield makes her most extended treatments of a single inner voice. These first-person confessional pieces represent a key phase in the development of Mansfield's characterization.

'Je ne Parle pas Français' is an important landmark in the modernist short story, and its importance is largely due to its method of characterization through voice. Raoul Duquette, the narrator of the story, is a sketch of the artist-as-parasite, a man who assesses his experiences purely in terms of their artistic usefulness. Duquette is a parody of the self-conscious artist and, in part, a self-parody by Mansfield. He frequently interrupts his story and draws attention to its self-conscious artifice, as when he describes 'a morsel of pink blotting-paper, incredibly soft and limp and almost moist, like the tongue of a little dead kitten, which I've never felt' (279). This artifice is extended to Duquette's relations with other people, since he believes that 'people are like portmanteaux' and imagines himself standing before them 'like a Customs official' seeing if they have 'anything to declare' (277). Accordingly, his attitude to Dick and Mouse is marked by a withdrawal of empathy, and this detachment, a satirical exaggeration of the writer's parasitism, has become habitual in Duquette. When he discovers that Dick and Mouse are suffering, he is elated: '"But you are suffering," I ventured softly, as though that was what I could not bear to see' (295). Innocent Mouse, deserted by Dick in Paris, becomes the subject of Duquette's predatory and soulless conjecturing: he contemplates her potential dependence on him, and, apparently, the possibility of becoming her pimp, but he has actually decided to abandon her.

The treatment of Duquette's self-consciousness represents an important parody: his spectator's attitude to life satirizes the art/life dichotomy that is often seen as a distinguishing mark of modernist writing. The manner in which the parodic element is expressed is illuminating, especially as it is achieved without overt omniscient commentary. John Middleton Murry found the effect of the story comparable to Dostoevsky, a comparison based on narrative point of view: Murry felt a compelling strangeness in Duquette, not 'because he has thought every-thing to a standstill, but because he is conscious of a piece out of him'.[6] Murry was uncertain in his praise, but his identification of Duquette's 'conscious[ness] of a piece out of him' is suggestive of the dialogic nature of the narrative. Just as Bakhtin indicates a 'reckoning with an absent interlocutor' in Dostoevsky, 'the intense anticipation of another's words', Duquette is con-tinually aware of an implied auditor's response and criticism of his words, and it is this internal dialogue which presents adverse aspects of the characterization as it is established.[7] The most prominent feature of this dialogical style is insistent affirmation which implies self-doubt and consciousness of criticism from 'an absent interlocutor'. When, for instance, Duquette compares his manner of evaluating people to the actions of a Customs official, he stridently affirms the thrill this involves for him: '"Have you anything to declare? Any wines, spirits, cigars, perfumes, silks?" And the moment of hesitation as to whether I am going to be fooled ... and then the other moment of hesitation just after, as to whether I have been, are perhaps the two most thrilling instants in life. *Yes, they are, to me*' (277; my emphasis). Duquette anticipates a lack of empathy in the reception of this self-analysis, and this reaction admits a critical position. The descriptive work is also interrupted by self-consciousness, as is the case with this fanciful reflection in a café:

> One would not have been surprised if the door had opened and the Virgin Mary had come in, riding upon an ass, her meek hands folded over her big belly...
>
> That's rather nice, don't you think, that bit about the Virgin? It comes from the pen so gently; it has such a 'dying fall'. I thought so at the time and decided to make a note of it. One never knows when a little tag like that may come in useful to round off a paragraph. (279; original ellipsis)

The semi-apologetic tone here – one of sarcasm combined with self-deprecation – reveals a desire to forestall the criticism which it simultaneously invokes. This kind of interior dialogue, which displays a continual anticipation of a critical stance, pervades the narrative, and results in an insecure tone, indicated locally by recurring stylistic emphasis and assertion, particularly in the form of exclamation marks and rhetorical questions. The entire narrative is problematic and unreliable, as it replicates the egotism of Duquette. The egotism is a parodic representation of an art/life dichotomy that obtains in some branches of modernist art, but since the narrative *engages* (at a surface level) with this dichotomous perspective, the story has a powerful ambivalence. The satirical undermining of Duquette and his narrative is subtly achieved through the interior dialogue, but there is no overt condemnation; the story's power lies in the tension between the narrative voice and its own self-doubts. A complex characterization is achieved in tandem with a disruption of narrative authority.

Mansfield's interest in characterization through voice – a dialogized style of writing most evident in 'Prelude' – is also evident in a series of experiments in dialogue and monologue. These are: 'The Festival of the Coronation' (1911), 'Stay Laces' (1915), and (all 1917), 'In Confidence', 'A Pic-Nic', 'Two Tuppenny Ones, Please', 'Late at Night', and 'The Black Cap'.[8] With the exception of the last two in the list, these pieces are straightforward dialogue interspersed with 'stage directions' in parentheses; they are mini-plays, in effect. 'The Black Cap' incorporates another characteristic of dramatic art, the monologue, and 'Late at Night' is pure monologue, with a handful of stage directions. The importance of these experiments lies in the fact that they show an identification between dialogue and monologue, and a particular interest in these modes immediately prior to the revision of *The Aloe* into the multi-voiced 'Prelude'.

Mansfield's dialogic experimentation with the short story form reaches its peak in 'Prelude', the narrative of which combines a variety of opposing and alternative voices. The story's effects are generated by the juxtaposition and conflict of these voices, and these are genuine short story effects, in their variety and their denial of an authoritative narrative centre: 'Prelude' is the final result of Mansfield's most ambitious literary project, the revised version of the novella *The Aloe*, a work originally conceived as a novel. The meticulous editorial process involved in trimming *The Aloe* by a third demonstrates emphatically Mansfield's aesthetic principle of excising all omniscient explanation. The revised version relies on action, symbolism, and dialogization of the narrative to convey the characterization and the thematic concerns.[9]

Throughout the story Mansfield expresses her themes through a subtle combination of different voices. This is clearly the case in the development of the various family tensions. Mrs Burnell's lack of maternal response is expressed in the opening paragraph, when her two youngest children are to be left behind: 'There was not an inch of room for Lottie and Kezia in the buggy. When Pat swung them on top of the luggage they wobbled; the grandmother's lap was full and Linda Burnell could not possibly have held a lump of a child on hers for any distance' (223). Linda Burnell's voice speaks here, and her scarcely concealed aversion to her own children inspires the unjustified assertion that she cannot entertain nursing one of them on her lap. Yet even in this sentence the familial pact to protect the unmaternal Linda Burnell from all maternal duties is implicit. The sentence, expressing the mother's concern, is offered as an irrefutable truism: 'Linda Burnell could not possibly have held a lump of a child'. As such, it could be expressed by the grandmother, by Beryl, or even by the children themselves. The ideology of presenting as normal the mother's 'unnatural' response finds a collective voice, and the assertiveness of this voice betrays an anticipation of dissent, that reckoning with an a absent interlocutor which here reveals the domestic problem as well as the fact of its concealment.

The effect of the mother's dialogue on her children is also suggested in the opening lines, with typical economy. The buggy is loaded with 'absolute necessities' which Linda Burnell will not allow out of her sight. Consequently there is no room for Lottie and Kezia: 'Hand in hand, they stared with round solemn eyes first at the absolute necessities and then at their mother' (223). The children's world-view is here fashioned by the concept of 'absolute necessities', material things which take precedence in the mother's eyes and which the children are required to assess in the same way. The commodification implicit in the mother's phrase is aptly summarized in the solution to the problem: like the tables and chairs Lottie and Kezia must wait to be transported later in the day. This phrase 'absolute necessities' thus suggests not only the mother's attitude, but also the children's sense of their own lack of value; the sight of the necessities inspires solemnity because it highlights for the children their own lack of utility and the absence of an emotional value-system in their domestic lives.

This kind of technique informs Mansfield's preoccupation in

the story with personality and indoctrination. The most significant aspect of this preoccupation concerns the evocation of male sexual predacity and female victimization. By means of psychological identification with her mother, Kezia's heritage of sexual trauma is suggested. This association is strongly made by Kezia's nightmare fears of rushing animals whose 'heads swell e-enormous' (228), an image which anticipates Linda Burnell's dream of the tiny bird which swells in her arms to be transformed into a huge baby with 'a gaping bird-mouth'. In this dream Linda's father has shown her the tiny fluffy bird and when her touch causes it to swell and transform, he breaks 'into a loud clattering laugh' (233). The imagery of sexual activity and reproduction is coloured by the cruel and knowing male figure who is presented as one playing a deceitful trick. There is a subtext here concerning the discrepancy between the idealism of romance and the burdensome reality of conception, a subtext which takes as its object of protest the misleading ideology of romance. It is presicely this ideology which dictates the action and aspirations of Beryl, as we shall see. The figure of the deceptive male also underpins Kezia's fear of aggressive animals, a fear which elicits a telling remark from the storeman. In response to her enquiry as to the difference between a sheep and a ram he explains: 'Well, a ram has horns and runs for you' (228). The sexually active male sheep confirms Kezia's incipient fears of male predacity, but it is the storeman's discourse which is revealing here. He offers a typical adult-to-child remark or semi-explanation in which the threat of being chased is tempered by ambiguity. 'Runs *for* you' is the ambiguous phrase which suggests the threat, but which also suggests the idea of a clockwork toy or a pet put in motion for a child's amusement.[10] The condescending discourse obscures the more sinister implication. This point is reinforced by Isabel's later reaction to the killing of the duck: as the headless creature waddles away she exclaims: 'It's like a little engine. It's like a funny little railway engine' (249). The response is emblematic of the absorption of the adult ideology: the reality of the action – and the castration motif which it carries – is distorted and sanitized by its resemblance to less sinister cultural codes.

The children also absorb and use adult discourse not specifically designed for their own consumption, and this, again, raises the issue of ideological power and conditioning. When Mansfield has the children play at being adults a serious investigation along these lines lies beneath the humorous vignette of childish mores. The passage, which is not introduced, also involves a tactic of shock-recognition, since we do not recognize until the fifth or sixth sentence that these are children speaking:

'Good morning, Mrs Jones.'
'Oh, good morning, Mrs Smith. I'm so glad to see you. Have you brought your children?'
'Yes, I've brought both my twins. I have had another baby since I saw you last, but she came so suddenly that I haven't had time to make her any clothes, yet. So I left her.... How is your husband?'
'Oh, he is very well, thank you. At least he had a nawful cold but Queen Victoria – she's my godmother, you know – sent him a case of pineapples and that cured it im-mediately. Is that your new servant?'
'Yes, her name's Gwen. I've only had her two days. Oh, Gwen, this is my friend, Mrs Smith.'
'Good morning, Mrs Smith. Dinner won't be ready for about ten minutes.'
'I don't think you ought to introduce me to the servant. I think I ought to just begin talking to her.' (244–5; original ellipsis)

The obvious irony of Linda Burnell's children glibly accruing members to their imaginary families provokes a wry smile, but it also uncovers the conditioning which distorts the issue here: no effort of endurance is required of these girls to add another doll to their nursery play, play that is socially acceptable and encouraged. The extract ends with an argument about the type of discourse applicable to a social inferior. Unquestioning but firm ideas are expressed about the language required to sustain a given hierarchical relationship. In this light the statement about Queen Victoria and the pineapples conveys a particular kind of indoctrination: the importance of being well connected is an attitude which the children have absorbed and the idea of social position and its concomitant wealth is linked in their minds with physical wellbeing. One might question the efficacy of the cure, but the children clearly find compelling the idea that Queen Victoria should be able to send cases of exotic fruit for the treatment of sick friends.

The use of voice to convey the characterization is most overt in the case of Stanley. His assessment of his handyman Pat, for instance, clearly reveals his egocentricity and self-assertion:

> 'I believe this man is a first-rate chap,' thought Stanley. He liked the look of him sitting up there in his neat brown coat and brown bowler. He liked the way Pat had tucked him in, and he liked his eyes. There was nothing servile about him – and if there was one thing he hated more than another it was servility. And he looked as if he was pleased with his job – happy and contented already. (240–1)

Typically, Stanley interprets behaviour only in so far as it impinges on his own feelings. This superficial attitude enables him to be content with a particular ideological obfuscation in his dealings with Pat: servility is wanted in deed, but an apparently egalitarian attitude must be presented, thereby obscuring the real relationship and easing Stanley's conscience. The meretricious nature of Stanley's discourse, and the social power it represents, is summarized in his plans for establishing a high profile at church. He delights in the thought of the *sound* of his responses and in the social kudos the occasion might embody:

> In fancy he heard himself intoning extremely well: 'When thou did overcome the *Sharp*ness of Death Thou didst open the *King*dom of Heaven to *all* Believers.' And he saw the neat brass-edged card on the corner of the pew – Mr Stanley Burnell and family. (241)

The irony of a self-seeking attitude to worship scarcely needs mentioning, other than to point out that this kind of concealed hypocrisy pervades the story and the familial relationships. There is, that is to say, an implicit conflict of voices even though the centripetal forces of indoctrination are predominant.

In a similar, but more complex way, Beryl's world-view is undermined by a conflict of discourses and influences. The language of romantic novels infuses her fantasy love intrigues: 'There is a ball at Government house.... Who is that exquisite

creature in *eau de nil* satin? Beryl Fairfield' (231; original
ellipsis). Kate Fullbrook, discussing 'The Tiredness of Rosabel',
has summarized Mansfield's assessment of this type of discourse:

> The young Katherine Mansfield recognized the *function* of trash
> romance for women (whose elements have not significantly changed),
> which invites dreams of being the perfect beneficiaries of the sexual
> system that in fact victimises them.[11]

Beryl's fantasizing is a response to the social pressure to marry,
a different discourse which dominates her letter to Nan Pym:
'I'll get to be a most awful frump in a year or two' (256). The
conflict of voices and pressures has opened a schizophrenic rift
in Beryl's personality, a rift which she recognizes in herself: 'It
was her other self who had written that letter. It not only bored,
it rather disgusted her real self' (256). The wretched Beryl is
conscious of a 'despicable' duplicity in her nature, and her
heart is rendered 'cold with rage' (258) in self-condemnation.
Mansfield's interest here is with the social forces which insist on
the need for a husband, but which also deny access to one for the
dependent spinster. These forces, irrational and destructive in
their effect on Beryl's personality, must be seen as doubly
damaging in the context of Linda Burnell's fear of childbirth:
marriage, far from being the promised state of fulfilment, is
presented as destructive of the female.[12]

The exposure of Beryl's fantasy as delusion conforms to a
pattern which recurs in Mansfield's work. The use of fantasy has
a special significance for the short story, and is related to the
notion of mystery, a common, but imprecise term in the theory
of the genre. Both mystery and fantasy have a direct relevance
to Mansfield's open-ended narratives. John Bayley has discussed
the role of fantasy in the genre, although this discussion requires
a degree of reformulation. Using Lawrence as an example
Bayley makes an uncomplicated assessment of fantasy as a tool
available to the short story writer for direct thematic development. Bayley claims that '[Lawrence] puts himself and his
desires into the tale in exaggerated form', thereby sketching,
with broad strokes, important themes and ideas. In 'The Fox',
for example, the killing of Banford is intelligible only in terms of
fantasy projection: 'The lack of a proper Lawrentian existence

in the frail and querulous Banford means that actual existence can be terminated as an act of the will by the hero on behalf of the author.'[13] I want to propose an adaptation of the role of fantasy, a partial reversal which is analogous to my appropriation of the mystery idea. Fantasy projection in the short story is a defence: it invariably conceals something, and so can be viewed as another formal restraint to be dismantled. (Beryl's fantasy-delusion in 'Prelude' is an obvious case in point.) There are clear affinities between the perceived compositional importance of fantasy and the short story's engagement with personal identity; and Katherine Mansfield's stories are particularly relevant here, as fantasy underpins much of her investigation into the nature of personality.[14]

The neglected story 'Honeymoon' is profitably approached with the overlapping concepts of mystery and fantasy in mind: the story concerns the fragmentation of personality through a subtext which undermines the fantasy idyll of the surface narrative.

By implication the story uncovers the seeds of destruction in the marriage of Fanny and George, clearly visible even on their Mediterranean honeymoon. The fact that the sojourn is a honeymoon is mentioned only in the title and not in the narrative itself, and this evokes a mystery of the most basic sort. A subtext is immediately installed concerning the reason for this concealment. The reason, actually, is suggested early in the narrative – which reproduces Fanny's restless impulsiveness – when a reluctance to mention the fact of her marriage manifests itself: 'These things seemed always to be happening to them ever since they they – came abroad' (534). This ellipsis is repeated a few lines later. The marriage, and the physical consummation it traditionally facilitates, are difficult for her to face, it seems. Fanny, like most of Mansfield's wives, appears to find her sexual relationship a source of distress.

Fanny's discourse of enthusiasm obviously masks, in its stridency, an inner fear and vacuousness. It also demonstrates an impercipience regarding the pecuniary machinations of George's world, a self-deluding willingness to be impressed by the surface gratifications he can offer. This is clear in her reaction to the cab which he has surely secured by means of a

cash advance: 'when they came out of the lace shop there was
their own driver and the cab they called their own cab waiting
for them under a plane tree. What luck! Wasn't it luck?'. Yet
even in her lack of comprehension about economic relations,
and the hegemony they construct, Fanny exhibits an instinctive
unease regarding George's brusque treatment of subordinates.
This unease, however, is swept aside by her awe-induced
subscription to George's world: 'Fanny sometimes felt a little
uncomfortable about the way George summoned cabs, but the
drivers didn't seem to mind, so it must have been all right'
(534). The superficial reasoning obscures the real relation.

Fanny does, however, allow her misgivings to surface,
misgivings which centre on the possibility of mental communion
in the marriage and, by extension, on the knowability of
personality:

'Do you feel,' she said, softly, 'that you really know me now? But
really, really know *me?*'
It was too much for George. Know his Fanny? He gave a broad,
childish grin. 'I should jolly well think I do,' he said, emphatically.
'Why, what's up?'
Fanny felt he hadn't quite understood. (536–7)

Fantasy, in the form of the honeymoon idyll, is a mask, a
defence against the underlying loneliness and lack of base in the
marriage. It is also an ideology of conformity, an ideology in the
sense of a false consciousness which is self-regenerating: the kind
of marital satisfaction which George offers depends upon the
sustention of superficialities and the concomitant denial of
psychological probing.

An important point concerning this story stems from its
relatively unsophisticated use of symbolism, which, uncharac-
teristically, is both stable and transparent. At least, the story
gives the *appearance* of such a lack of sophistication at first
glance: its final effect involves a rejection of the formal stability
it establishes at a surface level. A preliminary reading of
'Honeymoon' reveals that the undermining of the fantasy is
conveyed, primarily, through images associated with the sea.[15]
Fanny's unease and George's imperviousness are both pre-

visioned by a mysterious sea wind which blows over them and exhibits a greater affinity for her: 'a wind, light, warm, came flowing over the boundless sea. It touched George, and Fanny it seemed to linger over while they gazed at the dazzling water' (534). When George spots a swimmer in the sea he resolves to go swimming the very next day, a resolution which causes Fanny to fret over the dangers he will face: 'It was an absolute death-trap. Beautiful, treacherous Mediterranean' (535). Again it is she who is alert to the reality the sea represents.

The ominous connotations of sea imagery are expanded when the couple retire to their favourite hotel restaurant to take tea. The manager greets them, a man 'like a fish in a frock coat' whose 'mouth opened and shut as though he were ready for another dive under the water' (535–6). Having taken the order this fish-man extends the following invitation: '"perhaps de lady might like to look at de live lobsters in de tank while de tea is coming?" And he grimaced and smirked and flicked his serviette like a fin' (536). The couple's tête-à-tête (part of the romantic honeymoon fantasy) is disrupted by this distasteful intrusion and then by the 'funny-tasting' tea, tainted, claims George, by 'Lobster in the kettle' (537). At this point George's resolution to go swimming the next day is recalled, a resolution inspired by his glimpses of 'the reddened face' and 'the reddened arm' of a bather (534). The lobster-red imagery equates the bather with the lobsters for consumption in the restaurant. By implication George, who will bathe tomorrow, is identified as a victim to be devoured. (Both George and Fanny, of course, will be victims of the relationship that seems doomed to failure, but the focus is on her plight. This is because the story is mediated through her consciousness and, more importantly, because the force of destruction derives from George's attitude and her conditioned response to this.)

Other images suggest the superficiality and insubstantiality of the marriage. Initially we see the couple emerging from a lace shop. George's perception of Fanny is akin to an owner looking after a pet, a notion suggested when George implicitly compares her hand to a pet mouse he once kept: 'he caught hold of her hand, stuffed it into his pocket, pressed her fingers, and said, "I

used to keep a white mouse in my pocket when I was a kid"'
(534). The motif is recalled when Fanny's mouse-like nose
twitches in response to an aroma: 'they were passing a high wall
on the land side, covered with flowering heliotrope, and Fanny's
little nose lifted. "Oh George," she breathed. "The smell!"'
(535). Significantly, it is her nose that especially appeals to
George: 'he was just going to tell her how much he liked her
little nose, when the waiter arrived with the tea' (537). This is
George's response to Fanny's incipient fears about the lack of
depth and understanding in their relationship, a response which
confirms that she has genuine grounds for concern.

The death of the relationship is symbolized in the song they
hear while they drink their tea in the hotel restaurant, itself
'bone-white' (535), a conjoining image of marine erosion and
physical perishability. The fact that Fanny is moved (in a way
she cannot fully fathom) by the song, while George, characteristically, is impervious (his desire is to escape the 'squawk-
ing') illustrates, again, their incompatibility. The song, which
to Fanny's ear conveys a resigned acceptance of its own denial
(537), suggests the denial of Fanny's own personality. At this
point Fanny is almost shocked out of her acceptance of the
honeymoon fantasy and into the vacuum which lies behind it:

Is life like this too? thought Fanny. There are people like this. There
is suffering. And she looked at that gorgeous sea, lapping the land as
though it loved it, and the sky, bright with the brightness before
evening. Had she and George the right to be so happy? Wasn't it
cruel? There must be something else in life which made all these things
possible. (537–8)

Wrestling with her vision, Fanny turns to George, her ideologue,
apparently for guidance: her conditioned passivity disables her
from following the vision through on her own. It is a vision
beyond her blinkered husband, however. His lack of depth is
emphasized by his reactions to the song and to the sea which are
juxtaposed with Fanny's:

But George had been feeling differently from Fanny. The poor old
boy's voice was funny in a way, but, God, how it made you realize what

a terrific thing it was to be at the beginning of everything, as they were, he and Fanny! George, too, gazed at the bright, breathing water, and his lips opened as if he could drink it. How fine it was! There was nothing like the sea for making a chap feel fit. (538)

George's sudden sensation of fitness carries with it a suggestion of lust: '"I say," said George, rapidly, "let's go, shall we? Let's go back to the hotel. Come. Do, Fanny darling. Let's go now"' (538). George whisks Fanny off to their hotel, presumably to exercise his newly conferred conjugal rights. The vacuousness of the failure to communicate is compounded by the misplaced lust which brings the story full circle and reminds us of Fanny's implied squeamishness and inability to face the physical side of marriage.

As this reading of 'Honeymoon' suggests, the story lends itself to a straightforward interpretation, but there is another level to the piece which complicates its effects; the story is not simply an examination of gender roles, and its subversiveness also extends to its treatment of fictional form. Overall, the story has the air of an ironic send-up, and this means that the judgemental exposure of the honeymoon fantasy applies also to the story's mode of representation. Fanny's near-vision is so naive as to border on the farcical ('Is life like this too?'), and there is an obvious irony in her inability to perceive her real predicament, the ludicrous mismatch that is her marriage. But the narrative also reproduces the inadequacy of her perspective, and her struggle to recognize the palpably obvious is conveyed through the transparent symbolism, which is really superfluous. 'Honeymoon' is a deceptive text which, if taken at face value, provides material for a straightforward short story analysis, the 'rebuilding' method of exegesis which often focuses on symbolic detail to uncover oblique meanings. But it is precisely this kind of oblique expression – symbolic implication – which is satirized here as it embodies the naiveté of the central character; and this is an arresting formal dissonance in which the concept of a simple symbolic subtext is rejected. Beyond this there is a more serious point about ideological restriction. Fanny's predicament derives from a conditioned passivity, and is a state indicated by her intellectual inadequacy; since this inadequacy is reproduced through the story's transparent style, a connection is established between the undeveloped Fanny and the unsophisticated story convention. The dismantling of the 'fantasy' turns out to be a formal project, the restrictions of the stable literary type corresponding to those of the character. Both failures or inadequacies are determined by contextual forces: Fanny is restricted by patriarchal domination, while the transparent story mode which Mansfield satirizes conforms to the kind of simplistic short story which the modernists in general came to regard as unsuitable for the portrayal of personal identity.

The subversive nature of 'Honeymoon' – which applies both to its examination of gender roles and to its use of fictional form – is typical of Mansfield's work. The subversive nature of her writing, however, has not been fully recognized. Her critique of male oppression and female suffering has been located and discussed by several critics, but the broader political implications of Mansfield's identification of oppressive hegemonic structures have not been fully defined within the feminist project.[16] Mansfield's reputation as a 'delicate female stylist', engendered by her beguilingly homely or domestic choice of subject-matter, continues to obscure the radical nature of her political commentary.[17] When the seriousness of her sexual politics has been noted, it has sometimes been viewed in an unnecessarily negative light. Elaine Showalter, for instance, writes: 'In the short stories of Katherine Mansfield, the moment of self-awareness is also the moment of self-betrayal. Typically, a woman in her fiction who steps across the threshold into a new understanding of womanhood is humiliated, or destroyed. Mansfield's fiction is cautionary and punitive; women are lured out onto the limbs of consciousness, which are then lopped off by the author.'[18] Admittedly, the outcome of a Mansfield story often indicates defeat for a female character, but one can only consider this 'punitive' if one equates positive value only with a happy ending. An alternative way of evaluating the characteristic Mansfield outcome is suggested by the story 'Her First Ball', a piece which lays itself open, at first glance, to the description 'punitive', but in which a radical purpose is soon revealed.

'Her First Ball' is typically subversive, although its purport is potentially concealed by the subject. The events are straight-forward: Leila, attending her first ball, is overcome by her excitement at the romantic event, especially when dancing with the young men. An older, unattractive man then dances with her and points out that she will soon be old, unattractive and unwanted at such events. Her consequent brief disenchantment is soon effaced when 'a young man with curly hair bowed before her' and they dance (431).

A superficial reading of the piece might characterize it as being about youthful enthusiasm for romance which, in its intensity, is able to disregard the unpalatable truth of transience and age. Indeed, the story's action makes a strong reference to this traditional theme, a theme which the story adopts as a kind of disguise. A close reading, however, soon reveals the in-adequacy of the youth/age opposition: the story's deeper significance concerns a particular kind of social conditioning and the myopia it induces. The central point of comparison is that between male and female experience, rather than between youth and age. Leila's older, unattractive dancing-partner has been attending dances 'for the last thirty years', but points out that she 'can't hope to last anything like as long as that'. The physical deterioration that is no barrier for him will disqualify her from participating in this kind of social occasion (430). The *men* are also demarcated from the *girls*, not just in this adult/child terminological discrepancy, but also in the assert-ive/passive behaviour which the occasion requires from the two groups. Before the dancing the sexes stand separately, but the girls must await the collective move of the men who 'suddenly' come 'gliding over the parquet', seize the girls' programmes and write on them to claim their dances (428). This act of collective appropriation, with its suggestion of violation (the scribbling on the blank programmes), is a socially ordered gesture of oppression.

The hint of violation confers new meaning on Leila's position as newcomer to the social circuit. It is, of course, her impression of virginal innocence (which her older dancing-partner throws into sharp relief) that guarantees Leila's value on the dancefloor-marketplace. It is this quality which distinguishes her from 'the poor old dears' on the stage, those mothers looking on with aching hearts at their daughters, having used up their own allotment of that vital female currency of youth and virginity (430).

The most radical aspect of this analysis of sexual politics lies in the way it locates the self-perpetuating impetus of the dominant ideology of oppression. The indoctrinating structure of the dance channels less indoctrinated feelings in a particular direction. Thus Leila's quite natural attraction to the young men is translated into a sense of helpless awe by the social occasion which casts her in the role of passive commodity. The ideology of female passivity, in other words, provides an outlet for, and yet is reinforced by, heterosexual female response. The story's conclusion represents, on reflection, a disruption of expectation which underscores the feminist message. The youth versus age theme is strongly suggested by Leila's delight in the dance and her ability to forget her earlier disquieting conversation with the fat man ('she didn't even recognize him again' (431)). Yet, as the story has shown, her behaviour is not simply an expression of youth, but, more importantly, an expression of indoctrination, and this more sinister implication jars with the story's apparent conclusion: as in 'Millie' and 'Miss Brill' Mansfield extends and complicates the story convention of a simple concluding reversal, and it is this formal dissonance which reveals the real point.

The theory of ideological channelling illustrated by Leila's plight involves analysing a dominant ideology as a structure which draws sustenance from those contrary impulses which it is able to defuse. This is an idea which Mansfield invokes, possibly inadvertently, in many of her stories. One obvious local example occurs in 'Prelude' when the serving-girl Alice reflects bitterly on her position of subservience: 'she had the most marvellous retorts ready for questions that she knew would never be put to her. The composing of them and the turning of them over and over in her mind comforted her just as much as if they'd been expressed' (250). Alice ameliorates her situation by supplying her own ideology of personal gratification, a private system of satisfaction which effectively defuses her rebellious urge and facilitates her continuing conformity. The ideological restraints examined in the story as a whole are perpetuated by types of discourse which either obscure or make more palatable the nature of those restraints.

This aspect of a dominant social structure – its capacity to oppress those it simultaneously incites to rebellion – has been identified by Fredric Jameson as an integral part of dominant collective thought, the 'ideological function' of which can be 'understood as a process whereby otherwise dangerous and protopolitical impulses are "managed" and defused, rechannelled and offered spurious objects'.[19] An excellent example of this ideological function of collective thought is to be found in Mansfield's story 'The Garden Party'. A detailed reading of this piece clearly shows how Mansfield's political commentary is bound up with her development of the short story form.

'The Garden Party' focuses on Laura Sheridan's incipient growth towards an understanding of the disparate elements of experience, a growth which involves a move to reject the blinkers of her social conditioning. This conditioning is represented by the collective thought of the Sheridans, exemplified by the fragmented, classist and egocentric world-view of Laura's mother, Mrs Sheridan.

Mansfield's own comments on psychological presentation are revealing, not only in relation to 'The Garden Party', but also because of the affinity they show with the expressed opinions of other modernist writers. Just as Lawrence wanted to remove 'the old stable *ego* of the character' from his work, and Woolf complained against those literary 'gig-lamps symmetrically arranged',[20] Mansfield delivered her own iconoclastic blast against the inherent limitations of conventional fiction's handling of the psyche:

I was only thinking last night people have hardly begun to write yet... I mean prose. Take the very best of it. Aren't they still cutting up sections rather than tackling the whole of a mind? I had a moment of absolute terror in the night. I suddenly thought of *a living mind* – a whole mind – with absolutely nothing left out. With *all* that one knows how much does one not know? I used to fancy one knew all but some kind of mysterious core (or one could). But now I believe just the opposite. The unknown is far, far greater than the known. The known is only a mere shadow. This is a fearful thing and terribly hard to face. But it must be faced.[21]

'The Garden Party' deals with this perceived complexity of experience, and the author's summary of the story is instructive:

That is what I tried to convey in *The Garden Party*. The diversity of life and how we try to fit in everything, Death included. That is bewildering for a person of Laura's age. She feels things ought to happen differently. First one and then another. But life isn't like that. We haven't the ordering of it. Laura says, 'But all these things must not happen at once.' And Life answers, 'Why not? How are they divided from each other.' And they *do* all happen, it is inevitable. And it seems to me there is beauty in that inevitability.[22]

The story, then, treats Laura's incipient psychological growth and rejection of social conditioning, typified by the compartmentalizing of Mrs Sheridan. Interestingly, there is a close analogy between the falsity of the Sheridan way of life and the falsity perceived by Mansfield in conventional modes of character portrayal: the garden party syndrome hinges upon a particular ideological manipulation of experience, a manipulation comparable with the mental 'cutting up [of] sections' to which Mansfield objected.

The story is mediated through Laura's consciousness, but her discourse is tempered by a different discourse which expresses the ideology of Mrs Sheridan. It is this dialogized nature of the narrative which stages the ideological struggle. The apparently innocuous opening paragraph reveals the extent of Laura's indoctrination:

And after all the weather was ideal. They could not have had a more perfect day for a garden party if they had ordered it. Windless, warm, the sky without a cloud.... As for the roses, you could not help feeling they understood that roses are the only flowers that impress people at garden parties; the only flowers that everybody is certain of knowing. Hundreds, yes, literally hundreds, had come out in a single night. (487)

Laura's perceptions here are limited to a monomatic anthropomorphism: outer stimuli are interpreted in terms of her anticipated happiness as her apprehensive excitement for the party burgeons. Behind this discourse lies the dominant influence of Mrs Sheridan, the co-ordinator of the garden party syndrome. The world she represents promulgates the ideology that pecuniary power can create worthwhile and enjoyable social interaction in the shape of a successful party. This voice speaks through Laura here who reflects that a better day for the party could not have been *ordered*. The roses, too, are seen as understanding their utility value in cosmetic social terms.

Laura's conditioned response to the roses provides a link with the delivery of a tray of lilies. Her reaction to these flowers intimates, by way of contrast, her potential for growth beyond the closed Sheridan world. Ordered by Mrs Sheridan for the party, the lilies are intended to contribute to the day's atmosphere just as Laura imagines the roses will. *Potted* plants, however, would seem to be a stage too far for Laura:

> There, just inside the door, stood a wide, shallow tray full of pots of pink lilies. No other kind. Nothing but lilies – canna lilies, big pink flowers, wide open, radiant, almost frighteningly alive on bright crimson stems.
>
> 'O-oh, Sadie!' said Laura, and the sound was like a little moan. She crouched down as if to warm herself at that blaze of lilies; she felt they were in her fingers, on her lips, growing in her breast.
>
> 'It's some mistake,' she said faintly. 'Nobody ever ordered so many. Sadie, go and find mother.'
>
> But at that moment Mrs Sheridan joined them.
>
> 'It's quite right,' she said calmly. 'Yes, I ordered them. Aren't they lovely?' She pressed Laura's arm. (490)

Until the appearance of her mother, Laura is conscious of excess, and struggles with some unformed moral decision. Like the rest of the party's extravagant preparations the lilies, crammed together in pots, represent a distortion of experience: in their artificial proximity they are 'almost frighteningly alive'. Laura's unease is expressed in her sense of the lilies 'growing in her breast', a sensation indicative of a worrying conscience making itself felt. At this point Mrs Sheridan manages to stifle the independent analysis: pressing her daughter's arm she persuades her to toe the Sheridan line.

With the death of Mr Scott, the carter, Laura's tendency to mediate experience through her party mood is interrupted: 'we can't possibly have a garden party with a man dead just outside the front gate', she exclaims (493). External experience impinges, but Laura has not enlarged her understanding of life's diversity: one obsession is temporarily displaced by another. Mrs Sheridan is able to rechannel Laura's tunnel vision by means of strategic flattery: she places one of her own hats on her daughter's head and announces, 'the hat is yours. It's made for you' (494). Laura's vanity defeats her scruples. The passing-down of the hat signifies the heritage that Mrs Sheridan offers her daughter, and Laura is afforded a new glimpse of herself as a replica of her mother: 'Never had she imagined she could look like that' (495). Earlier, when on the phone to her friend Kitty, Laura has already shown herself her mother's daughter on points of style:

Mrs Sheridan's voice floated down the stairs. 'Tell her to wear that sweet hat she had on last Sunday.'
 'Mother says you're to wear that *sweet* hat you had on last Sunday.' (489)

Rather than merely parroting the parental opinion, Laura is happy to appropriate it, as indicated by her own emphasis on 'sweet'. The hat motif is here installed as a symbol of the transference of discourse, and continuing ideological control.

Mrs Sheridan's role as ideologue is developed through her 'brilliant idea' of sending Laura with a basket of scraps from the party to the grieving Scott family (496). Laura's preoccupation with the event outside her ken, and her submerged sympathy for a less privileged social stratum, is channelled into a pre-determined gesture of patronage. In this way an outlet is provided for Laura's incipient social non-conformity at the same time that this impulse is effectively undermined.

It is here that Jameson's characterization of ideology 'as a process whereby otherwise dangerous and protopolitical impulses are "managed" and defused, rechannelled and offered spurious objects' is particularly relevant. The Sheridan children's upbringing has been governed by just this sort of management: their youthful urge to explore and discover has been disarmed of its rebelliousness, while being falsely sated. As children, Laura and her brother Laurie were forbidden to set foot in the Scotts' neighbourhood 'because of the revolting language and of what they might catch' (the narrative here being fully dialogized with Sheridanese) (493). Their subsequent forays into the social unknown of the Scotts' neighbourhood are conditioned by this prejudice: 'since they were grown up, Laura and Laurie on their prowls sometimes walked through. It was disgusting and sordid. They came out with a shudder. But still one must go everywhere; one must see everything. So through they went' (493–4). This conditioned snobbishness restricts the need for contact to an easily satisfied dilettantism. 'One must go everywhere; one must see everything' insists the formulaic Sheridan discourse, even though the conclusion – 'disgusting and sordid' – has been predetermined by indoctrination. Laura and Laurie have their illusion of exploration and contact, even when the nett result is a confirmation of class division and impercipience.

Yet the potential for experiential growth remains present, a fact which Mrs Sheridan is conscious of, as is clear when Laura is on the point of departing for the Scotts'. There remains the potential danger of the encounter with vital experience in the form of death:

'Only the basket, then. And, Laura!' – her mother followed her out of the marquee – 'don't on any account –'
'What, mother?'
No, better not put such ideas into the child's head! 'Nothing! Run along.' (497)

Mrs Sheridan has realized that Laura may be asked, or may ask, to see the dead man laid out. Her unfinished admonishment expresses her desire that such an encounter be prevented, and this convincing expression of parental concern is subtly infused with the classist attitude: death, the great leveller, threatens to provide tangible proof of universal human frailty and, by extension, powerful evidence of the superficiality of class distinctions.

Laura does see the dead man, more by accident than design, and the incident triggers a confused moment of revelation in

which a more complex concept of experience than her upbringing has admitted impinges on her consciousness:

> His head was sunk in the pillow, his eyes were closed; they were blind
> under the closed eyelids. He was given up to his dream. What did
> garden parties and baskets and lace frocks matter to him? He was far
> from all those things. He was wonderful, beautiful. While they were
> laughing and while the band was playing, this marvel had come to the
> lane. (498–9)

The 'epiphany' is compromised. It embodies a dawning
awareness of the disparate elements of life and their random
simultaneity and, consequently, a partial progression beyond
rigid class distinctions. But the experience is mediated through
the (still persisting) Sheridan discourse, indicated here by a
certain wondering aestheticism. This recalls Laura's earlier
anthropomorphic reception of outer stimuli, conditioned by a
particular emotion. Here a different emotion arouses the same
aesthetic. Laura has arrived at the brink of a vision, but her
Sheridanese is inadequate for rendering the experience. When
she attempts to explain the revelation she finds her sentence
unfinishable: '"Isn't life," she stammered, "isn't life –"' But
what life was she couldn't explain' (499).

The epiphany is complex because it gathers positive and
negative forces around a single fulcrum. In one sense the very
nature of the near-vision – its revelation of the totality and
diversity of life, and the discrediting of class distinctions –
renders it unfit for précis. But it is only a partial vision, mediated
and compromised by a restricted language.

This ambiguity is superbly conveyed by the hat motif, which
makes its most significant contribution when Laura, still
wearing her party hat, views the body:

> He was wonderful, beautiful. While they were laughing and while the
> band was playing, this marvel had come to the lane. Happy...
> happy... All is well, said that sleeping face. This is just as it should be.
> I am content.
>   But all the same you had to cry, and she couldn't go out of the room
> without saying something to him. Laura gave a loud childish sob.
>   'Forgive my hat,' she said. (498–9; original ellipsis)

The hat, as we have seen, is emblematic of the Sheridan world. Here Laura considers it a solecism to her new, emerging conception of the world, and, in recognizing the need to apologize for it, she seems implicitly to be rejecting it and the world it represents. At the same time, however, the hat symbolizes the fallen Sheridan discourse, a notion confirmed here by Laura's concern at the impropriety of her headgear: the voice of Mrs Sheridan is heard once more making an irrelevant and superficial response. Even over the question of propriety, however, the ambiguity persists, since the party hat, being black, suggests funeral garb: it is half appropriate to the experience, as is fitting in relation to Laura's partial advancement. Laura's confused discourse encapsulates the ideological conflict, and the ambiguity of her apology indicates a limited, but important, debunking of the Sheridan voice. This ending also illuminates the issue of the 'paradoxical' and 'mysterious' nature of the short story form perceived by many commentators. Here the mysterious aura surrounding the death clearly emulates Laura's qualified enlightenment, a 'mystery' which the reader is required to see beyond. Laura, 'the artistic one' of the family (487), exemplifies the dual relationship to ideology which I have been tracing in other stories: just as literature can reveal the ideological restraints under which it labours, so does Laura's artistic capacity, for Mansfield, enable her to question and make a preliminary break with the restrictive context which still binds her.

It is important to note that there is a close relationship between the ideological restraints which Mansfield takes as her target and the restrictive fictional practices which she simultaneously disrupts. The symbolic hat, rather than connoting a single, fixed idea, reveals the ambiguity of Laura's situation: the literary device of a stable symbolism is rejected together with the false imposition of a social hierarchy. This coincidence of disruptive form and content clearly relates to the whole composition of a story, particularly in challenging the notion of unified development. The significant moment in Mansfield is an opening out of possibilities rather than a narrowing down, or a particular revelation. Yet the limiting conventions are played off against the radical gesture, as at the end of 'The Garden Party' where the scene is set for a clear dawning of awareness which does not come, Mansfield's point being that the anticipated epiphany would be reductive and simplistic. The conclusion of 'Bliss' uses the expectation of the conventional love-triangle to order a supposed moment of shock for Bertha Young, yet the discovery of her husband's adultery is really not the issue, and neither is there any sudden revelation: Bertha's homosexual tendencies, implicit throughout the narrative, are merely allowed to surface, in the process throwing her world into chaos. The ambiguity of the ending, and its symbolism, summarizes her impossible social position: the pressures of conformity, which deny her true feelings, are mirrored in the fictional expectations which Mansfield flouts. Mansfield's characters invariably experience a complex of external voices shaping their attitudes and behaviour, and this is what her cultivation of an impersonal style – her defeat of the personal – connotes: an insistence that individual behaviour is not a purely autonomous or straightforward phenomenon, to be rendered in a transparent story form, but rather a focus of confusion and conflict, requiring a polyphonous presentation.

CHAPTER 5

Wyndham Lewis: The Vorticist short story

In the stories of Joyce, Woolf and Mansfield, there is a substantial common ground in terms of method and effect; and, for each writer, formal dissonance is both a yardstick of generic innovation and a vital key to interpretation. All three writers, in their different ways, expand the short story form to incorporate and express a complex view of the interaction between individual experience and social organization. There is, however, a different side to the modernist preoccupation with personality and its social definition, a starker view typified in the short stories of Wyndham Lewis. This starker view is bound up with Lewis's aesthetic goals, and these are given direct formal expression in his major collection of stories, *The Wild Body*, published in 1927.

The collection displays the typical modernist preoccupation with literary form and artifice, but the use it makes of form and convention betrays an attitude to personality, and to society, which is quite different from that expressed in the works discussed so far. The book is representative of the dichotomous view of art as rarefied activity – satirized in Mansfield's 'Je ne Parle pas Français'. An analysis of the Wyndham Lewis collection, then, will contribute to a broader account of modernism, and, in the process, will provide an alternative test for the analytical approach to the short story propounded in previous chapters: where the stories of Joyce, Woolf and Mansfield make *overtly* disruptive gestures – designed to establish connections between text and context – we might expect the Wyndham Lewis stories to betray an opposite tendency, designed to buttress the authority and distinctiveness of the literary discourse. In a sense this is the case: these stories do not follow a principle of explicit formal dissonance in the effects they create, and this (comparative) lack of technical experimentation is an inevitable aspect of the bleak and static social vision conveyed. Yet there is an element of dissonance in these stories which, although not so pronounced as in the work of the other modernists, is equally crucial, usually as a means of exposing the contradictions implicit in Lewis's themes.

The importance of *The Wild Body* in the history of modernism lies in its relation to Vorticism. *The Wild Body* represents a systematic application of the Vorticist programme to the short story, and this fact alone makes it a key twentieth-century text, if Vorticism is accepted as the major movement it is sometimes claimed to be. Vorticism took as its aim the hugely ambitious project of uniting all the arts with a single world-view, and, given the extravagance of this intention, assessing the importance of the movement, particularly to the history of the visual arts, has been a contentious issue.[1] What is clear is that Vorticism was the only major artistic movement of the twentieth century to have originated in Britain, and this makes *The Wild Body* unique in the development of the short story since it is the principal expression of literary Vorticism in the genre. Purely in terms of literary history, then, the comparative neglect of *The Wild Body* is surprising: while book-length monographs on Lewis contain some helpful discussions of the stories, studies of the short story at large have ignored him completely.[2]

Another area of critical neglect is pertinent here: the role of literature in the Vorticist movement is sometimes overlooked in surveys of modernism. Lewis's Vorticist aesthetic entered his pictorial output with greater immediacy than it infiltrated his literary work, so its relevance to the development of his painting is more obvious. But this also suggests that Vorticist principles play a more enduring role in the development of his fiction, and, indeed, these principles can be discerned as important constituents of Lewis's writing long after 1914–15 when Vorticism first emerged.[3] Thus it is quite legitimate to view *The Wild Body* of 1927 as an expression of literary Vorticism. In fact the gestation period of the collection, from 1909 to 1927, emphasizes its relationship to the Vorticist movement, even when narrowly defined: the stories straddle the short lifespan often accorded to Vorticism (roughly 1914–19).[4] Many of the stories which were to form *The Wild Body* were published in earlier forms between 1909 and 1922, but they were reworked – their debt to anecdote and travel sketch effaced – to become fully-fledged fictional works in the completed volume.[5]

The ways in which these stories enact the Vorticist aesthetic – an aesthetic founded on a fundamental dichotomy between art and life – reveals the extent of Lewis's generic innovation, such as it is. But this art/life separation also accounts for the absence, in Lewis, of the disruptive gestures which link world and text in the stories of Joyce, Woolf and Mansfield. To account for Lewis's austere ethos, a brief outline of the Vorticist position is necessary here as a preface to more specific generic issues.

True art, for Lewis, has the quality of deadness, and avoids the flux and mutability of life. The eponymous character in the novel *Tarr* voices Lewis's conviction that 'deadness is the first condition of art'.[6] The Vorticist stance of detachment grows naturally out of this basis. Since art is distinct from life, it functions at a contemplative remove, and this detachment applies equally to the artist and to the nature of his art. The image of the vortex aptly illustrates this aesthetic basis: the still centre of the vortex represents the point of detachment from which the artist observes, and attempts to make sense of, the surrounding maelstrom of modern life.

Closely allied to the concept of the detached, still point is the use of dynamic form, a term which indicates the formative influences of Vorticism, in which the essential attributes of Futurism and Analytical Cubism are combined: the Futurists' interest in the dynamism of the modern world is reproduced, but is tempered by a tendency to formal analysis, as in Cubist art.[7] The cultivation of dynamic form therefore expresses the desire to depict the dynamism of the machine age in a way commensurate with the Vorticist dichotomy of life and art: if the artistic stance of analytic detachment is adhered to, this dichotomy can be preserved. Vorticist art attempts to achieve this by employing forms (i.e. 'dead' pictorial patterns) which convey the essence of dynamism. Dynamic form, in other words, is motion paralysed. The vortex itself is one such dynamic form, since the flux which surrounds the still central point is contained in a prescribed pattern, and the nature of this pattern encapsulates the stance of the Vorticist: the flux only has meaning in relation to the still point around which it must necessarily take shape, the still point which is synonymous with the detached stance of the artist.

Occasionally, the image of the vortex is used in direct pictorial fashion in Lewis's painting. The shapes in *Workshop* (1914–15), for instance, seem fashioned around a still central pivot, while in two figurative pieces of 1912 – *Le Penseur* and *The Vorticist* – a contemplative figure (pensive in the former, anguished in the latter) is actually part of a vortex.[8] However, it is usually more helpful to consider the vortex as an abstract model. Thus, Lewis employs dynamic forms in his paintings which incorporate the aesthetic concerns encapsulated in the image of the vortex, but which do not necessarily bear a direct physical resemblance to it. The model is, naturally, even more removed in Lewis's literary output: like other visual metaphors for the short story, the vortex has a value in locating guiding artistic principles, but it is an imprecise analogy for literary composition, and must be acknowledged as such.

The clearest indications of the Vorticist aesthetic in *The Wild Body* are given in two theoretical essays, 'Inferior Religions' and 'The Meaning of the Wild Body', both of which are part of the collection. These essays explain the principles that lie behind the stories, Vorticist principles adapted to a theory of short story composition. Most obvious is the emphasis on the dichotomy of mind and body:

First, to assume the dichotomy of mind and body is necessary here, without arguing it; for it is upon that essential separation that the theory of laughter here proposed is based. The essential us, that is the laugher, is as distinct from the Wild Body as in the Upanisadic account of the souls returned from the paradise of the Moon, which, entering into plants, are yet distinct from them. Or to take the symbolic vedic figure of the two birds, the one watching and passive, the other enjoying its activity, we similarly have to postulate *two* creatures, one that never enters into life, but that travels about in a vessel to whose destiny it is momentarily attached. That is, of course, the laughing observer, and the other is the Wild Body. (157)

The reference to the Hindu belief in the separateness of the soul is ironic, but it emphasizes Lewis's dichotomy, which hinges on the absurdity of the body. This absurdity is made all the more manifest by the inextricable linking of mind and body, of dumb matter with intellect. To be aware of the dichotomy and to laugh at it is all that can be achieved by way of redemption. This theory of laughter is the basis of Lewisan satire, derived from a profound Cartesian dualism. This kind of laughter is the assertion of the intellect, the mind's acknowledgement of its separate nature, and here the theory of laughter, or *satire*, parallels the separation of art and life: art is life considered at an intellectual remove, and a similar contemplative distancing can be achieved by the person who acknowledges the absurdity of the body and its intrinsic difference from the mind. Ker-Orr, the narrator of the stories, is just such a person. It is his self-knowledge that lifts him above the unconscious Wild Bodies of the stories: he acknowledges in himself the division that they are unconscious of:

I know much more about myself than people generally do. For instance I am aware that I am a barbarian. By rights I should be paddling about in a corracle. My body is large, white and savage. But all the fierceness has become transformed into *laughter*. (17)

Just as the separation of art and life leads to a stance of detachment in the Vorticist aesthetic, Ker-Orr's conscious understanding of the distinction of mind and body accords him a privileged position of detached observation, a position which directly parallels the position of the Vorticist artist. For the purposes of these stories, Ker-Orr is the centre of the vortex, a position sometimes alluded to overtly, as in his first sight of the character Carl in 'Beau Séjour': 'his grin of protest wandered in an aimless circle, with me for centre' (52). Ker-Orr speaks of his detachment from his physical self, a quality which validates his position as the withdrawn observer of the Wild Bodies in the collection: 'My sense of humour in its mature phase has arisen in this very acute consciousness of what is *me*.... This forked, strange-scented, blond-skinned gut-bag, with its two bright rolling marbles with which it sees, bull's eyes full of mockery and madness, is my stalking-horse. I hang somewhere in its midst operating it with detachment' (18).

Allied to the notion of detachment in the Vorticist aesthetic is the principle of dynamic form, and this has a crucial bearing on the structure of Lewis's stories. Dynamic form in the sense in which it is used in the stories does not apply to the structure of the prose in any specific syntactic, or semantic, sense; it applies, rather, to the activities of the characters under observation, activities which seem limited to certain predetermined patterns, and these patterns echo certain forms used by Lewis in his paintings to depict circumscribed human activity. This comparison depends upon a *narrative* reading of the visual work, it should be said, and does not indicate the presence of comparable technical effects operating in the two media. In the essay 'Inferior Religions' Lewis suggests that the rigid patterns of activity of the characters are comparable to the limited rituals and customs of a primitive religion, such as a ritualistic dance. He writes: 'we have in most lives the spectacle of a pattern as circumscribed and complete as a theorem of Euclid. So these are essays in a new human mathematic' (149). This reference to Euclidean geometry, unlike Joyce's in *Dubliners*, indicates a highly structured principle of composition. The term 'religious' in this context carries the implication of automatism and Lewis goes on in the essay to describe the automatism of some of the characters, noticeably by using machine imagery for the circumscribed activities of the Wild Bodies:

These intricately moving bobbins are all subject to a set of objects or to one in particular. Brotcotnaz is fascinated by one object, for instance; one at once another vitality. He bangs up against it wildly at regular intervals, blackens it, contemplates it, moves round it and dreams. He reverences it: it is his task to kill it. All such fascination is religious. The damp napkins of the inn-keeper are the altar-cloths of his rough illusion, as Julie's bruises are the markings upon an idol; with the peasant, Mammon dominating the background. Zoborov and Mademoiselle Péronnette struggle for a Pension de Famille, unequally. Zoborov is the 'polish' cuckoo of a stupid and ill-managed nest. (149)

The interaction of the characters determines the patterns of the stories, and these patterns involve the whole plot of a story. 'Brotcotnaz' is representative of the collection in adapting a particular short story convention – in this case the story with a reversal – and converting that notion of plot, or story 'shape' into a dynamic form amenable to the Vorticist project. The story concerns an aggressive innkeeper (the story's eponymous protagonist) and his battered wife. After frequent and severe beatings at the hands of her Wild Body husband, Madame Brotcotnaz is to be seen in the inn swathed in bandages, and perpetuating the myth of an illness – erysipelas – to account for her appearance. Nobody is fooled by this 'public' secret, but it enables her (together with her surreptitious quaffing of eau-de-vie) to keep going.

Ker-Orr affects a complete detachment from this state of affairs, and concentrates his attention on the external, physical fact of the couple's problem. His lack of apparent moral orientation is evident in the deliberate provocation of Madam Brotcotnaz. Without regard for her feelings, he probes her personal life in his single-minded investigation of the savage phenomenon of her marriage:

I approached the door of the débit in my noiseless *espadrilles* (that is, the hemp and canvas shoes of the country), and sprang quickly in after her. I snapped her with my eye while I shouted:
'Madame Brotcotnaz! Attention!'
She was behind the bar-counter, the fat medicine-glass was in the air, reversed. Her head was back, the last drops were trickling down between her gum and underlip, which stuck out like the spout of a cream-jug. The glass crashed down on the counter; Julie jumped, her hand on her heart. Beneath, among tins and flagons, on a shelf, she pushed at a bottle. She was trying to get it out of sight. I rushed up to her and seized one of her hands.
'I am glad to see you, Madame Brotcotnaz!' I exclaimed. 'Neuralgia again?' I pointed to the face. (133-4)

Ker-Orr deliberately takes her by surprise to catch her drinking, and then begins probing her about her most recent beating. If we are to give credence to the detached stance of the Vorticist artist, then we should not see any malice in this disregard of her two great secrets: this is merely the observing Ker-Orr in investigative mood. Monsieur Brotcotnaz's repeated beatings of his wife, and her acceptance of the situation, are presented as ritualistic aspects of an inferior religion. Brotcotnaz is solicitous and considerate to his wife after he has beaten her, but he seems helpless to stop mistreating her: she is the object of an obsession for him, an obsession which manifests itself as automatic violence. She too enters into the perpetuation of this ritual by her passivity, a complicity represented visually by the image of the couple dancing:[9]

> 'Is Madame fond of dancing? I asked.
> 'Why, yes. Julie can dance.'
> He rose, and extending his hand to his wife with an indulgent gallantry, he exclaimed:
> 'Viens donc, Julie! Come then. Let us dance.'
> Julie sat and sneered through her vinous mask at her fascinating husband. He insisted, standing over her with one toe pointed outward in the first movement of the dance, his hand held for her to take in a courtly attitude.
> 'Viens donc, Julie! Dansons un peu!'
> Shedding shamefaced, pinched, and snuffling grins to right and left as she allowed herself to be drawn into this event, she rose. They danced a sort of minuet for me, advancing and retreating, curtseying and posturing, shuffling rapidly their feet. Julie did her part, it seemed, with understanding. (138)

Despite her reticence Madame Brotcotnaz displays 'understanding' of the part she has to play in the minuet: the circumscribed dance mirrors the repeated acts of violence, for in both cases the couple are engaged in actions which involve a set and repetitive sequence of movements in relation to one another, and in both cases a grim acceptance is apparent. On the morning after a beating, we read, the couple 'are resigned, but none the less they remember the cross they have to bear' (139). The suggestion of martyrdom here clearly alludes to the notion of inferior religion. Why, though, do they *have* to bear this cross? The answer is that the pattern itself dominates the human figures who are powerless to escape the parameters of its form. The image of the dance makes this clear, its automatic and mechanical movement summarizing the couple's relationship.

This local image of the dance condenses the pattern of the human drama, and this larger pattern is the focus of the story. Ker-Orr feels that one day Brotcotnaz will surely kill his wife if things remain as they are. She does, in fact, sustain serious injury, but not at the hands of her husband. As the story ends she is in serious danger of losing one or more limbs, having been run over by a cart, and now the circumscribed pattern has been shattered, with no possibility of a resumption. The story concludes with a shift in the balance of power in the Brotcotnaz marriage, Madame Brotcotnaz dominant in the inn, which has now become her domain:

> She returned to the table and sat down, lowering herself to the chair, and sticking out her bandaged foot. She took the drink I gave her, and raised it almost with fire to her lips. After the removal of her arm, and possibly a foot, I realized that she would be more difficult to get on with than formerly. The bottle of eau-de-vie would remain no doubt in full view, to hand, on the counter, and Brotcotnaz would be unable to lay a finger on her: in all likelihood she meant that arm to come off. (144)

On the face of it we are presented with a simple ironic reversal, a straightforward shift in the domestic balance of power. This is stock story material, but it has been transformed through Lewis's emphasis on the behavioural pattern and its ultimate rupture: the 'reversal', rather than being a surprise, is the logical outcome of the story's dynamic, a pattern of aggression which must result in destruction, in a breaking apart. The concluding lines, as Ker-Orr departs, depict the rupture:

> 'To your speedy recovery, Madame Brotcotnaz,' I said.
> We drank to that, and Brotcotnaz came to the door. Julie remained alone in the débit. (144)

The simple symbolic image of Julie and Brotcotnaz apart, she remaining in the inn while he comes to the door, underlines not only her newly acquired control of the domestic scene, but also, and more importantly, the rupture of the pattern which previously had linked the couple, indoors, in an enclosed set of automatic responses. This concluding, and therefore resonant image of apartness forms a pointed contrast with the earlier minuet, but a separation that is the logical outcome of the earlier contact, and which emphasizes the mental division which remains unchanged. Lewis, then, adapts a stock story type for his own creative purpose: the disruption of form (the complication of 'reversal') is bound up with the story's analysis of a relationship. Superficially, this disruption appears to be at one with the kind of techniques that recur in the modernist short story, but there is, in fact, a crucial difference: where the other modernists link their disruptions to particularized contextual analysis, Lewis does not. For Woolf and Mansfield, for instance, the disruption of convention is often an implicitly feminist gesture, while in Joyce's *Dubliners* formal dissonance is intimately related to his critique of Irish social mores. In Lewis's work, however, there is no comparable sense of social intervention or context, and this means that the satirical element of his formal disruptions has a quite different effect: the satire is rootless, expressive, apparently, of an ahistorical and unchanging view of human interaction; this is a view conveyed by maintaining a creative balance in favour of the rigidities of literary form, rather than in favour of their deconstruction.

The existence of satire, however, indicates a strong element of commentary in the Lewis stories, despite the predicated objectivity of the Vorticist stance, and this is clearly so in the case of 'Brotcotnaz'. A comparison with the earlier version of the story, entitled 'Brobdingnag', indicates the importance of narrative pattern in the final version, and it is this pattern which implies judgement. In the early draft there is no resolution and the narrator is left to reflect on how the husband (Brobdingnag) might react: he imagines 'those nocturnal rites growing more savage and desperate', a development leading to a growth of insecurity, and the possible 'complete ruin' of Brobdingnag (296). There is no actual resolution, but rather a conjecture that the behavioural pattern will become more frenetic before burning itself out. In the rewrite this idea of rupture becomes pronounced and is transformed into the inevitable reversal of fortune, a development which suggests a kind of nemesis and, consequently, a degree of judgement. In fact there is an implicit judgement in the narrative stance and the ironic effects it produces.

The complexity of this kind of narrative stance is more apparent in 'The Death of the Ankou', a story which cultivates a deliberate ambiguity in this area. In retrospect 'The Death of the Ankou' leaves an impression of satirical scorn for superstitious folklore, but this impression requires an attentive reading of a story which seems ambiguous and unresolved at first glance.

The action begins with Ker-Orr reading a book of local Breton folklore, and focusing on the account of the blind Breton death god, the Ankou. An encounter with this apparition, so the legend has it, indicates imminent death. Looking up from his book Ker-Orr sees an apparition that he momentarily takes for the Ankou, and he experiences a fleeting sensation of superstitious mortal fear. In reality it is a blind beggar called Ludo that he sees, the central character of the story whom Ker-Orr subsequently tries to befriend. He seeks Ludo out at his cave and attempts to engage him in conversation. Discovering that Ludo is unwell, Ker-Orr remarks banteringly: 'Perhaps you've met the Ankou' (114). Taking this remark as terribly prognostic, Ludo's attitude soon changes. He refuses further intercourse with Ker-Orr and hurries off to conceal himself in his cave. When Ker-Orr next enquires about Ludo he discovers that he is dead, and there the story ends.

Superficially, the story might seem to adopt an open-ended attitude to the Ankou legend, or at least to the machinations of fate. This is how Timothy Materer, who defines the story as tragic rather than satiric, reads it:

The death-god had passed Ker-Orr by and, in its blindness, fixed instead on the object of his original fear. The effect of the story lies in what is left unsaid. No one knows for sure what Ludo dies of. He was simply felled by a random stroke from the Ankou; men are as blind to fate as Ludo was to the world around him.[10]

Ker-Orr's initial susceptibility to the primitive superstition of the death god would seem to corroborate this view. Yet such a reading would render 'The Death of the Ankou' an item unrelated to the *Wild Body* collection, unrelated to its principles of composition – even in opposition to these principles, for the Ankou myth is surely a prime example of an 'inferior religion'.

The story does, in fact, treat the Ankou myth as an inferior religion, even though it cultivates an aura of credibility to surround the myth, but this is an implicit aspect of the story's satirical purpose. The first clue to this purpose comes immediately after Ker-Orr's 'vision' of the Ankou: he at once rationalizes and explains this away as an aberration, and the terms used in this disclaimer are significant:

The blinded figure had burst into my daydream so unexpectedly and so pat, that I was taken aback by this sudden close-up of so trite a tragedy. Where he had come was compact with an emotional medium emitted by me. In reality it was a private scene, so that this overweening intruder might have been marching through my mind with his taut convulsive step, club in hand, rather than merely traversing the eating-room of a hotel, after a privileged visit to the kitchen. Certainly at that moment my mind was lying open so much, or was so much exteriorized, that almost literally, as far as I was concerned, it was inside, not out, that this image forced its way. Hence, perhaps, the strange effect. (110)

Ker-Orr's privileged position of detachment, we recall, is dependent on a rigid division between the mental and physical, or internal and external worlds. Here, however, not only are the two worlds allowed to merge, but they are actually transposed. A physical phenomenon is allowed to create an extravagant impression on Ker-Orr's mind only because his guard is down in this undisciplined fashion. This 'strange effect' is discredited as a 'private scene', for which we can legitimately read 'personal delusion'.

Susceptibility to this kind of superstition depends upon the defeat of the intellect, the common denominator of the other ritualistic inferior religions in the collection. Ker-Orr's lapse, however, creates an effect of ambiguity in the story which leads the reader on to a half-credulous stance towards the Ankou myth, a stance which has scope for development in the absence of clear narratorial guidelines. This aspect of the story is a deliberate cultivation by Lewis of a stock type of supernatural story, a type characterized by an air of uncertainty and implied meanings, and it is just this type of effect that Materer locates in his analysis, arguing that 'the effect of the story lies in what is left unsaid'. The final line of the story bolsters this effect with its laconic revelation of the action's dénouement: 'Later that summer the fisherman I had been with at the Pardon told me that Ludo was dead' (115). This bears a calculated resemblance to the discovery-after-the-event type of revelation which resonates with implied meanings at the end of so many supernatural tales, usually being the sole purpose of the composition. Poe's story 'A Tale of the Ragged Mountains' is a good example of this, where the backward spelling of a name confirms a supernatural connection between two characters ('Bedlo(e)' and 'Oldeb').[11] Yet this Lewisan ending is *too* brief to belong to this category. It poses as a stock device, yet satirizes that very device by its exaggerated brevity. The bare factual statement, rather than creating a chill, is a perfectly acceptable conclusion to the prosaic events of the narrative. Ludo himself has declared his illness, and the boy who looks after him has also attested to his poor health. Indeed, the death of a blind, cave-dwelling beggar in poor health, however regrettable, is scarcely cause for surprise. The factual statement of Ludo's demise represents the reassertion of Ker-Orr's intellect, and his acceptance of the logic of this outcome.

Lewis, in this story, satirizes the inferior religion of credulity in superstition and the supernatural, and he does so by undermining a stock technique. The reader, as well as the narrator, is drawn into a stance of credulity by an unguided, atmospheric narrative, before being shaken by an abrupt ending which invites an intellectual reassessment of the facts of the narrative. In this way an automatic response is elicited, first from Ker-Orr, and then from the reader, a response which parallels the pattern of the stock supernatural story as well as the pattern of the inferior religion in question.

The ambiguity cultivated in 'The Death of the Ankou' stems from a temporary lapse in the narrative stance, a failure on the part of Ker-Orr to preserve the Vorticist distinction between inner and outer worlds. Indeed, the satirical point of the story *depends* on the temporary collapse of Vorticist detachment, even though the cold intellectual eye is reasserted at the end. However, a compromise of the withdrawn position is implicit in this story (and in the others) since a satirical purpose depends upon some kind of involvement incompatible with complete detachment. This fact indicates a seminal contradiction in the Vorticist stance, a disjunction between detachment and commitment.

A way of accounting for this contradiction is suggested in Ortega y Gasset's famous essay 'The Dehumanization of Art', an essay which has a particular resonance in relation to *The Wild Body*. Ortega y Gasset, writing in the 1920s, discerned a new tendency in the artistic developments of his age, a tendency to short-circuit direct, realistic representation, and this is an attribute of modernist art which is now widely recognized. The tendencies discussed in this essay – the tendencies 'to dehumanize art, to avoid living forms, to see to it that the work of art is nothing but a work of art' – are particularly marked in early Lewis, who exemplifies the thesis that 'for the modern artist, aesthetic pleasure derives from ... a triumph over human matter'.[12] This detachment, however, does not preclude commitment: indeed the very dehumanization of character, linked as it is to a satirical intent, indicates a commitment to expose absurdity, and the very notion of absurdity depends upon the violation of an alternative order.

The question of commitment/detachment is complicated by Lewis's choice of the image of the physician to characterize the satiric stance of Ker-Orr. One of the few biographical details we are given about him is that his father is a doctor, and that this has been a traditional family profession (18). In 'A Soldier of Humour' Ker-Orr extends the motif of illness and cure when he hoists de Valmore with the petard of his own rabid nationalism, a passage examined below. The important thing about the physician motif is that it conjoins the conflicting elements of commitment and detachment: there is a withdrawn professionalism in the attitude of the physician, yet a simultaneous involvement and obligation to provide a cure. The early critical perspective of Ortega is particularly relevant to this question of gradations of detachment. In the essay cited, Ortega himself uses the stance of the doctor in defining the function of aloofness, or detachment. The witnessing of a man's death, from various standpoints, is employed to discuss representation in art: the role of doctor at this hypothetical scene is different in kind from that of wife and (more significantly, on the question of aesthetics) from that of reporter and painter:

The reporter, like the doctor, has been brought here for professional reasons and not out of a spontaneous human interest. But while the doctor's profession requires him to interfere, the reporter's requires him precisely to stay aloof; he has to confine himself to observing.... The painter...completely unconcerned, does nothing but keep his eyes open.... In the painter we find a maximum of distance and a minimum of feeling intervention.[13]

Ortega's purpose, in this account of artistic withdrawal, is to stress the emotional distance, and the subsequent transformation and objectification of the real event – its dehumanization – characteristic of 'the new artistic produce'. The point of invoking this early perspective here is that it provides an important preliminary angle on Vorticism. Ortega's scale of objectivity suggests that the stance of Ker-Orr does not really qualify as the basis of a fully dehumanized art, as a means of turning the real event 'into a theme of pure observation', which depends upon that 'maximum of distance' and 'minimum of feeling' which Ortega identifies with the painter's perspective.[14] Like Ortega's doctor, Ker-Orr betrays a professional involvement.

Ker-Orr's self-representation as physician, despite its ironic aspect, is nevertheless a serious analogy for his systematic exposure of the Wild Bodies he encounters. The dehumanization of character is thus a diagnosis by the contemplative Vorticist, who is also *in, and involved with*, the world. Indeed, Ker-Orr usually *provokes* the action, the behavioural patterns, which occur around him, and he acknowledges the subjectivity involved in his presentation:

I admit that I am disposed to forget that people are real – that they are, that is, not subjective patterns belonging specifically to me, in the course of this joke-life, which indeed has for its very principle a denial of the accepted actual. (17)

In 'forgetting' that people are real, Ker-Orr narrates a series of stories in which the characterization is aptly described as subjective patterning, and here Lewis's principle of composition coincides with Ortega's account of purpose in modern art being allied to the separation of idea and reality:

If, turning our back on alleged reality, we take the ideas for what they are – mere subjective patterns – and make them live as such…in short, if we deliberately propose to 'realize' our ideas – then we have dehumanized and, as it were, derealized them. For ideas are really unreal.[16]

Ker-Orr's observations are an extension of his own ideas: the centre of the vortex, in other words, gives form to, and controls, the surrounding patterns. Consequently, Ker-Orr feels that Monsieur and Madame Brotcotnaz 'danced a sort of minuet *for me*' (138; my emphasis), and, in 'Bestre', announces that he has 'become more conscious of myself and of my powers of personally provoking a series of typhoons in tea-cups' (80). (The typhoon (vortex) image is aptly chosen.)

The Ortega essay describes an artistic stance which the Lewis stories show both affinities with and differences from, and this unevenness underscores the contradictions implicit in Lewis's aesthetic. The separation of idea and reality is a strong impulse, yet the detachment of Ortega's painter, appropriate to the process of derealization, does not account for the involvement of Ker-Orr. The resulting contradiction between commitment and detachment is an essential feature of the effects produced by the stories.

'A Soldier of Humour' dramatizes this conflict between detachment and commitment which characterizes Ker-Orr's position as both recorder and instigator of the action. In this case Ker-Orr is the major participant in the action, which concerns his encounter with a Frenchman who reveres all things American, and who wishes to pass himself off as American as well. A fierce *verbal* battle between the narrator and this Monsieur de Valmore occurs in which Ker-Orr humiliates his interlocutor by subtly drawing attention to his French origins. De Valmore subsequently nurses a consuming hatred for Ker-Orr, an emotion born of a confused, but fervent, nationalism.

Despising Ker-Orr as an Englishman, and one against which he has a particular grudge, de Valmore subsequently attempts to ruin Ker-Orr's stay at the Spanish town of Pontaisandra (fictional), the place chosen by him for a language-learning sojourn. De Valmore's commercial dominance of the town enables him to turn the townsfolk against their visitor: the verbal battle clearly has different aspects, involving spoken argument, language and nationalism, and also language acquisition and power. Ostracized and out-manoeuvred, and with the purpose of his visit to Pontaisandra defeated, Ker-Orr prepares to leave. The tables are turned, however, with the arrival of a trio of Americans, friends of Ker-Orr. These three, under Ker-Orr's instructions, befriend de Valmore, the pseudo-American devotee of all that is genuinely American, as a prelude to the presentation of Ker-Orr as their highly esteemed companion, an assessment de Valmore is forced to accept.

Clearly, there is a large element of involvement for Ker-Orr in the action, which would seem incompatible with the detached role. It has already been pointed out, however, that Ker-Orr is no different from the Wild Bodies of the stories in embodying an absurdist mind–body separation. His claim to distinction lies in his acknowledgement of this separation, and it is by insisting on this self-knowledge that Ker-Orr attempts to preserve his theoretical position of detached observer. Significantly, Ker-Orr attempts this theoretical justification before relating the story's central incidents, as if to forestall any misinterpretation regarding his motives:

I could fill pages with descriptions of myself and my ways. But such abstractions from the life lived are apt to be misleading, because most men do not easily detach the principle from the living thing in that manner, and so when handed the abstraction alone do not know what to do with it, or they apply it wrongly. I exist with an equal ease in the abstract world of principle and in the concrete world of fact. As I can express myself equally well in either, I will stick to the latter here, as then I am more likely to be understood. So I will show you myself in action, manoeuvring in the heart of the reality. (19)

Ker-Orr distinguishes here between 'the abstract world of principle' and 'the concrete world of fact', a separation which is a reformulation of the split between the intellectual and

physical worlds. He indicates that the two must remain distinct
– he chooses between the abstract and the concrete – yet it is
difficult not to conclude that his intellectual life is implicated
in the emotive tussle which follows. A stance of fascinated
detachment is cultivated in relation to the whole episode, the
attitude of a scientist who just happens to be using himself as a
guinea pig in an intellectually absorbing experiment; but this
stance is disingenuous, and obscures the satirical purpose.

In this piece Ker-Orr's satiric eye scrutinizes the Wild Body
de Valmore, a man whose obsessive nationalism dictates his
automatic and unreasoning responses. Desiring to pass himself
off as American he is thwarted by the ineffaceable signs of his
French origins, a conflict apparent (though unexplained) on his
first appearance:

He was dressed with sombre floridity. In his dark purple-slate suit with
thin crimson lines, in his dark red hat-band, in his rose-buff tie,
swarming with cerulean fire-flies, in his stormily flowered waistcoat,
you felt that his taste for the violent and sumptuous had everywhere
struggled to assert itself, and everywhere been overcome. But by
what? That was the important secret of this man's entire machine, a
secret unfolded by his subsequent conduct. (23)

In passing it is worth noting that this conflict depends upon a
preconceived North American stereotype, and this precon-
ception, implicit in Ker-Orr's description, betrays a bigotry of
his own (and Lewis's) even though it is passed off as wry
detachment. Leaving aside, for a moment, the contradictions
implicit in the narrative stance, the purpose is to establish de
Valmore as a symbol of knee-jerk nationalism. The revelation
by Ker-Orr of his Englishness provokes de Valmore's great
hatred, even though he accepts it, outwardly, with a machine-
like passivity (23–4). Once stirred, however, his unreasoning
anger pursues its ferocious course unchecked, manifesting itself,
first of all, in automatic argument:

After another significant pause he brusquely chose a new subject of
conversation. It was a subject upon which, it was evident, he was
persuaded that it would be quite impossible for us to agree. He took a
long draught of the powerful fluid served to each diner. I disagreed
with him at first out of politeness. But as he seemed resolved to work
himself up slowly into a national passion, I changed round, and agreed

with him. For a moment he glared at me. He felt at bay before this dreadful subtlety to which his americanism exposed him: then he warily changed his position in the argument, taking up the point of view he had begun by attacking.

We changed about alternately for a while. It was a most diverting game. At one time in taking my new stand, and asserting something, either I had changed too quickly, or he had not done so quickly enough. At all events, when he began speaking he found himself *agreeing* with me. This was a breathless moment. It was very close quarters indeed. (27–8)

There is an obvious irony here: argument, notionally the tool of intellectual reasoning, is employed by de Valmore as the vehicle of his unreasoning national passion. He has no interest in the content of the discussions, only in the fact of disagreement. The automatism of his responses becomes more explicit as the episode develops:

He now with a snarling drawl engaged in a new discussion on another and still more delicate subject. I renewed my tactics, he his. Subject after subject was chosen. His volte-face, his change of attitude in the argument, became less and less leisurely. But my skill in reversing remained more than a match for his methods. At length, whatever I said he said the opposite, brutally and at once. (28)

The undisciplined emotion of nationalism is presented as the enemy of the intellect: intellectual activity is subsumed in the reductive ruling passion, and thereby negated. The course of the argument creates a pattern of assertion and denial, a circumscribed and repetitive pattern which is this story's version of dynamic form.

Although the story is about the absurdity of national passions, Ker-Orr nevertheless employs this force to his advantage to defeat de Valmore, and, moreover, he displays a degree of national prejudice in his own perceptions. There is, in other words, an involvement in his behaviour which undermines our sense of his detachment from events. An indication of sardonic involvement emerges from Ker-Orr's response to his American friends, as when he sends up their condemnation of their 'distinguished compatriot' de Valmore: '"I knew you'd look at the matter in that light," I said. "It's a rank abuse of authority; I knew it would be condemned at headquarters"' (41–2). Ker-

Orr implicitly ridicules the notion of American supremacy by his bantering talk of 'authority' and 'headquarters'. In one sense, this might convey a wry detachment from all manifestations of nationalism, yet Ker-Orr's manipulation of this 'authority' is indicative of an ambivalence which colours his attitude to the whole national feud in which he is embroiled. This ambivalence is indicated in the key image of himself as physician. When he has turned the tables on de Valmore, he describes a scene in which his analytical perspective is clearly tinged with vengeance:

> I...looked round in a cold and business-like way, as a doctor might, with the dignified enquiry, 'Where is the patient?' The patient was there right enough, surrounded by the nurses I had sent....I approached him with impassive professional rapidity, my eye fixed on him, already making my diagnosis. I was so carried away by the figure of the physician, and adhered so faithfully to the bedside manner that I had decided upon as the most appropriate for the occasion, that I almost began things by asking him to put out his tongue. Instead I sat down carefully in front of him, pulling up my trousers meticulously at the knee. I examined his flushed and astounded face, his bristling moustache, his bloodshot eyes in silence. Then I very gravely shook my head. (44)

The extravagant gestures of control and calm – the meticulous hitching of the trousers, for instance, is essential to this piece of theatre – betray a vengeful enjoyment over and above the detachment they ostensibly denote.

Ker-Orr's 'victory' over de Valmore is an ironic reversal which forms a neat pattern embodying the story's theme. The absurd nationalism manifests itself in violence, but Ker-Orr is able to use this very force against the original perpetrator. The narrative, in effect, comprises a pattern in which a force is turned in on itself. Nationalism is depicted as a circular dynamic force, a self-defeating dynamic form.[16] And yet the narrative stance itself is somehow complicit with this negation; the still point of Vorticist detachment collapses, the vortex implodes, destroying the theoretical platform of contemplative judgement.

This satirical portrait of nationalism is typical of Lewis in that it makes no clear contextual references. This absence of social

engagement is due, partially, to the subject-matter and (associated) narrative stance: Ker-Orr enjoys the stance of the cynical
and superior Englishman abroad, unwilling to understand the
native behaviour he can only ridicule. This is a timeless
relationship of social differentiation which also provides an
ideal situation for investigating the Vorticist position of (notional) detachment.

The lack, in Lewis, of detailed social analysis sits oddly with
his satirical observations which, ultimately, seem unsubstan-
tiated. There is a contradiction here, a repression, perhaps, of a
more committed social satire, and it is this which seems to
account for the confusion between detachment and commitment which characterizes Lewis's Vorticist vision. The precise
nature of this repressed commitment is debatable and it may be,
as Fredric Jameson argues of Lewis, that the repressed
'structural center of his work' is 'his implacable lifelong
opposition to Marxism itself'.[17]

However one defines this repression the significant thing is
the fact of the disjunction, which is important in the generic
context where a reading of formal dissonance is a particularly
valuable way of defining literary developments. In the absence
of overt political pronouncement 'A Soldier of Humour'
appears as a condemnation of nationalism in general, and the
core of this complaint is the tension between individuality and
the crowd impulse. The most important result of this tension is
the dissolution of the individual, a dissolution portrayed as the
automatic and mechanical behavioural patterns of human
beings as Wild Bodies. In 'A Soldier of Humour' a general
atmosphere of automatism is created in the description of the
workers in Bayonne where the mechanism seems to characterize
each and every aspect of their activity: 'In every way that man
could replace the implement that here would be done' (20). The
social implications of this devaluing of the workers are not
pursued: the process merely mirrors a general view of human
activity, represented by the dynamic forms of the different
stories. This view of human activity necessitates a fragmentary
means of characterization, a phenomenon which manifests itself
in different ways. At the most obvious level this affects the
external appearance of characters, as in the account of de

Valmore 'pull[ing] himself together as though the different parts of his body all wanted to leap away in different directions, and he found it all he could do to prevent such disintegration' (45). More important is the disintegration between characters, the failure to communicate, which implies the broader social disintegration which Lewis fails to address.

There is a fundamental link between short story form and the fragmented self in *The Wild Body*. We have seen how the automatism of de Valmore derives from a nationalistic impulse, and how this emotion determines the shape of the story's action: the circularity of the emotion necessitates the circularity of the form. Yet since it is this automatism that is the target of Lewis's satire, he is also, in a sense, attacking the circular form itself, a form which frustrates and denies possibilities. Language is the focus of these denied possibilities in the story, because it is through language that Ker-Orr and de Valmore, in their different ways, find means of attacking each other. Ker-Orr attempts to trick de Valmore into betraying his origins by addressing him in French, trying to 'trap him into using again his native speech' (26). Ker-Orr's tactic is to praise American dress sense, but in French, a gesture at once of conciliation and deceit: his words are at odds with his real intention. Natural verbal communication, in effect, is rendered impossible by de Valmore's disowning of his language, a denial of his own voice, which is the locus of the absurdity here. It is also significant that when de Valmore exacts his revenge on Ker-Orr it is language deprivation that is the most damaging effect: the estranged Ker-Orr has no one with whom to practise his Spanish, the main purpose of his stay. Yet even the process of language *acquisition* is used to represent a lack of exchange, and a denial of genuine dialogue. Indeed, for Ker-Orr, the business of learning Spanish is entirely self-serving, an activity in which he views his interlocutors as commodities, unworthy of a genuine exchange:

My neighbour…promised to be a little El Dorado of spanish; a small mine of gossip, grammatical rules and willingness to impart these riches. I struck a deep shaft of friendship into him at once and began work without delay. Coming from Madrid, this ore was at least 30 carat, thoroughly thetaed and castilian stuff that he talked. What I gave him in exchange was insignificant. He knew several phrases in french and english, such as 'If you please,' and 'fine day'; I merely confirmed him in these. Every day he would hesitatingly say them over, and I would assent, 'quite right,' and 'very well pronounced.' (37)

These local instances of dialogic failure, obviously indicative of the story's theme, are also representative of a broader failure of communication, a failure which is satirized yet simultaneously reproduced in *The Wild Body*. In 'A Soldier of Humour' a traditional plot reversal is modified to stand as a dynamic form with a satiric message, just as in 'Brotcotnaz' the peripeteia mirrors the circumscribed action. In 'The Death of the Ankou' the convention deceives and entices the reader into identifying with the emotion, or inferior religion, that is Lewis's target. In all three cases the structure of the composition emulates the attributes and behavioural patterns that are held up to ridicule, so that, effectively, the dynamic form in each case is something that is implicitly rejected. And, also in each case, the rigidities noted are an integral part of an uncompromising narrative stance: the ideal Vorticist detachment is compromised, but there is no mixing of discourse, no dialogizing of the narrative voice, as there invariably is in the stories of Joyce, Woolf and Mansfield. What we are left with is a negative aesthetic of rejection, a systematic diagnosis with no cure. This disjunction, in which satirical observation and generic allusion clash, is the basis of the literary effects produced, but it is a clash which also reveals the fundamental contradiction between detachment and commitment: the satirical observation prompts a degree of pointed, and therefore committed, analysis, but this is tempered by a detachment which paralyses the impulse to investigate a resolution. This is the essence of dynamic form, or paralysed motion, in Lewis's short stories.

This definition of dynamic form stems from the structural tension between characters – a *structural* tension because human conflict is expressed through an adaptation of conventional plot types. Lewis's development of confrontational characterization in his novels is described by Fredric Jameson as 'a veritable *agon*', a 'combative, exasperated, yet jaunty stance of monads in collision... in which matched and abrasive consciousnesses slowly rub each other into smarting vitality'. For Jameson this conflict implies some kind of exchange for which 'dialogue is too weak a term', and this leads him to accord Lewis 'a unique and original place' in the tradition of 'dialogical narrative'.[18] This view is based on the contrast between Lewis's stylized, external method of characterization and a conventional notion of the modern novel as being concerned primarily with exploring the individual consciousness.[19] This view of modernist narrative, as previous chapters have suggested, is vulnerable if subjected to close analysis, and, in any case, the Lewis short stories enact mechanized conflicts, lacking in vitality, and which deny the possibility of dialogue. Even so, there is something of Jameson's analysis in this area which is helpful in reading the short stories. He develops the idea of the agon by adopting the term 'pseudo-couple' from Beckett's novel *The Unnamable*. The device of the agon, or pseudo-couple, even if not conducive to genuine dialogue, is nevertheless the conflict that highlights the lack, and the very existence of this lack and its cultural implications may determine the kind of narrative that can be written.[20] For Jameson the pseudo-couple is 'a structural device for preserving narrative', a limited strategy which represents 'a curious structural halfway house in the history of the subject, between its construction in bourgeois individualism and its disintegration in late capitalism'. A compromise of this kind is necessary because 'the experience of collective relations and group dynamics [has not] yet been historically strong enough to generate the new postindividualistic narrative forms by which such compromise formations could be superseded'.[21]

The confrontational device is a process by which narrative 'is both enabled and strategically recontained' in a way which 'expresses the rage and frustration of the fragmented subject at the chains that implacably bind it to its other and its mirror image'.[22] This fragmentation of the self, although analogous to the dissolution of personal identity which recurs in modernist literature, is expressed in a more programmatic way, and no glimpse of a collective alternative is offered. Jameson's perspective does, however, suggest the context which is made manifest through Lewis's work: there is no sense of particularized social intervention – as is so common in the modernist story – but there is a sense of a broader philosophical context of existential despair. The important point is that the agon can be seen as a radical, but ultimately self-consuming gesture, and that this gesture is emulated in the form of Lewis's stories which, in their simultaneous dependence upon and adaptation of the conventional, plotted short story, offer a radical gesture which is limited and contained. Yet when the dynamic of the agon is disrupted, a point coincidental with the rejection of plot convention, the fictions resist both their redundant formal unity and the debilitation of the fragmented self. These effects, which are the essence of the value of Lewis's stories, are ultimately limited by the absence of alternative patterns. The effect is that of watching a spinning-top come to a halt: a pointless and hypnotic motion is arrested, but there is little else to see.

The rejection, in Lewis, of the unified short story is, then, a limited gesture. Unlike the other writers considered in this survey the disruption of pattern is not accompanied by any kind of dialogue or extension. Characters, or pairs of characters, are presented as self-contained units, and this self-containment is not necessarily presented in a negative light. Indeed the notionally detached narrative stance represents the kind of preservation of individuality that Lewis approves: it is only by reading the stories symptomatically that this state of affairs appears genuinely problematic, as an integral part of a contemporary crisis of self. Lewis's own response to his peers' treatment of individual personality is revealing in this area. He considered Joyce to be the primary literary exponent of 'the great *time-philosophy* that overshadows all contemporary thought', and the essence of this objection lies, as SueEllen Campbell has pointed out, in the effect this philosophy has had on character portrayal: 'Lewis... means by "time" everything opposite to what he means by space: time is what is *not* distinct personality, the conscious mind, vision, common sense, stability, order.'[23] In short, the fluid representation of personality common in modernist literature, a tendency which I have presented as a positive challenge to the limitations of short story form, was anathema to Lewis, and a strategy he would not employ: the resulting isolation of his characters provides its own judgement on literary Vorticism, and also locates another aspect commonly associated, in a negative sense, with the modern short story – an emphasis on solitary experience.

CHAPTER 6

Malcolm Lowry: expanding circles

If literary Vorticism is an effective cul-de-sac in modernist fiction, with *The Wild Body* representing a stage of impasse for the short story, a different way of examining individual experience in the genre, and a way out of the impasse, is suggested in the stories of Malcolm Lowry, a writer whose work, with its heightened self-consciousness, also bridges the perceived gap between modernism and postmodernism.

The circularity of individual experience encompassed by one branch of modernism – typified in the Vorticism of Wyndham Lewis – is reversed in Lowry and rendered in an expansive, positive manner. The texts discussed so far are all obviously located in the historical period (1900–30) usually associated with modernism in literature, while Lowry wrote his major work in the 1940s and 1950s. Yet, as Malcolm Bradbury has pointed out, Lowry takes some of his 'attitudes, colouring, and artistic assumptions from the climate of the 1930s, when the internationalist and experimental aspects of modernism survived... and had a direct continuity with the great modernists of the previous two or three decades'. An important aspect of this continuing tradition is its stress on 'technical expertise and ostentation',[1] a literary self-consciousness which is pronounced in Lowry and which anticipates the overt metafictional style of much postmodern fiction: his stories offer a bridge between the experimental short story of the early twentieth century and the continuing relevance of the genre, a topic examined in the concluding chapter.

This account of Lowry's contribution to the short story focuses on *Hear Us O Lord From Heaven Thy Dwelling Place*, the collection written in the early 1950s and published posthumously in 1961.[2] *Hear Us O Lord* also has a special significance in the Lowry canon, a significance that has not been fully acknowledged. Usually it is only *Under the Volcano* that is deemed, without serious qualification, to exhibit a highly sophisticated and innovative formal control. There is, however, a similar innovation operative in *Hear Us O Lord*. The design of each story suggests a sense of closure and this is an integral dynamic tendency of the short story form, even where such closure is resisted.[3] Yet the real significance of these stories lies in the way their structure simultaneously *cultivates* and *flouts* this generic tendency to closure. The principle of the closed circle is played off against a concept of *expanding* circles, or widening horizons, and this formal dissonance results in certain structural fault-lines, the points which reveal (and mirror) Lowry's thematic concerns. This method of composition depends upon the disruption of specific short story effects, notably the notion of sudden revelation, or epiphany, which Lowry restructures in 'The Forest Path to the Spring'. There are other 'single effect' techniques in the short story which Lowry utilizes and extends, particularly through his complex use of symbolism, and denial of a closed story form.

My argument is that the 'expanding circle' motif, which appears explicitly in key symbolic passages, also operates implicitly throughout the book, governing descriptions and even syntax. The motif provides a model for the proliferation of thematic interlinking and expansion – within the separate stories – giving free reign to Lowry's predilection for dense, associative prose.[4] This opening out of ideas enables him to relate his personal preoccupations to public themes by stretching the boundaries of a fictional form sometimes thought to be confined to the private and the insular. The historical specificity of these 'public' issues has not yet, nor is soon likely to become anachronistic.

The expanding process depends upon a dispassionate transformation by Lowry of his autobiographical inspiration, the blending of the private with the public, the personal with the impersonal; and, since failure in this regard is a charge often levelled at Lowry, this accomplishment needs to be defended.

Lowry's fundamental principle of composition – fictional self-projection – presents an obvious stumbling-block to the reader seeking a meaning beyond the individual authorial quest for self-definition. Successive critics have found the achievements of the short stories qualified, in varying degrees, by the (supposed) esotericism of their autobiographical content. Lowry's own rootlessness and paranoiac fears contribute to the (indisputable) sense of alienation which pervades his work, and these factors help to explain the series of outsiders and questing artistic misfits who are the protagonists of successive stories in *Hear Us O Lord*. Yet the self-projection is designed to reveal a general significance. The debate centres on the effectiveness of this design. A measure of success is suggested by the varied characterization, even where different protagonists share the same name. This indicates a control, through fragmentation, of the authorial persona, a deliberate fictionalization of the self-portrayal.[5] Lowry himself was in no doubt that the artistic struggle could provide an adequate vehicle for broader, societal themes. In a letter to his editor, Albert Erskine, he wrote: 'there is an artist, a poet in every man, hence he is a creature easy for anyone to identify themselves with: and his struggles are likely to be universal, even on the lowest plane'.[6]

While the counsel for the defence is examining the corpus delicti, the gravamen had best be admitted: short story theorists have questioned the very generic capacity of the story form to transcend insular effects. The isolation of successive protagonists in *Hear Us O Lord* provides, on the face of it, a corroboration of Frank O'Connor's conviction, in his influential *The Lonely Voice*, that the short story inevitably conveys an 'intense awareness of human loneliness' and Bernard Bergonzi's belief that 'the form of the short story tends to filter down experience to the prime elements of defeat and alienation'. This view of the genre's limitations effectively disqualifies the short story from the successful consideration of societal themes. For O'Connor the relationship between a society and an individual cannot be examined because the focus is always on 'outlawed figures wandering about the fringes of society',[7] while for Bergonzi the form is 'unhealthily limited, both in the range of literary experience it offers and its capacity to deepen our understanding of the world, or of one another'.[8] These observations may constitute a restatement, in sociological terms, of the formalist view mentioned earlier of closure as an informing generic feature. Considered in relation to *Hear Us O Lord* this takes us back to that damaging tendency in Lowry criticism to view his work as an interconnected web of esoteric references. If the very form of the short story prohibits the consideration of themes which place the isolated individual within a social context, then all we are left with are scraps of solipsistic self-indulgence, artistic failures written during Lowry's last years in British Columbia when, according to Richard Cross, 'the artist withdrew into an isolation so profound that he became progressively less capable of defining his characters in terms of a social matrix'.[9]

It is not my intention to lay bare a hitherto undiscovered 'social matrix' in Lowry, or to argue that the short story form never has a tendency towards isolating effects. Such a tendency would seem particularly relevant to Wyndham Lewis's *The Wild Body*, in which a concept of human isolation is expressed through a circumscribed form. The genre clearly can lend itself to the treatment of a single consciousness, just as Lowry's art oscillates around his own sensibility. The point is that Lowry organizes his stories specifically to extend the particular into the arena of the general, and this pattern of extension – an inductive process of composition – is coeval with an innovative expansion of the short story's formal possibilities. A progressive social vision, in other words, is conveyed through a principle of constructive formal dissonance; the same principle which orders the mainstream modernism of Joyce, Woolf and Mansfield, but which is lamentably absent in Wyndham Lewis. The lonely voice, for Lowry, is that of the visionary artist rather than that of the hermit.

Lowry's restructuration of the short story involves the kind of formal disruption which is seminal in modernist writing, the tension between old and new perceptions of form. This formal tension, for instance, is a key feature of 'The Forest Path to the Spring', a prime example of a closed, cyclic story in which broader thematic concerns are conveyed by elements which deny this closure. The story comprises a narrative cycle embracing the four seasons and involving an epiphanic experience for the questing narrator, whose dwindling conviction about his artistic vocation returns. This revelation is dependent upon the concomitant resolution of the problem of social integration: positive integration and artistic creation are shown to be mutually dependent. This connection is implicit in the story's composition by virtue of Lowry's certitude that the plight of the artist is an exemplary one, and is pointed by a pattern of symbolism. This symbolism is of a stable and easily identifiable character – unlike the ambiguous or fluid symbolism of Joyce or Mansfield – but there is a typically modernist complication in Lowry's technique in this area, an effect of 'overload' caused by a consciously excessive build-up of symbols.

The expanding circle motif in 'The Forest Path to the Spring', introduced here by the narrator's wife in a description of rain falling on water, is emblematic of the thematic cross-fertilization:

'You see, my true love, each is interlocked with other circles falling about it,' she said. 'Some are larger circles, expanding widely and engulfing others, some are weaker smaller circles that only seem to last a short while... The rain itself is water from the sea, raised to heaven by the sun, transformed into clouds and falling again into the sea.' (241; original ellipsis)[10]

This truism is redeemed by its symbolic resonance, the social aspect of which becomes evident as the story progresses. The ripples are suggestive of a widening of horizons, and here they inspire just such a development of thought: the sight of the ripples leads into a consideration of the entire water cycle.

In contrast to this model of thematic linkage, and its impulse to expansion, there is a formal principle of cyclic return and closure which shapes the story, a principle also conveyed by the motif of the water cycle. The overall structure – a retrospective account framed by scenes from a notional narrative present – parallels the return to the scene of the narrator's epiphany. Within the frame an account is given of the couple's spiritual growth and development through their first year at the inlet, a growth linked to the natural annual cycle and which culminates in the spring.

Even within sections the notion of cyclic return is operative. The second section covers the reactions of the narrator and his wife on first moving into the shack at Eridanus. Their relationship is shown, at the beginning and ending of the section, to be at a stage of total introversion, despite the interposed hint that this condition may need to be transcended. To begin with they are enjoying the archetypal honeymoon state: 'That is how selfish lovers are, without an idea in their heads for anyone save themselves.' To them 'the beach emptied of its cheery crowd seemed the opposite of melancholy' and living there permanently, the narrator reflects, 'would be almost tantamount... to renouncing the world altogether' (229, 233). There are hints of external impingement, and these are proleptic of later developments. The sight of ships carrying war cargo – even remote Eridanus witnesses evidence of the Second World War – pricks the narrator's social conscience and momentarily shatters the lovers' idyll: 'It's a hell of a time to live. There can't be any of this nonsense about love in a cottage', he reflects (231). A threat from *within* is also suggested when he conceives of his own shadow as 'the glowering embodiment of all that threatened us' (234). The section, a closed circle, ends as it begins, however, with the narrator's affirmation of the personal succour he draws from his wife: 'it seemed to me that until I knew her I had lived my whole life in darkness' (235).

The destructiveness of the reclusive impulse becomes manifest in subsequent sections, before a resolution is envisaged. This development occurs in phase with the succession of the seasons, so that winter provides the background to the trough of the crisis, while the solution emerges in the spring. The ferocious winter storms cause the lovers to 'lose all hope for terror at the noise', the sounds of 'elemental despair', and reduce them, at the depth of their insularity, to 'cl[i]ng[ing] to one another like two little arboreal animals in some midnight jungle – and we were two such animals in such a jungle' (255). This analogy emphasizes the asocial existence that has been cultivated to excess. The inability, at this stage, to sustain an outward-looking perspective is emphasized by the narrator's earlier remark concerning 'nonsense about love in a cottage' which has been emptied of its real purport and appropriated as 'a loving catchphrase' (243). During this 'winter' of the narrator's spiritual career he experiences a 'virulent and murderous' feeling which 'was like hatred of mankind', a state of mind which he finds 'turning inward and back upon myself, to devour my very self' (245, 246). The narrator's professional and personal selves are both being consumed here: the artist beset by misanthropy has lost his vocation, since he is external to the social medium in which his work must be defined. Isolation has resulted in a state of misanthropic limbo.

The self-negation of excessive self-interest and the rejection of community is summarized in Mauger's allegorical anecdote of the eagle drowned by the salmon: to avoid sharing the fish with a flock of crows the eagle attempts to fly off and is dragged beneath the sea by its booty (246).

Here, as elsewhere in the story, the negative is held in tension with the positive. Having recounted the details of his disturbing hatred, the narrator goes on fondly to consider his place in the Eridanus community, an ideal model of social organization; and, having done so, he re-evaluates the feeling of hatred which he now realizes is not for human beings but for 'the ugliness they made in the image of their own ignorant contempt for the earth' (248). Here the antinomy of nature and civilization, a tension which informs the collection as a whole and this story in particular, is merged thematically with the narrator's artistic/ spiritual quest. It is important to note that modern urban civilization is depicted as inimical to co-operative communal living (represented by the Eridanus community) as well as to the natural world. The healthy creating self depends upon an involvement with both social community and natural environment, though these profoundly linked ideas are really different sides of the same coin. This association ensures that the self-negating immersion in his idyllic surroundings can yet provide the narrator with the basis of a positive resolution to his quest. After redefining his hatred he turns to his wife and the solace of their marital cocoon, which now reveals its positive potential: 'I forgot all my hatred and torment the moment I saw my wife' (248). It is this solace that enables him to understand and empathize with the natural environment. She seems to him 'the eidolon of everything we loved in Eridanus' and so 'through her I myself became susceptible to these... currents of nature' (249).

The pattern of thematic expansion is complicated by the fact that each level which reveals symbolic correlatives must also be evaluated for its actual significance. In particular, this concerns Lowry's preoccupation with the natural environment, which is no idealistic romanticism. The consternation about the destructive aspect of civilization, 'creator of deathscapes', is more than the metaphorical analogue which, on one level, it palpably is (279). It is also a parallel theme in its own right. Lowry is concerned with the *literal* destruction of nature which is also the literal annihilation of human aesthetic perceptions. The ominous, encroaching city, the narrator feels, 'would almost suffocate all memory of the reality and wealth of such a life as ours' (254). The life-source itself, which for the narrator is inextricably tied to artistic creativity, is that which the encroaching city and the oil refinery threaten. The connection Lowry makes between conservation and the necessities of civilization places his thinking, here, in a continuing tradition of contemporary political ecology.

The chore of fetching water from the spring is the key event pertaining to the narrator's spiritual discovery. He recounts three separate occasions when, in the process of completing this task, he experiences a moment of revelatory insight, and these three moments represent a composite epiphany. The first of these moments, which I discuss later, draws a parallel between an explosive jazz break and a sensation of happiness which heralds the spiritual rebirth (257). The second involves the encounter with the mountain lion (264–6); the narrator's calm defusion of this mortal threat is shown to be emblematic of his resolution of the self-negating impulse. The final moment, like the encounter with the lion, occurs in the season of spring, the season of the narrator's renaissance when 'the very quality of the light was different' (261). The spring water provides an obvious symbol for spiritual rejuvenation and the path to the spring, according to this schema, clearly represents the pursuit of this sustenance. For the narrator, as for Lowry, this is the Proustian and Joycean quest, the search for the means of translating the past into art, and the incipient revelation involves a progression towards this capacity. This tripartite 'epiphany' tacitly challenges the notion of sudden revelation in the short story, and supplies, instead, a more comprehensive and extended awakening. The narrator, at the conclusion of his gradual revelation, is conscious of the path seeming progressively shorter and the job taking less and less time to complete, yet he also has 'a consciousness of a far greater duration of time having passed during which something of vast importance to me had taken place, without my knowledge and outside time altogether' (272). The plasticity of time and space signifies a new conception of personal time and history, a conception which will enable him 'to face th[e] past as far as possible without fear' and to 'transcend it in the present' because his 'new vocation was involved with using that past' (283). The accidental burning of his old work and the first shack emphasize this need to reconstruct the past 'like our new house, on the charred foundations and fragments of the old work and our old life' (274).

The various thematic threads coalesce when the circle image is echoed at the story's conclusion:

Each drop falling into the sea is like a life, I thought, each producing a circle in the ocean, or the medium of life itself, and widening into infinity, though it seems to melt into the sea, and become invisible, or disappear entirely, and be lost. Each is interlocked with other circles falling about it, some are larger circles expanding widely and engulfing others, some are weaker, smaller circles that only seem to last a short while. And smiling as I remembered my lesson I thought of that first time when we had seen the rain falling into a calm sea like a dark mirror, and we had found the cannister and decided to stay.

But last night I had seen something new; my wife had called me out of bed to the open window to see what she first thought was a school of little fishes breaking the still water just beneath, where the tide was high under the house. Then we saw that the whole dark water was covered with bright expanding phosphorescent circles. Only when my

wife felt the warm mild rain on her naked shoulder did she realize it
was raining. They were perfect expanding circles of light, first tiny
circles bright as a coin, then becoming expanding rings growing
fainter and fainter, while as the rain fell into the phosphorescent water
each raindrop expanded into a ripple that was translated into light.
(285–6)

The multi-significance of the expanding circle 'widening into
infinity' is fully embraced by the poetic progression of this
passage. The theme of social integration is suggested by the
notion of each droplet as a 'life' entering the ocean, or 'medium
of life itself' and producing 'interlocked' circles. This inter-
locking, suggestive of the need for communal assimilation, also
indicates the bridging of thematic interests. Here, as elsewhere,
the societal theme is shown to comprise the basis of the narrator's
artistic rebirth as it naturally develops into an image of artistic
inspiration. This is connoted by the natural light, earlier
invoked as emblematic of creative power (261), which here
brightly illuminates the 'expanding phosphorescent circles'.

The story concludes in a visionary, symbolic phase which
celebrates the positive potential of human creativity. The life-
source of natural light implied by the phosphorescent circles is
surpassed, as the rain stops, by the appearance of three
rainbows; and this is followed, significantly, by the 'beneficent
signaling' of a lighthouse, the 'highest symbol' of civilization,
which is fused with the inspirational signs of natural light (287,
280). Symbolic representations of social utility and artistic
creativity are conjoined. Approaching once more the all-
significant spring the narrator sees 'a deer swimming toward
the lighthouse' (287), a resonant image which depicts the
natural and the artificial in a converging, harmonious pro-
pinquity.

The overall impact of the story's conclusion is complicated by
a plethora of thematic 'tidying up'. This results in a sense of
congestion which overloads the limitations of the narrative
circuit, at least as far as it is conventionally perceived. Despite
the neatness and circularity of the story's design there is a
resonance about its dénouement which denies the formal
closure: the superabundance of symbolism which accrues

through the story disrupts any simple sense of finality. There is a conflict here with the couple's return to the spring, the event with which the story ends. Despite the sensation of closure, the peace and fulfilment of this ending, the final effect is not a straightforward affirmation of an idyllic lifestyle and the discovery of vocation it represents: the affirmation is tempered by the potentially destructive forces, internal and external, which are always in attendance.

The interrelated themes encompassed in the story – artistic inspiration, self-definition, social integration, environmental responsibility – represent a complex layering of ideas which projects a further widening of horizons beyond the text. This metaphorical density – an opening out and a denial of closure – contradicts the simplistic unity aesthetic which underpins much short story theory. Poe's doctrine of the 'single' and 'preconceived effect'[11] is severely strained, just as a conventional view of the visionary moment as the instantaneous revelation of character and/or situation is extended by the dispersed, composite epiphany.[12] It is this dissonance – the overt complication of a potentially simple narrative – that reinforces and clinches the topical content. The widening of horizons provides a corrective to the narrator's earlier isolation and to the insularity of the closed story form.

Lowry varies the nature of the artistic quest in this story by creating a protagonist who is a jazz composer, an occupation which has an interesting bearing on the present discussion, especially as a jazz analogy is used for the first moment of insight on the forest path. On this occasion the narrator thinks of a break by Bix Beiderbecke 'that had always seemed ... to express a moment of the most pure spontaneous happiness'. He considers, inconclusively at this stage, the possibility of translating this moment of happiness into his own life, and on the implications of trying to 'make a moment permanent' (257). This anticipates his later reassessment of personal time and history.

There is a tacit parallel here between the jazz break and the epiphany in the short story, and this is another indication of the formal experimentation that is implicit in the story. It is interesting to note that Lowry's artistic cross-reference effectively anticipates Julio Cortázar's observation that 'the efficacy and *meaning* of a story rel[y] on those values that make poetry and jazz what they are: tension, rhythm, inner beat, the unforeseen within fore-seen parameters'.[13] Lowry's description of the Beiderbecke break is aptly conveyed as 'the unforeseen within fore-seen parameters', a formulation that is equally apposite in relation to Lowry's extension of the short story's parameters.

A similar tension to that discernible in 'Forest Path' informs 'Elephant and Colosseum', another story concerning a circular quest in which the narrator is confronted with a significant reminder of his past which conveys to him how that past may be used as artistic inspiration in the present.

The writer Kennish Drumgold Cosnahan, a Manxman based in the USA, is on a European tour in search of the publishers of his autobiographical novel, *Ark from Singapore*. His trip has been hastened by the need to visit his dying mother on the Isle of Man. In terms of these objectives the trip is a failure: his mother dies before he arrives and the publishing houses of Europe collectively show no interest in his work. Cosnahan is isolated and anonymous. He is redeemed, however, by a visionary encounter with the elephant Rosemary, the 'heroine' of *Ark from Singapore* and the creature he himself had nursed many years ago on the voyage fictionalized in his novel. The encounter triggers a revelation which offers the solution to his personal and professional crisis. The story is structured around this moment of epiphany – or 'anagnorisis' as Cosnahan, out-Joyceing Joyce, calls it[14] – and it is through this revelation that Cosnahan finds meaning in his vocation as artist, receives absolution of his guilt over his dead mother, and perceives a tangible bridge between life and art as the professional and personal themes are merged. The plot itself, though structured as a closed unit, betrays a wry detachment from conventional notions of order. This is no pilgrimage to a spring at an Edenic inlet: Cosnahan's epiphanic encounter with Rosemary is pure serendipity, a happy chance on an afternoon of aimless time-killing. The irony is encapsulated by the portentous use of 'anagnorisis' to describe the effect of the encounter.

The symptoms of Cosnahan's malaise are isolation and anonymity; and the diagnosis is that his (thwarted) need for recognition is a false surrogate for a genuine vocation. In his isolation Cosnahan's literary powers have dried up, a point aptly symbolized by his loss of language power in everyday situations. He has difficulty, as a poor linguist, in communicating in a foreign city, and his phone conversation with his brother is rendered incomprehensible by a crossed line (141). This symbolic isolation is Cosnahan's punishment for his pursuit of ego-enhancing recognition, which is the wrong kind of social definition. When he considers the trappings of literary fame (which he has enjoyed in the USA) he perceives that these include acrimonies and jealousies disruptive of social contact (140). Moreover, the superficial trappings of the literary life have a deleterious effect on a writer's creativity by diverting genuine artistic endeavour. This censure applies especially to notices and reviews, the commercially decisive elements in the writer's career, which wield an unwarranted and enervating power:

Reading these later eulogies produced in Cosnahan a bizarre mental commotion as of some endless mirrored reduplication, as if it were not merely that all these reviews had been written before of countless other books, but that for a moment he felt like an eternal writer eternally sitting in the eternal city, eternally reading precisely the same sort of notices from which he always derived precisely the same eternal feelings of mingled pleasure, pain, gratitude, sadness, amusement, dismay and beautiful vain-glory. (118)

The meretricious publishing game is a closed circle of eternal puffery, a system which restrains the writer from finding a genuine purpose, and which obscures the vital connections with external experiences. (This erroneous 'idea' of writing is exemplified by the literary efforts of the quartermaster Quattras.)

From the beginning of the story there are intimations of the need for positive social integration. Despite his sense of alienation Cosnahan yet has a glimmering awareness of the social ramifications of his actions, even of such minor events as the settling of his café bill:

Since it wasn't merely the milk he would be paying for (any more than anyone who bought that book would only pay for the spiritual nourishment it contained) but the commanding site of the Restaurant Rupe Tarpea upon the Via Veneto, to say nothing of the three other sidewalk restaurants on the other three corners created by the crossroads with the Via Sicilia and *their* rent, or their exquisitely dressed female occupants eating ices, to whose charming activities he felt he would be expected also, obscurely, to contribute; as naturally he would be paying also for the view, should he turn around, of the gateway of the Porta Pincia, and finally for the Via Vittoria Veneto itself, with its sidewalks ten feet broad, and its plane trees casting dappled shadows on either side as it swept in great curves down toward the invisible Piazza Barberini. (114–15)

This passage is representative of the story as a whole: the tone is ironic, yet the expanding perspective has a serious formal significance. If the thought of inadvertently paying to watch the consumption of ice-cream is a comic touch, there is also evidence here of the recurring impulse to make connections between events and occurrences on various levels. In this case Cosnahan examines the social implications of his actions, and this expensive scene of grandeur is later recalled when he gives a beggar-woman 50 lire, 'half the price of his milk' (152). The earlier reflections on pecuniary power are implicit in this image of social inequality which inspires a feeling of meanness in Cosnahan.

The reflections at the café, however, merely anticipate Cosnahan's eventual sense of integration, and are not sustained: seduced by a sensation of luxury he forgets his unease in an

expansive feeling of great riches and peace, that purring roaring feeling, yet somehow quiet as a Rolls Royce engine, of life being at a sort of permanent flood, as if there had never been a first world war, let alone a second one, which was like an evocation of 1913, of those truly pre-war days from which he retained only this curious yet powerful sensation, when with his parents he must have visited London or Dublin, or at least Weston-super-Mare, at the age of five. (115)

The apparently 'expansive feeling' is actually one of regression, infantile and socially naive. His mind retreats from the social implications of the episode, becomes disconnected from historical context, and finds succour in the sensation of opulent comfort his circumstances inspire. This is a state of moral stasis, an equivalent condition to the torpor resulting from Cosnahan's preoccupation with the trappings of the literary life. As a whole this passage recalls the ripples on the water witnessed by the narrator of 'Forest Path', but here the reflecting mind does not see the expanding horizons as the significant part of the model, and focuses on its own concentric position in relation to the 'ripples' in a way which recalls the Vorticist stance of Wyndham Lewis. Indeed, Cosnahan's struggle for his sense of social integration is part of the story's struggle against the kind of circumscribed form – evident in *The Wild Body* – which is implicated in the isolating effects the short story form can produce.

The metaphorical pattern of 'Elephant and Colosseum' is complicated by the association of supernatural power and literary creativity. Cosnahan's erstwhile mystical powers have waned since the publication of his novel, just as his excessive preoccupation with success has occluded his creative energies (127). The supernatural theme is inextricably tied to the question of personal history: Cosnahan recalls that he has been 'conscious of something peculiar in his nature' ever since the Christmas his mother (herself a witch) 'presented him with a gray suède [*sic*] elephant' (126). This toy elephant, symbol of his inherited supernatural/literary powers, is encompassed within Rosemary's multi-significance at the moment of anagnorisis.

In literary terms Cosnahan's 'magical' powers (and those desired by Lowry himself) comprise the ability to forge art from life, and, as the necessary counterpart in this two-way process, to define himself by writing. Cosnahan's vision restores his powers (a symbolic rediscovery of his personal past) and sets him up to write again. His problems have been 'exorcised' just as he once had the capacity to exorcise possessed dwellings on the Isle of Man.[15] Revitalized, and feeling like 'some old magician who had just recovered his powers', Cosnahan realizes that 'he really *was* a magician' and that the 'source' of his 'future salvation' will be his transformation 'into a conscious member of the human race' (174). This consciousness of social integration, 'his sense of kinship deepening', is an integral part of his regeneration, just as his former powers of exorcism and water-divining both have a community serving function (173).

A further enrichment of the story's symbolic density is occasioned by the Manx motif which has an obvious generalizing tendency (the Isle of *Man*). Thus the Manx faces that Cosnahan is disappointed not to encounter, in his misplaced quest for recognition ('where is Quayne, and where is Quaggan? where is Quillish? where is Qualtrough?' (134)), become representative of a human totality at the story's conclusion:

Man was Quayne, and man was Quaggan, man was Quillish, man was Qualtrough, man was Quirk and Quayle and Looney, and Illiam Dhone, who had been hanged. And yet lived – because he was innocent? (174)

The names have acquired a general significance which emphasizes the tempering of egocentricity involved in Cosnahan's new concept of personality. The story of Illiam Dhone, who survived being hanged, provides another analogy for Cosnahan's vocational reprieve, and also relates the new objective to the broader horizon of social purpose. Illiam Dhone recalls the Manx 'monarch martyr' Illiam Dhôan whose plight, 'which no Manxman ever really forgets, shot... before his pardon arrived', is another symbolic marriage of personal circumstance and social undertaking (132).

The elephant Rosemary has a complex symbolic function in gathering together the story's thematic strands. When Cosnahan chances upon this key 'character' in his novel, art and life, past and present, merge on the narrative level. Rosemary also provides the summation of the supernatural theme as her appearance implicitly invokes Cosnahan's mother and, through his mother, his own inherited powers: she recalls their gifts to each other of a lapis lazuli elephant and the suede one. Cosnahan's epiphanic reverie makes these connections explicit: 'Rosemary was changing into a lapis lazuli elephant. And the lapis lazuli elephant changing into a portrait of a young elephant, on the cover of a novel named *Ark from Singapore*' (169). Rosemary is also an embodiment of the interweaving of different levels of experience: her all-encompassing significance, her inherent 'juxtaposition of the grotesque and the sublime', is emulated in the epiphany she inspires in Cosnahan who experiences 'a hundred ideas, a hundred meanings...spiraling up from the same depths, from the same source in his mind' (162, 171). The echo, here, of the expanding circle motif is not to be overlooked. The serio-comic tone in which the story is cast is an attempt to conjoin different levels of experience in this way.

As with 'Forest Path' the formal closure is denied by the symbolic overload which resonantly widens the story's horizons, an effect centred on the metaphorical multivalency of Rosemary. At one level a symbol of Cosnahan's personal regeneration, Rosemary is really no one thing, especially as she also embodies the impersonal context that must underpin that regeneration. Before his epiphany Cosnahan implicitly undercuts the personal aspect of the symbol by dismissing an anthropomorphic view of Rosemary's significance: 'If it so happened then that an elephant showed you a love or intelligence you were wont to say was "almost human," as usual you were flattering to yourself' (163). This single symbol which conjoins so many portentous ideas gives the piece a complexity of texture which its surface narrative might not seem to warrant, but, once more, the dissonance is very much to the point, since it reiterates, formally, the need to make connections and to grow beyond the insular and the superficial.

The shorter stories in *Hear Us O Lord* – 'The Bravest Boat', 'Gin and Goldenrod', 'Present Estate of Pompeii' – evince the same impulse to thematic extension that I have been tracing. In these three stories, however, though the expanding horizon principle is evident, it is not structurally disruptive. The result is a more conventional (and less arresting) fictional texture.[16]

The element of formal conflict is more pressing in 'Strange Comfort Afforded by the Profession', a story explicitly about literary artifice in which the notion of closure is extended to breaking-point. Sigbjørn Wilderness, on a quest for his spiritual brethren, supposes himself to be continuing a great literary tradition. The narrative is constructed around the citation of letters and biographical details pertaining to Keats, Shelley,

Gogol and Poe; and these are strategically juxtaposed with Wilderness's despairing letter which is the final (and longest) artefact quoted. Wilderness exhibits a continuing uncertainty as to what to make of the literary miscellany, and this is a curiously impassive response to a body of texts testifying to artistic suffering and isolation. The 'relatively pleasureable fit of coughing' which Wilderness experiences at the story's end suggests his role as a modern suffering (tubercular) Keats (113); but the romantic conception of the suffering artist is dissipated by the ambiguous assessment which Wilderness makes of Poe's letter, and also of his own. The inconclusiveness of the story replicates the writer's continual self-conscious evaluation of the public use to be made of private experience; and this is not a mercenary tendency, merely evidence of the continuing need of the writer to define himself in social terms.

'Through the Panama', which takes this impulse to an extreme, represents the pinnacle of Lowry's experiment with the story form. The metafictional paradigm which informs the collection is recontained within another chinese box; and this extended self-consciousness – or meta-metafiction – shatters the closed circle convention by explicitly destroying the narrative artifice which obtains in the other stories. The discourses of author and character in the story, Sigbjørn Wilderness and Martin Trumbaugh, are almost undifferentiated, and these voices are juxtaposed with a split-column layout which begins and ends with annotations taken directly from the marginal text of Coleridge's *Ancient Mariner* but which develops, in a parody of Coleridge's commentary, into a history of the Panama Canal. The 'single effect' doctrine is overtly flouted here.

The artistic self-consciousness is most explicit in the passage about the lock-keepers of ascending power, a model which directly links the expanding circle motif to the process of fictional composition and which admits the author's own manipulative presence in 'this celestial meccano', operated

at the touch of that man sitting up in the control tower high above the topmost lock who, by the way, is myself, and who would feel perfectly comfortable if only he did not know that there was yet another man sitting yet higher above him in *his* invisible control tower, who also has a model of the canal locks before him, carefully built, which registers electrically the exact depth of everything *I* do, and who thus is able to see everything that is happening to me at every moment – and worse everything that is *going* to happen. (61)

This fragmentation is really the logical extension of what Lowry does in the other stories; but whereas in 'Elephant and Colosseum' and 'Forest Path' meaning is generated by stretching story conventions to a point of resonating tension, here the conventions are shattered by the expanding motif. This is the unforeseen rupturing its foreseen parameters. The story's meaning, however, is still partly determined by those parameters, which offer a yardstick in the implicit debate on the value of literary composition.

The marriage of formal innovation and thematic content, both governed by the expanding circle principle, has a pervasive bearing on the collection, and this is true even at the level of syntax. Lowry's prose has the occasional tendency to ramble in apparently undisciplined and unwieldy sentences, but in *Hear Us O Lord* such 'expanding syntax' is sometimes used organically in an effort to unite the disparate threads of the topical content. The following passage from 'Forest Path' is a good example of this:

As the mist rolled up towards us, beginning to envelop us, the sun still trying to maintain itself like a platinum disc, it was as if the essence of a kind of music that had forever receded there, that seemed evoked from the comments of my wife as she looked through this window, out on to this porch in the first days when we'd just meant to spend a week, or in the autumn when we still stayed on, while she was making the coffee, talking to herself partly for my benefit, describing the day to me, as if I had been like a blind man recovering his sight to whom she had to teach again the beauties and oddities of the world, as if it became unlocked, began to play, to our inner ear, not music but having the effect of music, not sentimental at all, but fresh and innocent, and only moving because it was so happy, or because happiness is moving; or it was like a whispering of the ghosts of ourselves. (278)

This free-flowing passage elides the story's various themes. Artistic regeneration for the composer (represented here by the healing 'music') is linked to the prerequisite reassessment of personal history – 'a whispering of the ghosts of ourselves' – in a passage which also alludes to the first observation of the expanding circles, to the symbolism of natural light as inspiration, and to the narrator's dependence on his wife as a medium. An even longer paragraph of this nature occurs in 'Elephant and Colosseum' (138). This passage, too long to quote here, summarizes Cosnahan's initial state of moral stasis by conjoining images of social injustice, professional frustration and personal ineffectuality.

The nature of the formal project in *Hear Us O Lord* provides a corrective to the view of Lowry as a writer enervated by self-absorption, a view which the stories seem, superficially, to reinforce. The Lowryan quest which informs the book depends upon its personal roots, and there is a conviction and consistency in the collection about the need for an impersonal extension of this basis which challenges the 'bewilderment about the potential public meanings of his own type of creativity' which Malcolm Bradbury, articulating a widely held view, has discerned in Lowry.[17] Admittedly, there is no detailed social fabric in *Hear Us O Lord* and its public themes are of a general rather than a specific nature. Yet the extension of the single consciousness (the examination of which the story form invites) into contact with broader areas is an important development in its generic context.

The densely associative narrative style in which the thematic interlinking is conducted precludes any exegetical dismantling which dilutes the richness: in *Hear Us O Lord* it is impossible to accord differing degrees of importance to the personal or the impersonal, the public or the private, since the ubiquitous expanding circle paradigm insists on their interdependence.

CHAPTER 7

Conclusion: contemporary issues

Each of the major modernist figures discussed in the preceding chapters found the short story form amenable to his or her own personal literary innovations, and this indicates that the genre is of particular importance as a vehicle for modernist expression. Key features of modernist writing – particularly the cultivation of paradox and ambiguity, and the fragmented view of personal identity – find a well-suited outlet in the adapted materials of the conventional short story. Perhaps the most surprising discovery of this survey is the disjunction between the modernists' problematizing of the genre, and the continuing simplistic assumptions of short story theory: while there is a general consensus that figures such as Joyce and Mansfield have had a major impact on the development of the short story, that impact has not been properly registered in the generic theory, governed as it is by a simplistic emphasis on single effects, narrative stability and formal unity.

The overt literary artifice of the short story, its emphasis on technique, tallies with the concerns of the modernists, their pursuit of social ends through formal experimentation. The importance of form – not as an aesthetic end in itself, but as the means of defining broader, contextual goals – demands an interpretive methodology which acknowledges the interrelation between form and content, by viewing 'form as the structure of a ceaseless self-production, and so... as "structuration"'.[1] The modernists' restructuration of the short story form – their positive adaptation of formal convention and narrative technique – has been the focus of this survey: Joyce subverts the single-effect story in delineating his ambiguous internal dramas;

Woolf's experimentation repudiates an ordered approach to
fiction and the hierarchical world-view it embodies; similarly,
Mansfield's rejection of ordered techniques – such as stable
symbolism – can also be a rejection of a fixed social hierarchy,
as in 'The Garden Party'; even Wyndham Lewis, the least
radical of the authors discussed, utilizes a conventional story
'shape' for his own satirical purposes; Lowry, most ambitious of
all, cultivates the conventional closure he simultaneously flouts,
a gesture bound up with the attempt to conjoin individual
experience with broader social need.

The one thing all of these writers have in common is a
deliberate utilization of the short story's formal properties, and
the methodological implications of this are important, because
the literary effects of these stories are best located by discovering
the conscious manipulation of generic properties, rather than
by reading systematically against the grain. Effectively, the
approach I have followed indicates how the Machereyan fault-
line reading, outlined in the opening chapter, can be less
oppositional than one might expect. Fredric Jameson gives an
account of the fault-line reading which clearly sets in opposition
the Marxist critic's social analysis and the perceived restrictive
practices of the writer:

A Marxist negative hermeneutic, a Marxist practice of ideological
analysis proper, must in the practical work of reading and interpretation be exercised *simultaneously* with a Marxist positive
hermeneutic, or a decipherment of the Utopian impulses of these same
still ideological cultural texts.[2]

Jameson has, with some justification, been criticized for his
commitment to the category of 'Utopia', but this Utopia/
ideology duality, despite its weaknesses, still provides a very
useful framework for extricating the political impulse of a work
from any potentially obfuscating formal limits.[3]

Yet in defining these fault-lines, as they are evident in the
short stories of the major British modernists, it is clear that
formal dissonance is an integral part of their purpose, and so
rather than simply opposing the Utopian impulse of their
themes to specific formal limitations, it is also possible, and

usually more appropriate, to acknowledge that these Utopian impulses are themselves bound up with the disruption of formal restraints. There are, of course, always external factors operating negatively on literary form: the political confusion of Wyndham Lewis, for instance, is reflected in a limited means of characterization which should be read symptomatically. A negative hermeneutic is also required, initially, to indicate how social taboo may have demanded that the homosexual content of 'Bliss' be silenced, and reduced to covert presentation. But, despite the limitation on the story's discursive content, the form of the story simultaneously disrupts a limiting story type – the story which ends with a single discovery – a disruption which also undermines the social expectation of a heterosexual norm.

Again and again the modernist short story utilizes and restructures literary form to make this kind of commentary. One of the most complex examples of this is Joyce's 'A Little Cloud', which offers a detailed character portrayal, primarily by undermining the stability of the narrative type it resembles. The point of view of the character Chandler colours the structure of the story itself which, superficially, reinforces the construction he puts on the action: it mimics the tri-part structure of a learning or initiation plot which progresses from delusion or immaturity through disabusement/revelation to enlightenment. But the structure also undercuts Chandler's version: the final scene is a cruel *parody* of enlightenment and decisive action, and this undermines the process of learning implied in the story's structure. The structure of the story, then, exposes the self-delusion it nominally reinforces, which is another way of saying that the story creates its effects by exaggerating its own techniques, its very fictiveness: its total form stages a debate concerning the adequacy of a straightforward narrative progression, which here replicates the character's own delusion. The nature of this delusion provides the focus of Joyce's social intervention: a critique of the ideology of marital contentment and stability – (Chandler's confusion stems from his inability to fit into, or break out of, this social system) – and a simultaneous critique of Chandler's unthinking reverence of literary creativity, a preoccupation (satirized through his vacuous discourse) which prevents him dealing with his domestic problems.

Another representative modernist story is Woolf's 'The Evening Party', which undermines its own frame-tale structure as Woolf rehearses an encounter between an idealized narrator and the 'uncircumscribed spirit' of life. An integral part of this encounter is pointed by the story's allusion to slavery and exploitation as an index of a modern fragmented consciousness, a disjointedness also implicated in the hierarchical literary canon of the professor present at the party. For Woolf, it is the fragmentation caused by hierarchical categorization which distances her from the 'luminous halo' of life, and within this hierarchical, fragmented consciousness, a restrictive approach to literary language is clearly related to broader issues of ideological control.

The question that arises from these readings of 'social intervention' is, to what extent are these worthwhile and purposive interventions, rather than simply abstract, theoretical links? Put another way, the question here concerns how far the materials of the short story lend themselves to serious contextual analysis. When, for instance, Mansfield appears to develop the short story in a way which is closely allied to her analyses of sexual and social politics, *how* can this project be seen as more than an intellectual exercise? Consider Laura's struggle against her bourgeois domestic conditioning in 'The Garden Party'. This struggle and its tensions are expressed through the complex and fluid symbolism of the hat, a significant extension of what is, notionally, a stable feature of short fiction. But what is the special generic significance of this kind of gesture?

The problem here centres on the exaggerated literary artifice of the short story, which clearly foregrounds the process of formal restructuration as the means of making contextual intervention. But this self-consciousness might be seen as a contradiction in terms: by drawing attention to its own literary artifice the modernist short story explicitly closes off the possibility of imitating 'reality', of creating an illusory version of the social world it describes, and this might be said to emphasize a gulf between world and text. I want to suggest that, to the contrary, this literary self-consciousness is actually a good way of making connections between world and text, and the remainder of this chapter will offer some speculations on this issue.

The connection I am making is a vital one between literary form and social context, a connection which is often challenged. The discussion of isolation in the previous chapter addressed one such challenge to the communicative power of the short story. The example of Lowry shows how isolation can be used to explore positive, communal themes, and also how such a project is bound up with the simultaneous cultivation and negation of circularity in the short story: to put it another way, this is an ambivalent development of fictional closure, a matter of significance which is discussed below. The problem of isolation, however, has not yet been adequately solved. At one level, for instance, it could be argued that there is nothing in *Hear Us O Lord* which necessarily disproves the belief that 'in the short story we are presented with characters in their essential aloneness, not in their taken-for-granted social world': the proposed exemplary status of individual experience remains contentious.[4] But this notion of exemplary behaviour suggests an idealistic, allegorical principle – a kind of leading by Utopian example – and this is at odds with the negativity of social exclusion: the positive social value of isolation is re-visionary, in a way that is analogous to the positive, progressive aspect of fiction which innovates through a disruption of convention. The stance of the isolatee reveals its potential by virtue of an oppositional stance: the value in the position of the isolatee, or outsider, depends on a constructive condemnation of the social structure from which he or she is excluded. Thus Kate Fullbrook can discern an 'outlaw' tendency in Mansfield's characterization, as well as in her artistic stance, a method designed to reveal social hypocrisy and which 'lies at the core of the rebellious author's work'.[5]

The notion of subversion in the short story is actually implicit in O'Connor's *The Lonely Voice*, even though it is obscured by some of his formulations. When he identifies 'a submerged population group' as a feature of the short story, he approaches an understanding of the radical potential of characterization in the genre, but he closes off this potential by concluding that the submerged population group invariably suffers 'defeat inflicted by a society that has no sign posts, a society that offers no goals and no answers'. But O'Connor understands the crucial point that the distinctiveness of the short story is determined by 'ideological' factors, and, in a brief but seminal discussion, he points out how the short story has flourished best in unstable and developing cultures, in which a cynicism and lack of credence in unproven models of social organization is often displayed by an author.[6]

This attitude of social alienation, if it is indeed a prominent feature of the modern short story, suggests a radical contemporaneity inherent in the genre. It is interesting to note the frequency with which commentators have discerned some connection between a perceived instability of modern life and the short story form, a connection typified by V. S. Pritchett's assertion that the short story 'is the glancing form of fiction that seems to be right for the nervousness and restlessness of contemporary life'.[7] Nadine Gordimer's formulation of this 'glancing form', mentioned in chapter 3, suggests an integral perspicacity and insight: she writes of 'the quality of human life, where contact is... like the flash of fireflies, in and out, now here, now there, in darkness. Short-story writers see by the light of the flash; theirs is the art of the only thing one can be sure of – the present moment.'[8] The ways in which the structure of the short story is able to reflect the conditions of contemporary life is the crucial issue here, and one can begin by observing a parallel between fragmentary experience and the incompleteness of the literary form. Valerie Shaw notes that 'the twentieth-century short story arises precisely out of a sense that life can only be rendered in fragments and compressed subjective episodes'.[9] This remark, with only a slight leap of imagination, could be said to apply to the modernist short story, and the way it reveals an attitude to contemporary experience through a highly self-conscious process of structural fragmentation; yet what we need to explore further are the particular properties the short story has in this connection. Nadine Gordimer offers a preliminary signpost:

What about the socio-political implications of the short story's survival? Georg Lukács has said that the novel is a bourgeois art form whose enjoyment presupposes leisure and privacy. It implies the living room, the armchair, the table lamp... From this point of view the novel marks the apogee of an exclusive, individualist culture;... Here... it would seem that the short story shares the same disadvantages as the novel. It is an art form solitary in communication; yet another sign of the increasing loneliness and isolation of the individual in a competitive society. You cannot enjoy the experience of a short story unless you have certain minimum conditions of privacy in which to read it; and these conditions are those of middle-class life. But of course a short story, by reason of its length and its *completeness*, totally contained in the brief time you give to it, depends less than the novel upon the classic conditions of middle-class life, and perhaps corresponds to the breakup of that life which is taking place. In that case, although the story may outlive the novel, it may become obsolete when the period of disintegration is replaced by new social forms and the art forms that express them.[10]

Gordimer's remarks are wide-ranging, betraying a writer's reliance upon intuition, and to follow up Gordimer's point we need to expand upon her remarks comparing the expectations involved in the reception of novels and short stories. Again Frank O'Connor provides a good reference point: his conviction that the short story 'function[s] as a private art intended to satisfy the standards of the individual, solitary, critical reader' is problematic, and is at one with his belief that the 'process of identification between the reader and the character', inevitable in the novel, is absent from the short story, with the result that no connection is offered 'with society as a whole'.[11] Richard Kostelanetz agrees with O'Connor that the lack of identification 'is certainly more often true of short stories than of longer works of fiction', and this is an intuition with which most readers would probably concur.[12] Yet O'Connor's interpretation of this fact is certainly questionable. To begin with, it is difficult to understand what he might mean by the *standards* of the *solitary* reader, because standards of any sort must be defined by social context (in a social vacuum there is nothing to measure up to, or to fail to measure up to). The further problem, however, is O'Connor's assumption that an identification between fictional character and reader must result in social connection; one can certainly argue that it is precisely this identification which debilitates the social intervention that fiction can make.

In his *Resisting Novels* Lennard Davis suggests that the novel, rather than a vehicle of moral and intellectual enlightenment, may in fact be 'part of the process that got us to the world of the "minimal self" in the first place'.[13] The argument is that the novel is a defence, an apparent way out of the isolation which it actually reinforces: 'the comfort of overcoming loneliness through reading', writes Davis, 'is fraught with the tension inherent in the loneliness of reading, the isolation of the act, and the inaccessibility of the fictional characters'. 'In making friends with signs we are weakening the bond that anchors us to the social world.'[14] The charge here is that the desire for action or change may be satisfied and defused by the passive aesthetic fulfilment of reading.

Leaving aside the vulnerability of this as an out-of-context generalization, it does identify a possible effect of containment resulting from identification – the isolating effect of entering the world of the novel, and withdrawing from daily life. If identification is, at least potentially, capable of eliciting asocial behaviour, then O'Connor's formula for social connection seems dubious. It may well be that by failing to encourage the type of identification which Davis and O'Connor both discern as an integral effect of the novel, the short story actually eschews the isolation that reading may produce: the lack of empathic characterization can be seen as just one part of the self-consciousness of the form, its preoccupation with its own artifice. This self-consciousness precludes the creation of an illusory novel-world: the effects of the short story, to be grasped fully, require an acknowledgement of artifice and a consciousness of technique in the reader. 'In modern short stories', as Kostelanetz points out, 'the reader observes the scene instead of participating in it.'[15]

This is not, I hasten to add, an elitist prescription for literary appreciation: I am not suggesting that the short story can only be read ater the acquisition of certain 'rules' of reception.[16] On the contrary, a consciousness of technique, far from being the sole province of the literary critic, may be an inevitable aspect of the whole business of creating and receiving certain kinds of narrative in our culture. Joan Didion has made a direct comparison between the composing of short stories and the manner in which individuals perceive the world: she claims that 'all of us make up stories' as we apply a process of selection and revision to our perception of experience, and that it is only this process of giving our experiences a 'dramatic shape' that enables us to cope with the plethora of stimuli, the 'incessant clatter' which 'all of us have... going on in our heads, all the time'.[17] The essence of this claim is, in the words of William Saroyan, that 'the short story *is*, of itself, central to the human experience'.[18] The remarks of Didion and Saroyan, however, apply as much to the tradition of the oral tale as they do to the modern short story, so one cannot push this connection too far. But it does seem possible that narrative artifice may be a subconscious aspect of a contemporary world-view, a necessary tool for survival in developed western countries, where media proliferation threatens to overwhelm the individual with a cacophony of data. The point, however, is to remark upon this connection between the technical methods of the short story – a deliberate distancing from 'reality' – and the way in which we make sense of the world, a connection which both undercuts the notion of sophistication in literary artifice, and reinforces the association between the short story form and the nature of modern experience. Michael Chapman makes a similar point when, acknowledging that 'the short story... announces boldly its deflection from models of social interaction', claims that it is consequently 'an ideal medium through which to demystify literature'.[19]

Joan Didion's parallel between story composition and the revisionary individual perception of experience obviously has a direct relevance to fictional closure, how the representation of experience is packaged. Susan Lohafer also considers the relationship between diurnal reality and the short story form, and finds herself 'tempted' to make the claim 'that, for both author and reader, the impetus to closure on the story level is really an internalized expectation of patterns we've noted in life: problems followed by solutions, meetings followed by partings, the unknown yielding to the known, and the known giving way to the unknown.'[20] This is not a simplified aesthetic of unified closure, but rather an account of expectations which may or may not be fulfilled in a story, but which nevertheless order its composition and its reception:

We'll keep on reading if our appetite stays ahead of our ability to assimilate, so that, in our reading, even more intensely than in our living, we experience the impetus to closure. Ideally there is a point at which the need to have more and the need to assimilate reach equilibrium. Perhaps we never hit the point exactly, for this may be one of those balances of nature which are always in the process of righting themselves. But the art of the short story is manifest in the guiding of the balance arm to rest – briefly, illusorily – for the sake of our need.[21]

This suggests that a consciousness of closure is operative in all short stories, even those which are open-ended. The continual resistance to closure in the modernist short story – its repudiation of simple order and pattern in experience – complicates this view, however. Yet it is inevitably true that a piece of short fiction makes its point in a closed, manageable narrative period, even if that point concerns the irreducible ambiguity of life. Consequently there is a principle of closure in relation to the mode of communication, though not necessarily in the matter communicated, and this tension, or formal dissonance, has been noted in previous chapters. Now we can really see how this kind of dissonance reveals the social context, which in this case can be defined as a crisis of identity: the anti-closural gesture is a repudiation of conventional fictional representations of experience, but the short story still indicates a need to simplify and order the way in which life is portrayed, in a general sense. This Catch-22 may be a necessary defence against the 'incessant clatter' which Didion sees an endemic in modern life.

This view of 'modern life', like the other impressions of modernity cited so far, is equally as relevant to the modernist era, narrowly defined, as it is to late twentieth-century life. I want to consider now how more specifically contemporary issues are represented by the kind of fictional techniques which were developed by the modernists. The purpose of this discussion, rather than to arrive at any definitive and detailed conclusion, is to make a preliminary investigation of topics which seem to establish clear links between the short story form and contemporary context. This discussion implicitly makes a case for the continuing relevance of the modernist story, since it is underpinned by a notion of the genre defined by modernist practice.

Frank Kermode, in his *The Sense of an Ending*, argues (like Didion) that ending in fiction replicates the way in which we need to impose a closed structure on experience in order to make sense of it. The suggestive example he uses is the fiction of representing the ticking of a clock with the sound 'tick-tock': the final sound organizes and gives form to the preceding temporal structure, and this is seen as a model for the organization of time in fictional plots. The real value of Kermode's book lies in the way he indicates the relationship between this closural tendency in our perceptions and our fictions, and a wider cultural tendency: that of 'apocalyptic thought'. Kermode, writing in the early 1960s, argues that although a sense of impending apocalypse is continually disproved by history (each age has its own version of imminent catastrophe), apocalyptic thinking still governs contemporary thinking, which is characterized by a sense of crisis, rather than an identifiable temporal end: 'although for us the End has perhaps lost its naive *imminence*, its shadow still lies on the crises of our fictions; we may speak of it as *immanent*'. Writing about 'The Modern Apocalypse' of the nuclear age, Kermode suggests that there is a danger in seeing this new crisis in a directly teleological way, as imminent rather than immanent, because the notion of imminent apocalypse is the kind of myth which, 'uncritically accepted, tends like prophecy to shape a future to confirm it'. Again there is a direct relationship here to fictional practice, which, if perceived as fixed, can lead to such aberrations as Wyndham Lewis's cult of deadness, a cult which, for Kermode, saw liberal thought as the enemy of its para-digmatic rigidity.[22] The political implications of fiction, for Kermode, are more acceptable if a process of transition, and historical flexibility, is applied to fictional composition. My survey, which has seen modernist innovation as the essence of its social justification, is in agreement with this broad stance. Yet a quarter of a century after the publication of Kermode's book there is a new, apparently imminent apocalypse which is beginning to dominate contemporary thinking, the impending catastrophe of ecological destruction, which history is only serving to confirm rather than disprove.

However, to assess the contemporary relevance of Kermode's views about apocalypse, particularly in relation to short fiction, we need to consider his own example. A fit object for this discussion is a collection of short stories by Martin Amis, *Einstein's Monsters*, a book which is specifically about nuclear weapons and nuclear war. These stories display an intense angst about, and anticipation of, nuclear holocaust: they prophesy that which they dread, and in doing so they clearly fall into Kermode's category of dangerous mythological thinking.

Einstein's Monsters begins with a polemical introduction entitled 'Thinkability', in which factual descriptions of nuclear warheads – statistics of incomprehensible and awesome power – are overlaid by Amis's own emotive reactions and impressions. The intention is clearly to evoke an impression of imminent apocalypse threatened by these weapons which 'are biblical in their anger'.[23] Amis wants us to see beyond statistics and really worry about the nuclear age in individual, human terms:

> I am sick of them – I am sick of nuclear weapons. And so is everybody else. When, in my dealings with this strange subject, I have read too much or thought too long – I experience nausea, clinical nausea. In every conceivable sense (and then, synergistically, in more senses than that) nuclear weapons make you sick. What toxicity, what power, what range. They are there and I am here – they are inert, I am alive – yet still they make me want to throw up, they make me feel sick to my stomach; they make me feel as if a child of mine has been out too long, much too long, and already it is getting dark. This is appropriate, and good practice. Because I will be doing a lot of that, I will be doing a lot of throwing up, if the weapons fall and I live. (8–9)

The question is whether Amis is caught in the kind of paradigmatic 'apocalyptic thinking' which Kermode sees as restricted to fatal prediction only, or whether he is successful in his attempt to achieve the reverse by overcoming passivity and inspiring positive condemnation. It is precisely the 'thinkability' of the apocalypse which Amis wants to reject by demonstrating that all aspects of nuclear holocaust are, in 'human' terms, unthinkable, and that, consequently, all attempts to plan aspects of nuclear conflict – civil defence as well as military strategy – are the products of 'subhuman' thinking. The introductory essay introduces the theme which governs the collection: the repudiation of opposition and violence, usually at an individual level where a character's attitude to conflict has a clear allegorical relationship to the contemporary situation evoked in the essay.

The opening story, 'Bujak and the Strong Force' (alternatively titled 'God's Dice'), is an allegory of disarmament in which the physically imposing character Bujak progresses from an attitude of physical assertiveness to pacifism, a growth of intellectual strength which is accompanied by the waning of his awesome physical strength. There is a decisive scene in which Bujak comes home to find his mother, daughter and granddaughter assaulted and murdered by two men who are still on the premises, asleep. The murderers, who have come to London from Scotland to commit their crime – across a national border – symbolize a nuclear assault. Amis makes this clear by applying to them the terminology he also uses to describe nuclear weapons themselves. While Bujak is away, 'energetic actors, vivid representatives of the twentieth century – Einstein's monsters – were on their way south' (44). The test for Bujak is to resist the urge to wreak a terrible, personal revenge on the two men, an urge he overcomes. The story's narrator asks Bujak why he showed this restraint, and the answer he receives is the key to the allegorical message:

'Why didn't you kill the sons of bitches? What stopped you?'
'Why?' he asked, and grinned. 'What would have been the reason?'
'Come on. You could have done it, easy. Self-defence. No court on earth would have sent you down.'
'True. It occurred to me.'
'Then what happened? Did you – did you feel too weak all of a sudden? Did you just feel too weak?'
'On the contrary. When I had their heads in my hands I thought how incredibly easy to grind their faces together – until they drowned in each other's faces. But no.'
But no. Bujak had simply dragged the men by the arms (half a mile,

to the police station in Harrow Road), like a father with two frantic children. He delivered them and dusted his hands.

'Christ, they'll be out in a few years. Why *not* kill them? Why not?'

'I had no wish to add to what I found. I thought of my dead wife Monika. I thought – they're all dead now. I couldn't add to what I saw there. Really the hardest thing was to touch them at all. You know the wet tails of rats? Snakes? Because I saw that they weren't human beings at all. They had no idea what human life was. No idea! Terrible mutations, a disgrace to their human moulding. An eternal disgrace. If I had killed them then I would still be strong. But you must start somewhere. You must make a start.'

And now that Bujak has laid down his arms, I don't know why, but I am minutely stronger. I don't know why – I can't tell you why. (48–9)

Bujak, rather than retaliating to the pre-emptive strike, chooses to lay down his arms, feeling that there is nothing to be gained from adding to the carnage. The narrator's gain in strength, which we are required to interpret, indicates hope arising out of the start that has been made on the path to disarmament.

The allegorical content is overt, unambiguous, and Utopian in its anti-apocalyptic drive. But this will not further our investigation into fictional closure until it is linked to the formal method of the story. The first point to be made here is that the overall design of overt allegory represents a deliberately artificial recreation of experience (something which is common in committed political fiction). This shaping of material into a pre-given form is accompanied, however, by an opposite opening-out tendency which results in a productive, resonant ending:

Einsteinian to the end, Bujak was an Oscillationist, claiming that the Big Bang will forever alternate with the Big Crunch, that the universe will expand only until unanimous gravity called it back to start again. At that moment, with the cosmos turning on its hinges, light would begin to travel backward, received by the stars and pouring from our human eyes. If, and I can't believe it, time would also be reversed, as Bujak maintained (will we move backward too? will we have any say in things?), then this moment as I shake his hand shall be the start of my story, his story, our story, and we will slip downtime of each other's lives, to meet four years from now, when, out of the fiercest grief, Bujak's lost women will reappear, born in blood (and we will have our conversations, too, backing away from the same conclusion), until Boguslawa folds into Leokadia, and Leokadia folds into Monika, and Monika is there to be enfolded by Bujak until it is her turn to recede, kissing her fingertips, backing away over the fields to the distant girl with no time for him (will that be any easier to bear than the other way around?), and then big Bujak shrinks, becoming the weakest thing there is, helpless, indefensible, naked, weeping, blind and tiny, and folding into Roża. (49–50)

Leaving aside the accuracy, or otherwise, of the physics, the point here is that existence is placed in a (literally) universal perspective: this ending of poetic closure develops an Einsteinian concept – the inseparability of time and space – in order to widen the relevance of Bujak's development. The image of Bujak's 'lost women' going back to the womb emphasizes the point of human interdependence, and the reverence of human life which is the wellspring of Amis's pacifism. The names refer to Bujak's granddaughter, daughter, and wife, each folding into one another, before he in turn folds into his own mother. There is a suggestion here of a human totality analogous to that evoked at the end of Lowry's 'Elephant and Colosseum', and in this sense the story concludes positively. But Amis's motif of interdependence is double-edged, because the infinite regression also suggests ultimate human failure, the potential catastrophic reversal of the post-Einsteinian, nuclear world. Thus there appears to be a deliberate inconclusiveness to the piece: despite the closural gesture – that motif of individual regression – the ending is finally open. Implicitly, a choice is outlined between progression and destruction, a choice which aptly summarizes Amis's overall message. It seems clear that Amis, in this story at least, is able to write an ending in which the suggestion of closure *does* imply imminent apocalypse, but an ending which permits him, simultaneously, to appeal for an alternative.

The tension between closure and non-closure at the end of this story echoes the ambiguity which is a key ingredient of the ending in so many modernist stories. It also seems possible that the notion of a fully closed-off ending is actually incompatible with the exploratory, multi-accentual nature of narrative. D. A. Miller makes this point in his book on closure in the traditional novel, *Narrative and its Discontents*: 'the narratable is stronger than the closure to which it is opposed in an apparent binarity. For the narratable is the very evidence of the narrative text, while closure (as, precisely, the nonnarratable) is only the sign that the text is over.' But, since the narratable 'can never generate the terms for its own arrest', an artificial imposition of termination is required, 'an act of "make-believe," a postulation that closure is possible'.[24] This is in accord with the arguments adduced earlier concerning the necessarily revisionary element of fictional composition, the means of making sense of the world. Miller's point also indicates the possibilities for complicating closure which are inherent in fictional composition, and which have a prominent function in the short story.

The ambiguous role of closure becomes even more prominent in the postmodernist short story, where the predominance of metafiction has given rise to a large body of navel-contemplating texts which offer much commentary on their role in the contemporary world. It is, however, beyond the scope of the present work to undertake an extended survey of the bewildering field of postmodernism, or, indeed, to offer any serious conclusions concerning this complex phenomenon. I will, however, offer a reading of what seems to me to be a representative postmodernist short story, merely to speculate on how the related issues discussed in this chapter – fictional closure, story form, and social context – may be altering their matrix. Such speculation is, inevitably, imprecise, but I still resist the cautionary impulse, since it seems right to offer a sketch of how the modernists' innovations in the short story continue to influence fictional practice, even while these innovations appear to have become subverted, in turn, themselves.

The story I have chosen for this preliminary investigation is 'The Balloon' by Donald Barthelme, a text which illuminates the present discussion on fictional closure and contemporary crisis. This story, which is representative of Barthelme's art, is a metafiction about the exegesis of its title image which is, itself, a metaphor for the fictional artefact. The story concerns the inflation of a large balloon, on the narrator's instructions, above Manhattan, and the subsequent attempts of the New Yorkers to explain, understand, and appreciate this artefact. Like many postmodern fiction writers, Barthelme cultivates a sense of contemporary confusion, although his stories are usually posited on the implicit struggle of his characters to make sense of this confusion: in 'The Balloon' the effort of interpreting the world is elided with the business of literary criticism.

In evoking a fragmented, dissonant modern world, Barthelme employs a decentred narrative which will embrace, without apparent discrimination, a multitude of contemporary voices and influences. There is, however, a narratorial frame to the story which cuts across the exploratory nature of the piece: the style of resonant openness is supplanted by an exaggerated, traditional closed ending. The impoverished, single interpretation of the balloon as 'a spontaneous autobiographical disclosure',[25] heralds the deflation of the balloon (the object), and an obvious simultaneous deflation of the story.

The exaggerated closure is an ironic gesture, a parody of the commodification of experience in literature, the end-oriented reshaping of events to conform to an authorial grand design. The conspicuous end contradicts the narrative assertion that 'it is wrong to speak of "situations," implying sets of circumstances leading to some resolution, some escape of tension' (16). By extension, the irony is directed against the reification of contemporary life, a recurring Barthelmean concern. In *The Shape of Art in the Short Stories of Donald Barthelme*, Wayne Stengel points out 'the clash between the soft, undifferentiated form of the balloon and the hard-edged contours of the city buildings and skyscrapers on which it rests', suggesting that this illustrates one 'of the many conflicts between fluid content and solidified form that appear throughout the story'.[26] This conflict between the rigid, alienating cityscape and the fluidity of the art object is replicated in the clash between openness and closure in the writing.

The balloon (the object) is also an extravagant Barthelmean joke at the expense of rigid symbolic organization in literature. The balloon takes this impulse to an absurd extreme in standing as a symbol for the whole story. When, in the narrow conclusion, the balloon is discussed in more conventionally representational terms – as a recognizable symbol – its deflation occurs.

Specifically, it is phallic symbolism which the story satirizes, at its conclusion. This narrow significance of the balloon is anticipated earlier in the piece when we are informed that 'the purpose of the balloon was not to amuse children' (17). Finally we are informed that the inflation of this massive dirigible had to do 'with sexual deprivation' (22), and it is implied that its deflation accompanies the end of this deprivation. The excessiveness of the balloon as phallic symbol creates an absurdist effect, not just in terms of scale, but also through the amorphousness of the balloon: it is 'phallic' not by virtue of its shape, but simply because it expands.

An important source of irony is the further contradiction between the predominant openness of the narrative to contemporary discourses, and the impoverished closure of these discourses. One example of this is the story's invocation of sales-talk: Barthelme's awareness of the conditioning capacity of publicity is clearly displayed by his understanding of the interpretive difficulty presented by a dirigible *not* displaying an advertising slogan: 'Had we painted, in great letters, "LABORATORY TESTS PROVE" or "18% MORE EFFECTIVE" on the sides of the balloon, this difficulty would have been circumvented' (18). The irony is obvious: incomplete and apparently meaningless advertising phrases communicate unambiguously in the modern world.

If Barthelme's narrative style is mainly an inconsistent collage of contemporary voices, we can view it, as Charles Molesworth suggests, as the narrative voice of the mass media.[27] This linguistic collage is a contemporary representation of heteroglossia, the combination and conflict of a variety of cultural texts and voices, which, in Bakhtinian terms, is a positive source of progress, because such conflict involves the debunking of unitary forces. This tendency allows language to thrive because 'discourse lives ... on the boundary between its own context and another, alien, context', yet it seems possible that this notion of heteroglossia has become, in the postmodern era, a source of confusion, a dilution of meaning.[28] In his novel *Snow White*

Barthelme reveals the threat of communication breakdown which pervades his work when he writes: 'The moment I inject discourse from my universe of discourse (u. of d.) into your u. of d., the yourness of yours is diluted.'[29]

Yet this problem of communication is not to be solved by recourse to the rigidities of fictional convention: the disruption of closure retains its positive aspect. This principle extends to the interpretation of the balloon (the object) which provokes and embraces a diversity of interpretation and experience. An indication of this is given in the account of a man who might erroneously apply a preconceived interpretation to the balloon: 'One man might consider that the balloon had to do with the notion *sullied*, as in the sentence *The big balloon sullied the otherwise clear and radiant Manhattan sky*' (18). The linguistic structure, however, does not fit the experience because 'the underside of the balloon was a pleasure to look up into'. Consequently, 'while this man was thinking *sullied*, still there was an admixture of pleasurable cognition in his thinking, struggling with the original perception' (19).

In extrapolating the tendency to flout the closed short story, at least before the final paragraph, Barthelme is able to make some broad social and cultural suggestions.

Amongst the New Yorkers an interpretive consensus is ultimately reached that there can be no consensus; they are happy in agreeing to disagree: 'It was suggested that what was admired about the balloon was finally this: that it was not limited or defined' (21). This formal freedom has a sociological implication:

This ability of the balloon to shift its shape, to change, was very pleasing, especially to people whose lives were rather rigidly patterned, persons to whom change, although desired, was not available. The balloon, for the twenty-two days of its existence, offered the possibility, in its randomness, of mislocation of the self, in contradistinction to the grid of precise, rectangular pathways under our feet. The amount of specialized training currently needed, and the consequent desirability of long-term commitments, has been occasioned by the steadily growing importance of complex machinery, in virtually all kinds of operations; as this tendency increases, more and more people will turn, in bewildered inadequacy, to solutions for which the balloon may stand as a prototype, or 'rough draft.' (21)

There is an implicit comment here on the ideological restraints of fiction presented and received in formulaic fashion. A collective identity of sorts is suggested unfettered by preconceived or end-structured representations of experience. Barthelme's rejection of limiting fictional conventions is here explicitly identified with ideological conditioning in society at large. The specific charge here is against the 'bewildered inadequacy' occasioned by specialization, the alienation and fragmentation which follow in the wake of an increasingly mechanized world. The crucial concluding paragraph, in substituting personal angst for social possibility, seems to confirm these intimations about the tragedy of development, the impoverishment paradoxically caused by the proliferation of stimuli.

It may well be that 'The Balloon' epitomizes a kind of postmodernism which consciously replicates a state of communication breakdown. For Fredric Jameson this kind of work is symptomatic of a cultural moment in which 'stylistic innovation is no longer possible'.[30] Innovation, according to this view, has been supplanted by a collage of contemporary discourses, a non-judgemental fusion of disparate sources: this element of postmodernism might lead one to assess it in terms analogous to Marshall Berman's characterization of pop modernism as a movement that 'never developed a critical perspective which might have clarified the point where openness to the modern world has got to stop'.[31]

These comments on postmodernism, however, are too brief to carry much weight in themselves; they merely stake out the kind of territory that a different book might describe. What is of interest to me from this brief analysis is the light it might shed on the modernist project: of particular significance here are the claims that several critics have made concerning the lack of a critical perspective in postmodernism at large, an undiscriminating openness to the modern. The charge cannot be authoritatively upheld or rejected here, but the significant, and depressing, thing is how this *account* of postmodernism presents it as diametrically opposed to the impulses of modernism from which it derives. The modernists' formal developments of the short story generate effects concerned, primarily, with where openness to the modern world has got to stop. The availability of such 'judgements' derives from a stress on artifice and its capacity to *re*-present the social world. Yet an even greater emphasis on literary artifice in more contemporary literature may be seen to have precluded judgement altogether. In postmodern short stories like 'The Balloon' the formal dissonance of the modernists may have become not merely the governing principle of composition, but the sum total of the comment on offer: is this a fictional style which pushes to an extreme the connection between literary form and social context, where a crisis of organization and direction is common to both?

Notes

1 THE SHORT STORY: THEORIES AND DEFINITIONS

1 The notion of a new genre is sometimes opposed: Warren S. Walker, for instance, challenges the idea of the modern short story as a new genre by arguing that its roots lie in the oral tale. See 'From Raconteur to Writer: Oral Roots and Printed Leaves of Short Fiction', in *The Teller and the Tale: Aspects of the Short Story*, edited by Wendell M. Aycock (Lubbock, Texas, 1982), pp. 13–26. For discussions of the modern short story as a new phenomenon see note 6 below.

2 L. P. Hartley, 'In Defence of the Short Story', in *The Novelist's Responsibility* (London, 1967), pp. 157–9 (p. 157).

3 Susan Lohafer, *Coming to Terms with the Short Story* (Baton Rouge, 1983), p. 159.

4 The term 'genre', it should be said, is used in this survey to connote generic *forms* (novel, short story, novella), rather than generic *styles* (romance, thriller, metafiction), which cross the boundaries of form.

5 Lohafer, *Coming to Terms with the Short Story*, p. 103.

6 Mary Louise Pratt dates the emergence of the modern short story between 1835 and 1855 in 'The Short Story: The Long and the Short of It', *Poetics*, 10 (1981), 175–94 (182). H. E. Bates considers 1809, the year in which both Gogol and Poe were born, to be the key date. See *The Modern Short Story* (1941; rep. London, 1988). Ian Reid discusses the form's nineteenth-century origins in chapter two of *The Short Story* (London, 1977). Commentators on the modern short story in England have frequently taken 1880 as the starting-point for their survey: see Clare Hanson, *Short Stories and Short Fictions: 1880–1980* (London and Basingstoke, 1985); Suzanne Carol Ferguson, 'Formal Developments in the English Short Story: 1880–1910', unpublished doctorial dissertation, Stanford

University, 1967; Joseph M. Flora, ed., *The English Short Story: 1880–1945* (Boston, Mass., 1985). One useful way of indicating new developments in short fiction is to trace the growth of the genre in the literary magazines of the 1880s and 1890s, particularly in *The Yellow Book*. Some of the historical surveys contain speculation on this issue. See particularly Hanson, *Short Stories and Short Fictions*, pp. 11–19.

7 Pratt, 'The Short Story: The Long and the Short of It', 180–1.

8 E. M. Forster, *Aspects of the Novel* (1927; rep. Harmondsworth, 1981), p. 25.

9 Norman Friedman, 'What Makes a Short Story Short?', *Modern Fiction Studies*, 4 (1958), 103–17, in *Short Story Theories*, edited by Charles E. May (Ohio, 1976), pp. 131–46 (p. 133).

10 Anthony Burgess, 'On the Short Story', *Les Cahiers de la Nouvelle: Journal of the Short Story in English*, 2 (1984), 31–47 (38).

11 Elizabeth Bowen, 'The Faber Book of Modern Short Stories', in *Short Story Theories*, ed. May, pp. 152–8 (p. 153).

12 G. B. Stern, *Long Story Short* (London, 1939).

13 Bernard Fonlon, 'The Philosophy, the Science and the Art of the Short Story', *Abbia: Revue Culturelle Camerounaise*, 34–7 (1979), 427–38 (431).

14 Pratt, 'The Short Story: The Long and the Short of It', 183.

15 See, for instance, Hanson, *Short Stories and Short Fictions*, p. 55.

16 This term has also incurred difficulties: Joseph Gibaldi disputes the common use of 'novella' and suggests that 'short novel' or 'novelette' would be preferable. 'Novella', he argues, is 'the term for a definite period genre, specifically that tradition of short prose fiction that flourished between the fourteenth and seventeenth centuries, for which Boccaccio's *Decameron* served as the supreme model.' See 'Towards a Definition of the Novella', *Studies in Short Fiction*, 12 (1975), 91–7 (92).

17 Judith Leibowitz, *Narrative Purpose in the Novella* (The Hague, 1974), pp. 12, 16.

18 Ibid. See, especially, pp. 12–17.

19 Ibid., p. 64.

20 The task of definition has been further complicated by the growth of the very short story – the 'minimal fiction' or the 'short-short story', as it is variously defined. See, for instance, the anthology *Sudden Fiction: American Short-Short Stories*, edited by Robert Shapard and James Thomas (1986; rep., Harmondsworth, 1988). The 'Afterwords' (pp. 227–58) by well-known writers attempt to define the short-short story, but often only serve to confuse the generic issue, as when Paul Theroux comments that 'in most cases it contains a novel' (p. 228).

21 Michael Chapman, 'The Fiction Maker: The Short Story in Literary Education', *CRUX: A Journal on the Teaching of English*, 18 (1984), 3–20 (4).

22 Ibid., 5.

23 Valerie Shaw, *The Short Story: A Critical Introduction* (London and New York, 1983), pp. 134, 135.

24 Edgar Allan Poe, 'Review of *Twice-Told Tales*', *Graham's Magazine*, May 1842, reprinted in *Short Story Theories*, ed. May, pp. 45–51 (p. 48).

25 Ibid., p. 48.

26 Shaw, *The Short Story: A Critical Introduction*, p. 13.

27 Ibid., pp. 12, 15.

28 A picture, of course, cannot always be taken in all at once, and may also employ foregrounding devices – pattern, juxtaposition of colours – which invite a particular order of perception. But in a painting there can be no fixed, temporal order of assimilation as there always must be in a sequence of words.

29 Shaw, *The Short Story: A Critical Introduction*, pp. 14–15.

30 Other analogies between painting and the short story are made by William Peden, 'Realism and Anti-Realism in the Modern Short Story', in *The Teller and the Tale*, ed. Aycock, pp. 47–62 (p. 49), and John Bayley, *The Short Story: Henry James to Elizabeth Bowen* (Brighton, 1988), p. 43. One textbook on the short story stresses the supposed affinity by opening each chapter with a famous picture in order to 'illustrate' different aspects of the short story. (See *Four Elements: A Creative Approach to the Short Story*, edited by Anne Sherrill and Paula Robertson-Rose (New York, 1975).) The final chapter, on 'The Organic Whole' of the short story, is prefaced by a reproduction of Edvard Munch's litho 'The Scream' which, it is said, derives its force from 'a total impression' just as the story writer 'creates an *organic whole*, in which parts are dependent on one another' (p. 117).

31 Avrom Fleishman, 'Forms of the Woolfian Short Story', in *Virginia Woolf: Revaluation and Continuity*, edited by Ralph Freedman (Berkeley, Los Angeles and London, 1980), pp. 44–70.

32 Johannes Hedberg, 'What is a "Short Story"? And What is an "Essay"?', *Moderna Språk*, 74 (1980), 113–20 (119).

33 Rüdiger Imhof, 'Minimal Fiction, or the Question of Scale', *Anglistik & Englischunterricht*, 23 (1984), 159–68 (167). 'Frame Tale' is from John Barth's *Lost in the Funhouse* (Harmondsworth, 1972).

34 John Wain, 'Remarks on the Short Story', *Les Cahiers de la Nouvelle: Journal of the Short Story in English*, 2 (1984), 49–66 (51).

35 'Katherine Anne Porter: An Interview', *Paris Review*, 29 (1963), 101.
36 *The Letters and Journals of Katherine Mansfield*, edited by C. K. Stead (Harmondsworth, 1981), p. 247.
37 A. E. Coppard, *It's Me, O Lord!* (London, 1957), p. 33.
38 Cay Dollerup, 'Concepts of "Tension", "Intensity" and "Suspense" in Short-Story Theory', *Orbis Litterarum: International Review of Literary Studies*, 25 (1970), 314–37.
39 Reid, *The Short Story*, pp. 6, 8.
40 Eileen Baldeshwiler, 'The Lyric Short Story: The Sketch of a History', *Studies in Short Fiction*, 6 (1969), 443–53, reprinted in *Short Story Theories*, ed. May, pp. 202–13 (p. 208).
41 John Gerlach, *Toward the End: Closure and Structure in the American Short Story* (Alabama, 1985), p. 6.
42 Ibid., p. 160.
43 A. L. Bader, 'The Structure of the Modern Short Story', *College English*, 7 (1945), 86–92, reprinted in *Short Story Theories*, ed. May, pp. 107–15 (p. 110).
44 Lohafer, *Coming to Terms with the Short Story*, p. 26.
45 Ibid., p. 86.
46 Hanson, *Short Stories and Short Fictions*, pp. 83, 120, 127.
47 Kafka makes this objection in a letter of 25 October 1915. See Franz Kafka, *Letters to Friends, Family, and Editors*, translated by Richard and Clara Winston (London, 1978), pp. 114–15 (p. 115).
48 Kafka, *The Trial*, translated by Willa and Edwin Muir (1935; rep. Harmondsworth, 1981), pp. 235–7.
49 Frank Kermode, *The Genesis of Secrecy: On the Interpretation of Narrative* (Cambridge, Mass., 1979), p. 28.
50 Ferguson, 'Formal Developments in the English Short Story', pp. 4, 5.
51 Baldeshwiler, 'The Lyric Short Story', p. 202.
52 Ibid.
53 Hanson, *Short Stories and Short Fictions*, pp. 55–81.
54 See *The Story: A Critical Anthology*, edited by Mark Schorer (New York, 1950), p. 433. Quoted and discussed by Thomas A. Gullason in 'Revelation and Evolution: A Neglected Dimension of the Short Story', *Studies in Short Fiction*, 10 (1973), 347–56 (347).
55 Elizabeth Bowen, *After-Thought: Pieces About Writing* (London, 1962), p. 79.
56 See, for instance, *Introduction to the Short Story*, edited by Robert W. Boynton and Maynard Mack (1965; second edition, New Jersey, 1972); *Studies in the Short Story*, edited by Virgil Scott and David Madden (1968; fourth edition, New York, 1976); *The Shape of*

Fiction: British and American Short Stories, edited by Leo Hamalian and Frederick R. Karl (1967; second edition, New York, 1978).
57 The phrase is from *Stephen Hero* (1944; reprinted, London, 1969), p. 216.
58 Hanson, *Short Stories and Short Fictions*, p. 55.
59 Ibid., p. 56.
60 Ibid., pp. 78, 81.
61 See Wayne C. Booth, *The Rhetoric of Fiction* (second edition, Chicago and London, 1983).
62 Shaw, *The Short Story: A Critical Introduction*, pp. 136, 137, 193–4.
63 Julio Cortázar, 'On the Short Story and its Environs', translated by Naomi Lindstrom, *The Review of Contemporary Fiction*, 3 (1983), 34–37 (34, 37).
64 János Szávai, 'Towards a Theory of the Short Story', *Acta Litteraria Academiae Scientiarum Hungaricae*, 24 (1982), 203–24 (204, 205).
65 William B. Warde (Jr.), 'The Short Story: Structure of a New Genre', *South Central Bulletin*, 36 (1976), 155–7 (156).
66 John Gerlach, *Toward the End*, p. 111.
67 Bayley, *The Short Story*, pp. 15, 31.
68 Ibid., p. 36.
69 Terry Eagleton, *Criticism and Ideology* (1976; reprinted, London, 1986), p. 184. Eagleton is here employing Marxian terms from *The Eighteenth Brumaire*.
70 Bayley, *The Short Story*, p. 26.
71 Eudora Welty, 'The Reading and Writing of Short Stories', *The Atlantic Monthly*, 183 (February and March 1949), 54–8 and 46–9, reprinted in *Short Story Theories*, ed. May, pp. 159–77 (p. 164).
72 Reid, *The Short Story*, p. 65.
73 Hanson, *Short Stories and Short Fictions*, p. 36.
74 *The Stories of Katherine Mansfield*, edited by Antony Alpers (Auckland, Melbourne, Oxford, 1984), p. 307.
75 Ibid., p. 315.
76 Walter E. Anderson, 'The Hidden Love Triangle in Mansfield's "Bliss"', *Twentieth Century Literature*, 28 (1982), 397–404.
77 Marvin Magalaner's reading of the story in *The Fiction of Katherine Mansfield* (Carbondale and Edwardsville, 1971), pp. 78–9, contrasts with Anderson's. Magalaner finds the symbolism 'confusing' (79) precisely because it appears to represent the shifting feelings of different characters (this is its strength, in my view).
78 *The Stories of Katherine Mansfield*, p. 308.
79 Ibid., p. 315.
80 For details of magazine publication of *Jude* see Richard Little

Purdy, *Thomas Hardy: A Bibliographical Study* (1954; reprinted, Oxford, 1979), pp. 87–8.

81 John Goode, *Thomas Hardy: The Offensive Truth* (Oxford, 1988), pp. 139, 140. These brief references to Goode's book, it should be noted, do not do full justice to the sophistication of his argument at this point.

82 Michael Sprinker, *Imaginary Relations: Aesthetics and Ideology in the Theory of Historical Materialism* (London, 1987), p. 269. See pp. 178n, 179n for a summary of the political interpretations of Althusser.

83 'A Letter on Art in Reply to André Daspre', in Louis Althusser, *Essays on Ideology* (London, 1984), pp. 173–9 (pp. 173–4). For a critical view of the passage quoted see Terry Eagleton, *Criticism and Ideology*, p. 84.

84 Althusser, *Essays on Ideology*, p. 178.

85 Gregory Elliott, *The Detour of Theory* (London and New York, 1987), p. 177.

86 Louis Althusser and Etienne Balibar, *Reading Capital*, translated by Ben Brewster (1970; reprinted, London, 1986), p. 28.

87 Fredric Jameson, *The Political Unconscious: Narrative as a Socially Symbolic Act* (1981; reprinted, London, 1986), p. 81.

88 Ibid., p. 56.

89 Etienne Balibar and Pierre Macherey, 'On Literature as an Ideological Form', *Oxford Literary Review*, 3 (1978), 4–12, reprinted in *Untying the Text: A Post-Structuralist Reader*, edited by Robert Young (1981; reprinted, London, 1987), pp. 79–99 (p. 87).

90 C. A. Hankin, *Katherine Mansfield and Her Confessional Stories* (1983; reprinted, London and Basingstoke, 1988), p. 66.

91 Eagleton, *Criticism and Ideology*, p. 177.

92 See the 'Ideology of Modernism' in Georg Lukács, *The Meaning of Contemporary Realism*, translated by John and Necke Mander (London, 1963), pp. 17–46.

93 The continuing lack of sophistication in short story theory is surprising. In this connection mention should be made of a collection of brief essays, *Re-reading the Short Story*, edited by Clare Hanson (London and Basingstoke, 1989), which appeared after this work was originally drafted. The collection includes preliminary attempts to discuss the genre in terms of feminism (Mary Eagleton), psychoanalysis (Clare Hanson), and reader-response theory (David Miall). One would like to see the ideas broached in these short pieces extended in longer, more rigorous works.

2 JAMES JOYCE: THE NON-EPIPHANY PRINCIPLE

1 The quotation is from Homer Obed Brown, *James Joyce's Early Fiction: The Biography of a Form* (Cleveland, 1972), p. 7.

2 See Richard Ellmann, *James Joyce* (revised edition, Oxford, 1983), pp. 230–1.

3 Undated letter to Constantine Curran, 1904, *The Letters of James Joyce*, volume I, edited by Stuart Gilbert (London, 1957), p. 55.

4 This is Stanislaus' account of a conversation with Joyce. See Stanislaus Joyce, *My Brother's Keeper*, edited by Richard Ellmann (1958; reprinted, London, 1982), p. 116. Joyce's comments refer to 'my poems', but the connection with his accounts of *Dubliners* is clear.

5 *The Letters of James Joyce*, volume II, edited by Richard Ellmann (London, 1966), p. 134.

6 Ibid., I, pp. 63–4.

7 Florence L. Walzl, 'Dubliners', in *A Companion to Joyce Studies*, edited by Zack Bowen and James F. Carens (Westport and London, 1984), pp. 157–228 (p. 170).

8 See Robert Scholes, 'Grant Richards to James Joyce', *Studies in Bibliography*, 16 (1963), 139–60 (145–6).

9 *Letters*, II, pp. 141–3 (p. 143).

10 Robert Scholes, 'Grant Richards to James Joyce', 146.

11 *Letters*, II, pp. 135–8 (p. 137).

12 Robert Scholes, 'Grant Richards to James Joyce', 146–7.

13 *Letters*, I, pp. 61–3.

14 An indication of Joyce's opinion of Richards is evident in the letter to Stanislaus of 25 September 1906 (*Letters* II, 164–8), in which he exhibits dismissive contempt for Richards' critical acumen: 'where the hell does he get the meaningless phrases he uses?' (166).

15 Casebooks on *Dubliners* usually quote these letters in introductory sections, as is the case with *James Joyce's 'Dubliners'* (Belmont, 1969), edited by James R. Baker and Thomas F. Staley, and the Macmillan casebook *'Dubliners' and 'A Portrait'* (London, 1979), edited by Morris Beja.

16 In 1914 Richards did, eventually, agree to publish the collection. A thorough account of the publishing difficulties is given by Richard Ellmann, *James Joyce*. See especially pp. 214–31.

17 Phillip F. Herring includes a useful note on Joyce's Euclidean sources in *Joyce's Uncertainty Principle* (Princeton, 1987), pp. 3–4.

18 Gerhard Friedrich, 'The Gnomonic Clue to Joyce's *Dubliners*', *Modern Language Notes*, 72 (1957), 421–4 (422).

19 See David R. Fabian, 'Joyce's "The Sisters": Gnomon, Gnomic,

Gnome', *Studies in Short Fiction*, 5 (1968), 187–9 (188); and James Leigh, 'The Gnomonic Principle in *Dubliners*', *The Lamar Journal of the Humanities*, 9 (1983), 35–40 (36).

20 Robert Adams Day, 'Joyce's Gnomons, Lenehan, and the Persistence of an Image', *Novel*, 14 (1980–1), 5–19 (9).

21 Hugh Kenner, *The Pound Era* (1972; reprinted, London, 1975), pp. 34–9. For a discussion of Hugh Kenner's gnomonic criticism see Bernard Benstock, 'The Kenner Conundrum: Or Who Does What With Which to Whom', *James Joyce Quarterly*, 13 (1975–6), 428–35. A useful account of Kenner's discussions of 'Eveline' is Sidney Feshbach's '"Fallen on His Feet in Buenos Ayres": Frank in "Eveline"', *James Joyce Quarterly*, 20 (1982–3), 223–7.

22 Subsequent page references in the text are to *Dubliners* (the corrected text, London, 1967).

23 Edward Brandabur, *A Scrupulous Meanness: A Study of Joyce's Early Work* (Urbana, 1971), pp. 88–9.

24 Joseph C. Voelker, '"Chronicles of Disorder": Reading the Margins of Joyce's *Dubliners*', *Colby Library Quarterly*, 18 (1982), 126–44 (126, 128, 144).

25 Phillip F. Herring, *Joyce's Uncertainty Principle*, p. 7.

26 See Richard Ellmann, *James Joyce*, pp. 220–1. See also Robert Scholes, 'Grant Richards to James Joyce', and 'Further Observations on the Text of *Dubliners*', *Studies in Bibliography*, 17 (1964), 107–22.

27 Scholes, 'Further Observations on the Text of *Dubliners*', 117–18.

28 Herring, *Joyce's Uncertainty Principle*, pp. 7–8.

29 Ibid., pp. 3–4, 17.

30 Scholes has argued that Joyce used the term 'epiphany' in a precise sense, and that critics ought to follow his lead. Joyce's epiphanies were recordings of actual experiences, over seventy of which were written between 1900 and 1904. The forty which survive are published in *The Workshop of Daedalus* (Evanston, 1965), edited by Robert Scholes and Richard M. Kain. Several of these epiphanies were reworked for inclusion in *Stephen Hero*, *A Portrait* and *Ulysses*, but, as Scholes argues, not one of these real-life epiphanies occurs in *Dubliners*. (See Robert Scholes and Florence L. Walzl, 'The Epiphanies of Joyce', *PMLA*, 82 (March 1967), 152–4.)

31 Scholes and Walzl, 'The Epiphanies of Joyce', p. 153.

32 Morris Beja, *Epiphany in the Modern Novel* (London, 1971), pp. 93–4.

33 Zack Bowen, 'Joyce and the Epiphany Concept: A New Approach', *Journal of Modern Literature*, 9 (1981), 103–14 (104, 105–6).

34 L. J. Morrissey, 'Joyce's Narrative Strategies in "Araby"', *Modern Fiction Studies*, 28 (1982), 45–52 (47, 46).

35 John Gordon, *James Joyce's Metamorphoses* (Dublin, 1981), pp. 13, 17.

36 Morris Beja, 'One Good Look at Themselves: Epiphanies in *Dubliners*', in *Work in Progress: Joyce Centenary Essays*, edited by Richard F. Peterson, Alan M. Cohn and Edmund L. Epstein (Carbondale, 1983), pp. 3–14 (p. 10).

37 In their essay on 'Araby' John Brugaletta and Mary Hayden offer a different interpretation of the juxtaposed scenes, arguing that the boy *imagines* the crucial conversation with Mangan's sister. Brugaletta and Hayden deny any chronological break between the two scenes because this 'violates the integrity of the passage', and so they feel that Mangan's sister either suddenly appears in the back room unannounced and unexplained, or her presence is imagined by the boy. Because the former explanation is too implausible they conclude that the latter is the case. See John J. Brugaletta and Mary H. Hayden, 'The Motivation for Anguish in Joyce's "Araby"', *Studies in Short Fiction*, 15 (1978), 11–17 (13).

38 *Stephen Hero*, p. 216.

39 Gérard Genette, *Narrative Discourse*, translated by Jane E. Lewin (1980; reprinted, Oxford, 1986), pp. 186, 189, 194.

40 See Maurice Harmon, 'Little Chandler and Byron's "First Poem"', *Threshold*, 17 (1962), 59–61.

41 Robert Boyle discusses the tri-part structure in his essay 'A Little Cloud', in *James Joyce's 'Dubliners': Critical Essays*, edited by Clive Hart (London, 1969), pp. 84–92.

42 For a discussion of the initiation story see Mordecai Marcus, 'What is an Initiation Story?', in *Short Story Theories*, ed. May, pp. 189–201.

43 Martin Dolch, 'Eveline', in *James Joyce's 'Dubliners'*, ed. Baker and Staley, pp. 96–101 (p. 99). Dolch's chart is reproduced in Herring, *Joyce's Uncertainty Principle*, p. 35.

44 Clive Hart, 'Eveline', in *James Joyce's 'Dubliners'*, ed. Hart, pp. 48–52.

45 M. M. Bakhtin, *The Dialogic Imagination*, edited by Michael Holquist, translated by Caryl Emerson and Michael Holquist (Austin, 1983), p. 276.

46 Ibid., p. 272.

47 Hugh Kenner, *The Pound Era*, pp. 34–9.

48 Brandabur discusses this possibility in *A Scrupulous Meanness*, pp. 67–73.

49 Jennie Skerl, 'A New Look at Vladimir Propp's Narrative

Grammar: The Example of Joyce's "Eveline"', *Essays in Literature*, 8 (1961), 151–71 (164, 166).

50 For Propp's functions, see *Morphology of the Folktale*, translated by Laurence Scott (second edition, 1968; reprinted, Austin, 1988), pp. 25–64.

51 See Brandabur, *A Scrupulous Meanness*, pp. 57–8, 73–82. Brandabur adopts D. H. Lawrence's use of the division of the psyche into separatist and sympathetic aspects, a division Lawrence discusses in *Psychoanalysis and the Unconscious*. See '*Fantasia of the Unconscious*' and '*Psychoanalysis and the Unconscious*' (Harmondsworth, 1971), p. 240.

52 Suzanne Katz Hyman, '"A Painful Case": The Movement of a Story Through a Shift in Voice', *James Joyce Quarterly*, 19 (1981–2), 111–18 (114).

53 Herring, *Joyce's Uncertainty Principle*, p. 67.

54 V. N. Vološinov, *Marxism and the Philosophy of Language*, translated by Laidislav Matejka and I. R. Titunik (1973; reprinted Cambridge, Mass., and London, 1986), p. 144. The disputed authorship of this book – Vološinov or Bakhtin – seems unresolvable. For a discussion of the disputed texts see Katerina Clark and Michael Holquist, *Mikhail Bakhtin* (Cambridge, Mass., and London, 1984), pp. 146–70.

55 The two quotes are from John William Corrington, 'Isolation as a Motif in "A Painful Case"', *James Joyce Quarterly*, 3 (1965–6), 182–91 (184); and Hyman, '"A Painful Case": The Movement of a Story Through a Shift in Voice', 115.

56 Herring, *Joyce's Uncertainty Principle*, pp. 41–55 (p. 41).

57 Etienne Balibar and Pierre Macherey, 'On Literature as an Ideological Form', p. 81.

3 VIRGINIA WOOLF: EXPERIMENTS IN GENRE

1 Baldeshwiler, 'The Lyric Short Story', in *Short Story Theories*, ed. May, pp. 202–13 (p. 202).

2 Ibid., p. 210.

3 Hanson, *Short Stories and Short Fictions*, p. 34. See pp. 34–54 for a discussion of early twentieth-century 'tale-tellers', Kipling, Somerset Maugham and 'Saki'.

4 The essays widely known under these titles are in Virginia Woolf, *Collected Essays*, edited by Leonard Woolf, 4 vols. (London, 1966–7); volume I (1966), pp. 319–37, and volume II (1966), pp. 103–10.

5 The edition of the stories used is *The Complete Shorter Fiction of*

Virginia Woolf, edited by Susan Dick (new edition, expanded and revised, London, 1989). Subsequent references are given in the text. I have followed Dick's dating of the stories – some dates are conjectural – which she explains in the useful notes to this edition, together with the publication history (pp. 293–313).

6 *Collected Essays*, II, p. 106.
7 Ibid., I, pp. 330; 337.
8 Ibid., II, p. 106.
9 Ibid., I, p. 334.
10 Ibid., I, p. 330.
11 Jean Guiguet makes an affirmative reading of the epiphany in *Virginia Woolf and Her Works*, translated by Jean Stewart (London, 1965), p. 333. Here it is suggested that a complete reversal is effected in the characterization of Miss Craye.
12 The innovatory nature of Woolf's style has increasingly been seen by critics as inextricably bound up with her challenge to patriarchal structures. 'Mr Bennett and Mrs Brown' is discussed in this light in the following: Beth Rigel Daugherty, 'The Whole Contention Between Mr Bennett and Mrs Woolf, Revisited', in *Virginia Woolf: Centennial Essays*, edited by Elaine K. Ginsberg and Laura Moss Gottlieb (New York, 1983), pp. 269–94; Rachel Bowlby, *Virginia Woolf: Feminist Destinations* (Oxford, 1988), pp. 1–16.
13 *Collected Essays*, I, p. 330.
14 *The Diary of Virginia Woolf*, edited by Anne Olivier Bell, 5 vols. (London, 1977–84; reprinted, Harmondsworth, 1979–85), volume III, p. 218.
15 *Collected Essays*, I, p. 334.
16 Harvena Richter, 'Hunting the Moth: Virginia Woolf and the Creative Imagination', in *Virginia Woolf: Revaluation and Continuity*, edited by Ralph Freedman (Berkeley, Los Angeles and London, 1980), pp. 13–28 (pp. 27–8).
17 Nadine Gordimer, 'The Flash of Fireflies', in *Short Story Theories*, ed. May, pp. 178–81 (p. 180).
18 See William C. Dowling, *Jameson, Althusser, Marx: An Introduction to 'The Political Unconscious'* (London, 1984) for an account of Jameson's concept of primitive communism as a 'mode of *perception*' (p. 22), as set out in *The Political Unconscious*.
19 Bakhtin, *The Dialogic Imagination*, p. 300. Bakhtin's use of the term 'heteroglossia' is usefully defined in the glossary to this edition as the 'base condition governing the operation of meaning in any utterance'. Contextual forces – social, historical, and so on – determine meaning and ensure that 'all utterances are heteroglot

in that they are functions of a matrix of forces'. Consequently, 'heteroglossia is as close a conceptualization as is possible of that locus where centripetal and centrifugal forces collide' (428).

20 Ibid., p. 298.
21 Ibid.
22 Ibid., p. 284.
23 Virginia Woolf, *Books and Portraits*, edited by Mary Lyon (1977; reprinted, St Albans, 1979), p. 139.
24 *The Essays of Virginia Woolf*, edited by Andrew McNeillie (London, 1986–   ), volume II, p. 167.
25 Virginia Woolf, *Books and Portraits*, p. 142.
26 Ibid., p. 143.
27 Bakhtin, *Problems of Dostoevsky's Poetics*, edited and translated by Caryl Emerson (Manchester, 1984), pp. 212, 215.
28 Ibid., pp. 212, 213.
29 Ibid., pp. 217, 226, 227.
30 Susan Dick conjectures that the story was originally drafted in 1918. See *The Complete Shorter Fiction*, p. 298.
31 Vološinov, *Marxism and the Philosophy of Language*, p. 118.
32 Bakhtin, *The Dialogic Imagination*, p. 272.
33 *Collected Essays*, II, p. 106.
34 See Makiko Minow-Pinkney, *Virginia Woolf and the Problem of the Subject* (Brighton, 1987), p. 25.
35 *Collected Essays*, II, p. 106.
36 Avrom Fleishman, 'Forms of the Woolfian Short Story', in *Virginia Woolf: Revaluation and Continuity*, ed. Freedman, p. 64.
37 *Collected Essays*, II, p. 106.
38 'The Sphinx Without a Secret', in *The Complete Works of Oscar Wilde* (1966; reprinted, London and Glasgow, 1977), pp. 215–18 (p. 218).
39 *Collected Essays*, I, pp. 327–8.
40 Ibid., p. 328.

4 KATHERINE MANSFIELD: THE IMPERSONAL SHORT STORY

1 *Journal of Katherine Mansfield*, definitive edition, edited by John Middleton Murry (1954; reprinted, London, 1984), p. 195.
2 Saralyn R. Daly, *Katherine Mansfield* (Boston, 1965), pp. 82, 85.
3 Page references given in the text are to *The Stories of Katherine Mansfield*, ed. Alpers. Proclaimed 'Definitive Edition' on the dustjacket, this is the nearest thing to a scholarly edition of the stories yet published. One should be aware, however, of the criticism it has provoked. See particularly Sophie Tomlinson's

review, 'Mans-Field in Bookform', *Landfall*, 39 (1985), 465–89. For the dating of the stories I have followed the bibliographical account given in the 'Commentary' in the Alpers edition, pp. 543–78. (Some of the dates are conjectural.)

4 David Daiches makes this objection in *New Literary Values: Studies in Modern Literature* (Edinburgh and London, 1936), p. 93.

5 *The Letters and Journals of Katherine Mansfield*, ed. Stead, p. 213.

6 See *The Letters of John Middleton Murry to Katherine Mansfield*, edited by C. A. Hankin (London, 1983), pp. 114–15 (115).

7 Bakhtin, *Problems of Dostoevsky's Poetics*, p. 205.

8 Some early experiments in dialogue are also to be found in 'Katherine Mansfield's Juvenilia', edited by Margaret Scott, *Adam International Review*, 370–5 (1973), 42–72. The story 'Pictures' (1919–20) was also originally written in dialogue form as 'The Common Round', *New Age* (31 May 1917).

9 Sylvia Berkman's discussion of the revision of *The Aloe* is particularly valuable. See *Katherine Mansfield: A Critical Study* (London, 1952), pp. 84–98.

10 The same ambiguity is evident in *The Aloe*, where the phrase is '*goes* for you'. See *The Aloe*, edited by Vincent O'Sullivan (London, 1985), p. 13.

11 Kate Fullbrook, *Katherine Mansfield* (Brighton, 1986), p. 38.

12 Sex and childbirth as predation and oppression in Mansfield is examined by Fullbrook, ibid. Sylvia Berkman's early study introduced this line of critical thought: see *Katherine Mansfield: A Critical Study*.

13 Bayley, *The Short Story*, pp. 123, 125.

14 Mansfield's use of fantasy is discussed intermittently in C. A. Hankin, *Katherine Mansfield and Her Confessional Stories*, and Fullbrook, *Katherine Mansfield*.

15 The importance of sea imagery in other Mansfield stories, often as representative of the harsh reality of experience, has been examined by Marvin Magalaner, especially in relation to 'At the Bay'. See *The Fiction of Katherine Mansfield*, pp. 40–3.

16 For an account of Mansfield's subversive feminist content see Fullbrook, *Katherine Mansfield*.

17 This is Fullbrook's apt summary of a prevailing critical view. Ibid., p. 127.

18 Elaine Showalter, *A Literature of Their Own: British Women Novelists From Brontë to Lessing* (revised edition, 1982; reprinted, London, 1988), p. 246.

19 Fredric Jameson, *The Political Unconscious*, p. 287.

20 D. H. Lawrence, letter to Edward Garnett, 5 June 1914, *The Letters of D. H. Lawrence*, volume II, edited by George Zytarak

and James Boulton (Cambridge University Press, 1981), p. 183; Virginia Woolf, 'Modern Fiction', in *Collected Essays*, II, pp. 103–10 (106).

21 *Letters and Journals*, p. 213.

22 Ibid., p. 259.

5 WYNDHAM LEWIS: THE VORTICIST SHORT STORY

1 Richard Cork makes large claims for the importance of Vorticism in the development of abstract art in *Vorticism and Abstract Art in the First Machine Age*, (London, 1976). For a challenge to this account see Reed Way Dasenbrock, *The Literary Vorticism of Ezra Pound and Wyndham Lewis: Towards the Condition of Painting* (Baltimore and London, 1985), especially pp. 61–5. See also Michael Durman and Alan Munton, 'Wyndham Lewis and the Nature of Vorticism' in *Wyndham Lewis: Letteratura/Pittura*, edited by Giovanni Cianci (Palermo, 1982), pp. 101–18.

2 Recent historical surveys that omit discussion of Lewis include Walter Allen's *The Short Story in English* (Oxford, 1981), Clare Hanson's *Short Stories and Short Fictions*, and *The English Short Story*, ed. Flora.

3 See Dasenbrock, *The Literary Vorticism of Ezra Pound and Wyndham Lewis*, for an excellent account of the gradual infiltration of Lewis's Vorticist painting aesthetic into his literary work. Dasenbrock shows how this aesthetic is involved in Lewis's literary output right through to the 1950s.

4 Richard Cork argues for this narrow definition. See particularly *Vorticism and Abstract Art*, pp. 508–57.

5 The edition used is *The Complete Wild Body*, edited by Bernard Lafourcade (Santa Barbara, 1982). In addition to the 1927 versions of the stories this edition also contains early drafts and other relevant primary material, together with publication details. Page references here are given subsequently in the text. See also Lafourcade's essay on the evolution of the stories, 'The Taming of the Wild Body', in *Wyndham Lewis: A Revaluation*, edited by Jeffrey Meyers (London, 1980), pp. 68–84.

6 *Tarr* (revised edition, 1928; reprinted, Harmondsworth, 1982), p. 312.

7 See Cork, *Vorticism and Abstract Art*, p. 246.

8 See Walter Michel, *Wyndham Lewis: Paintings and Drawings* (London, 1971), p. 58, for an explanation of the dating of *Workshop; The Vorticist* and *Le Penseur* are reproduced in plate 10.

9 The image of the dance recurs in Vorticist art, and was particularly important to Lewis. See Cork, *Vorticism and Abstract Art*, p. 39.

10 Timothy Materer, *Wyndham Lewis the Novelist* (Detroit, 1976), p. 44.

11 G. B. Stern makes excellent serious use of the supernatural discovery-after-the-event convention in a story from her collection *Long Story Short*, 'With Wings as Eagles'. The supernatural conclusion of the piece is used ingeniously to parallel the self-delusion of the central character.

12 José Ortega y Gasset, 'The Dehumanization of Art', translated by Helene Weyl in '*The Dehumanization of Art*' and Other Essays on Art, Culture, and Literature (Princeton, 1948; rep. 1972), pp. 1–54 (pp. 14, 23).

13 Ibid., pp. 16–17.

14 Ibid., p. 20, 17.

15 Ibid., p. 38.

16 There is an interesting parallel between 'A Soldier of Humour' and one of Lewis's most famous paintings, *The Crowd* (1914–15), which can be read as a critique of nationalism. The painting appears to depict stick figures – sometimes merged together to form impersonal blocks like tall modern buildings – which figures are being marshalled (by a general on the lower left) towards a large wheel (symbolizing the treadmills of war, or of factory life, or both) on the upper right.

The circumscribed form which dehumanizes the characters, and which also controls their movement, supplies a dual satirical observation, directed simultaneously at the impersonality of modern urban living, and against the destructiveness of the nationalistic impulse which engenders war. For a reproduction of the painting see Michel, *Wyndham Lewis: Paintings and Drawings*, plate 6, p. 59.

17 Fredric Jameson, *Fables of Aggression: Wyndham Lewis, the Modernist as Fascist* (1979; reprinted Berkeley, Los Angeles and London, 1981), p. 18.

18 Ibid., pp. 37, 37–8.

19 See ibid., pp. 39–40. Jameson's argument is based on the conviction that 'the most influential formal impulses of canonical modernism have been strategies of inwardness, which set out to reappropriate an alienated universe by transforming it into personal styles and private languages'. For Jameson 'such wills to style have seemed in retrospect to reconfirm the very privatization and fragmentation of social life against which they meant to protest' (p. 2).

20 Jameson borrows the term 'pseudo-couple' from Beckett in order to distinguish this new 'relational category from the conventional pairing of lovers or partners, or siblings or rivals'. The new term is used 'to convey the symbiotic "unity" of this new "collective" subject, both reduplicated and divided all at once'. See ibid., p. 58.
21 Ibid., p. 59.
22 Ibid., pp. 36, 61.
23 Wyndham Lewis, *Time and Western Man* (London, 1927), p. 129; SueEllen Campbell, *The Enemy Opposite: The Outlaw Criticism of Wyndham Lewis* (Athens, Ohio, 1988), p. 135.

6 MALCOLM LOWRY: EXPANDING CIRCLES

1 Malcolm Bradbury, *Possibilities: Essays on the State of the Novel* (Oxford, 1973), p. 181.
2 Douglas Day discusses the evolution of the stories in *Malcolm Lowry* (Oxford and New York, 1973; reissued, 1984), pp. 423–59. Particularly helpful here is Tony Bareham's list of the stories which gathers together the relevant bibliographical information, in *Malcolm Lowry* (London and Basingstoke, 1989), pp. 92–3.
3 I have opted to consider each of the fictions in the collection a 'story' despite the fact that the three longer pieces are sometimes termed 'novellas'. This terminology is discussed in the opening chapter.
   The generic importance of closure is examined in more detail in the final chapter.
4 Each story is approached as a separate work which generates its own effects, even though the book is sometimes seen as a cycle of interlinked pieces. Such an approach, which, I feel, obscures the generic specificity of the stories, is also made problematic by the uncertain genesis and posthumous publication of the collection. For an alternative view of the book's unity, and more detail on its development, see Bareham, *Malcolm Lowry*, pp. 90–101.
5 I disagree here with Dale Edmonds who considers the inconsistency in the characterization of Sigbjørn Wilderness to be an 'indefensible lapse'. See 'The Short Fiction of Malcolm Lowry', *Tulane Studies in English*, 15 (1967), 59–80 (72).
6 Letter to Albert Erskine, spring 1953, *Selected Letters of Malcolm Lowry*, edited by Harvey Breit and Margerie Bonner Lowry (1967; reprinted, Harmondsworth, 1985), p. 330.
7 Frank O'Connor, *The Lonely Voice* (1962; reprinted, London, 1963), pp. 19, 18.
8 Bernard Bergonzi, 'An Appendix on the Short Story', in *The*

Situation of the Novel (1970; reprinted, Harmondsworth, 1972), pp. 252, 256.

9 Richard K. Cross, *Malcolm Lowry: A Preface to His Fiction* (London, 1980), p. 96.

10 '*Hear Us O Lord From Heaven Thy Dwelling Place*' and '*Lunar Caustic*' (Harmondsworth, 1979, reprinted 1984), p. 241. Page references to this Penguin edition are given in the text.

11 Edgar Allen Poe, 'Review of *Twice-Told Tales*' in *Short Story Theories*, ed. May, pp. 45–51 (p. 47).

12 Valerie Shaw makes the conventional claim that 'most worthwhile short stories do contain a definite moment at which understanding is attained'. See *The Short Story: A Critical Introduction*, pp. 193–4.

13 Julio Cortázar, 'On the Short Story and its Environs', 34–7 (37).

14 Anagnorisis, in Greek tragedy, is the key moment of revelation, with regard to character and/or situation, which leads to plot resolution. This is an implicit extension, perhaps not by design, of Joyce's 'epiphany' concept, formulated in *Stephen Hero* and which is usually deemed to inform the revelatory moment in *Dubliners* (see chapter 2). Cosnahan's invocation of anagnorisis extends the epiphany concept by relating it to formal design, a point which adds weight to my argument that the density of the epiphany in *Hear Us O Lord* has a crucial bearing on the resonant formal effect.

15 For Lowry, too, the working out of a perennial author's dilemma is a personal exorcism of sorts, and although all his writing can be viewed in this way, it is worth considering the special generic capacity the short story may have in this respect, in the light of Julio Cortázar's incisive comment that 'in any memorable short story you get this polarization, as if the author had wanted to get rid, as quickly and utterly as possible, of this being harbored within him, exorcising it the only way he could: by writing it'. Cortázar, 'On the Short Story and its Environs', 35.

16 I discuss these three stories briefly in 'Expanding Circles: Inductive Composition in *Hear Us O Lord*', in *Malcolm Lowry, Eighty Years On*, edited by Sue Vice (Macmillan, 1989), pp. 70–91 (pp. 85–6).

17 Bradbury, *Possibilities*, p. 182.

7 CONCLUSION: CONTEMPORARY ISSUES

1 Eagleton, *Criticism and Ideology*, p. 184.

2 Jameson, *The Political Unconscious*, p. 296.

3 John Frow makes the valid criticism that Jameson glosses over the importance of historical specificity in his commitment to the

concept of Utopia. See *Marxism and Literary History* (1986; reprinted, Oxford, 1988), pp. 35–8. This objection does not, of course, prevent the appropriation of the concept to describe particular historical moments.

4 Charles E. May, 'The Nature of Knowledge in Short Fiction', *Studies in Short Fiction*, 21 (1984), 328–38 (333).

5 Fullbrook, *Katherine Mansfield*, p. 32.

6 O'Connor, *The Lonely Voice*, pp. 18, 20, 19–20.

7 V. S. Pritchett, *Collected Stories* (1982; reprinted, Harmondsworth, 1984), p. xi.

8 Gordimer, 'The Flash of Fireflies', p. 180.

9 Shaw, *The Short Story*, p. 43.

10 Gordimer, 'The Flash of Fireflies', p. 181.

11 O'Connor, *The Lonely Voice*, pp. 14, 17.

12 Richard Kostelanetz, 'Notes on the American Short Story Today', in *Short Story Theories*, ed. May, pp. 214–25 (p. 217).

13 Lennard J. Davis, *Resisting Novels: Ideology and Fiction* (New York and London, 1987), p. 6.

14 Ibid., pp. 134, 161.

15 Kostelanetz, 'Notes on the American Short Story Today', p. 217. For an alternative view of the literary effects of the short story see Julio Cortázar, 'On the Short Story and its Environs', where it is argued that 'the great short story...seizes hold like an hallucination...to fascinate the reader, tear him away from the suddenly pallid reality around him, plunge him more intensely, more overwhelmingly, inward' (35).

16 Fredric Jameson seems to be guilty of this suggestion in a discussion of genre as 'something like a social contract in which we agree to respect certain rules about the appropriate use of the piece of language in question'. See *The Ideologies of Theory: Essays 1971–86*, volume II, *The Syntax of History* (London, 1988), p. 116.

17 Joan Didion, 'Making up Stories', *Michigan Quarterly Review*, 18 (1979), 521–34, (524).

18 'The International Symposium on the Short Story', Part Two, *Kenyon Review*, 31 (1969), 57–94 (62).

19 Chapman, 'The Fiction Maker', 8, 10–11.

20 Lohafer, *Coming to Terms With the Short Story*, p. 96.

21 Ibid., p. 98.

22 Frank Kermode, *The Sense of an Ending* (1967; reprinted, Oxford, 1968). The following pages are cited in this paragraph: pp. 45, 5, 6, 94, 110.

23 Martin Amis, *Einstein's Monsters* (London, 1987), p. 8. Subsequent references are given in the text.

24 D. A. Miller, *Narrative and its Discontents: Problems of Closure in the Traditional Novel* (1981; reprinted, Princeton, 1989), pp. 266–7.
25 Donald Barthelme, *Unspeakable Practices, Unnatural Acts* (London, 1969), p. 22. Subsequent references are given in the text.
26 Wayne B. Stengel, *The Shape of Art in the Short Stories of Donald Barthelme* (Baton Rouge and London, 1985), p. 165.
27 Charles Molesworth, *Donald Barthelme's Fiction: The Ironist Saved From Drowning* (Columbia and London, 1982), p. 36.
28 Bakhtin, *The Dialogic Imagination*, p. 284.
29 Barthelme, *Snow White* (London, 1968), p. 46.
30 Fredric Jameson, 'Postmodernism and Consumer Society', in *Postmodern Culture*, edited by Hal Foster (1983; reprinted, London, 1985), pp. 111–25 (p. 115).
31 Marshall Berman, *All That is Solid Melts Into Air: The Experience of Modernity* (1982; reprinted, London, 1987), p. 32.

Bibliography

PRIMARY WORKS

Amis, Martin, *Einstein's Monsters* (London, 1987)

Barth, John, *Lost in the Funhouse* (Harmondsworth, 1972)

Barthelme, Donald, *Snow White* (London, 1968)

  Unspeakable Practices, Unnatural Acts (London, 1969)

Joyce, James, *Dubliners* (1914; corrected text, London, 1967)

  The Letters of James Joyce, volume I, edited by Stuart Gilbert (London, 1957)

  The Letters of James Joyce, volume II, edited by Richard Ellmann (London, 1966)

  Stephen Hero (1944; reprinted, London, 1969)

Kafka, Franz, *The Trial*, translated by Willa and Edwin Muir (1935; reprinted, Harmondsworth, 1981)

Lawrence, D. H., *The Letters of D. H. Lawrence*, volume II, edited by George Zytaruk and James Boulton (Cambridge University Press, 1981)

Lewis, Wyndham, *Blasting and Bombadiering* (1937; reprinted, London, 1982)

  The Complete Wild Body, edited by Bernard Lafourcade (Santa Barbara, 1982)

  Tarr (revised edition, 1928; reprinted, Harmondsworth, 1982)

  Time and Western Man (London, 1927)

Lowry, Malcolm, '*Hear Us O Lord From Heaven Thy Dwelling Place*' and '*Lunar Caustic*' (Harmondsworth, 1984)

  Selected Letters of Malcolm Lowry, edited by Harvey Breit and Margerie Bonner Lowry (1967; reprinted, Harmondsworth, 1985)

Mansfield, Katherine, *The Aloe*, edited by Vincent O'Sullivan (London, 1985)

  '*The Aloe*' With '*Prelude*', edited by Vincent O'Sullivan (Manchester, 1983)

The Collected Letters of Katherine Mansfield, edited by Vincent
O'Sullivan and Margaret Scott, 4 vols. (Oxford, 1984–)
The Collected Stories of Katherine Mansfield (Harmondsworth, 1982)
The Critical Writings of Katherine Mansfield, edited by Clare Hanson
(London and Basingstoke, 1987)
Journal of Katherine Mansfield, definitive edition, edited by John
Middleton Murry (1954, reprinted, London, 1984)
'Katherine Mansfield's Juvenilia', edited by Margaret Scott, *Adam
International Review*, 370–5 (1973), 42–72
The Letters and Journals of Katherine Mansfield: A Selection, edited by C.
K. Stead (Harmondsworth, 1981)
The Stories of Katherine Mansfield, edited by Antony Alpers (Auck-
land, Melbourne, Oxford, 1984)
Stern, G. B., *Long Story Short* (London, 1939)
Wilde, Oscar, *The Complete Works of Oscar Wilde* (1966; reprinted,
London and Glasgow, 1977)
Woolf, Virginia, *Books and Portraits*, edited by Mary Lyon (1977;
reprinted, St Albans, 1979)
Collected Essays, edited by Leonard Woolf, 4 vols. (London, 1966–7)
The Complete Shorter Fiction of Virginia Woolf, edited by Susan Dick
(new edition, London, 1989)
The Diary of Virginia Woolf, edited by Anne Olivier Bell, 5 vols.
(London, 1977–84; reprinted, Harmondsworth, 1979–85)
The Essays of Virginia Woolf, edited by Andrew McNeillie (London,
1986–), volume II

SHORT STORY CRITICISM

Allen, Walter, *The Short Story in English* (Oxford, 1981)
Aycock, Wendell M., ed., *The Teller and the Tale: Aspects of the Short
Story* (Lubbock, Texas, 1982)
Backus, Joseph M., '"He Came into Her Line of Vision Walking
Backwards": Nonsequential Sequence-Signals in Short Story
Openings', *Language Learning*, 15 (1965), 67–83
Bader, A. L., 'The Structure of the Modern Short Story', *College
English*, 7 (1945), 86–92, reprinted in *Short Story Theories*, edited
by Charles May, pp. 107–15
Baldeshwiler, Eileen, 'The Lyric Short Story: The Sketch of a
History', *Studies in Short Fiction*, 6 (1969), 443–53, reprinted in
Short Story Theories, edited by Charles May, pp. 202–13
'Katherine Mansfield's Theory of Fiction', *Studies in Short Fiction*, 7
(1970), 421–32
Bates, H. E., *The Modern Short Story* (1941; reprinted, London, 1988)

Bayley, John, *The Short Story: Henry James to Elizabeth Bowen* (Brighton, 1988)

Bergonzi, Bernard, 'An Appendix on the Short Story', in *The Situation of the Novel* (1970; reprinted, Harmondsworth, 1972), pp. 251–6

Bowen, Elizabeth, *After-Thought: Pieces About Writing* (London, 1962) 'The Faber Book of Modern Short Stories', in *Short Story Theories*, edited by Charles May, pp. 152–8

Boynton, Robert W., and Maynard Mack (eds.), *Introduction to the Short Story* (1965; second edition, New Jersey, 1972)

Burgess, Anthony, 'On the Short Story', *Les Cahiers de la Nouvelle: Journal of the Short Story in English*, 2 (1984), 31–47

Chapman, Michael, 'The Fiction Maker: The Short Story in Literary Education', *CRUX: A Journal on the Teaching of English*, 18 (1984), 3–20

Cook, Dorothy E., and Isabel S. Monro, *Short Story Index* (New York, 1953)

Coppard, A. E., *It's Me, O Lord!* (London, 1957)

Cortázar, Julio, 'Some Aspects of the Short Story', translated by Naomi Lindstrom, *The Review of Contemporary Fiction*, 3 (1983), 24–33
'On the Short Story and its Environs', translated by Naomi Lindstrom, *The Review of Contemporary Fiction*, 3 (1983), 34–7

Didion, Joan, 'Making up Stories', *Michigan Quarterly Review*, 18 (1979), 521–34

Dollerup, Cay, 'Concepts of "Tension", "Intensity" and "Suspense" in Short-Story Theory', *Orbis Litterarum: International Review of Literary Studies*, 25 (1970), 314–37

Ferguson, Suzanne Carol, 'Formal Developments in the English Short Story: 1880–1910', unpublished doctoral dissertation, Stanford University, 1967

Fleishman, Avrom, 'Forms of the Woolfian Short Story', in *Virginia Woolf: Revaluation and Continuity*, edited by Ralph Freedman (Berkeley, Los Angeles and London, 1980), pp. 44–70

Flora, Joseph M., ed., *The English Short Story: 1880–1945* (Boston, Mass., 1985)

Fonlon, Bernard, 'The Philosophy, the Science and the Art of the Short Story', *Abbia: Revue Culturelle Camerounaise*, 34–7 (1979), 427–38

Friedman, Norman, 'What Makes a Short Story Short?', *Modern Fiction Studies*, 4 (1958), 103–17, in *Short Story Theories*, edited by Charles May, pp. 131–46

Gerlach, John, *Toward the End: Closure and Structure in the American Short Story* (Alabama, 1985)

Gibaldi, Joseph, 'Towards a Definition of the Novella', *Studies in Short Fiction*, 12 (1975), 91–7

Gordimer, Nadine, 'The Flash of Fireflies', in *Short Story Theories*, edited by Charles May, pp. 178–81

Gullason, Thomas A., 'Revelation and Evolution: A Neglected Dimension of the Short Story', *Studies in Short Fiction*, 10 (1973), 347–56

'The Short Story: Revision and Renewal', *Studies in Short Fiction*, 19 (1982), 221–30

Hamalian, Leo and Frederick R. Karl (eds.), *The Shape of Fiction: British and American Short Stories* (second edition, New York, 1978)

Hanson, Clare, *Short Stories and Short Fictions: 1880–1980* (London and Basingstoke, 1985)

ed., *Re-reading the Short Story* (London and Basingstoke, 1989)

Hartley, L. P., 'In Defence of the Short Story', in *The Novelist's Responsibility* (London, 1967), pp. 157–9

Hedberg, Johannes, 'What is a "Short Story"? And What is an "Essay"?', *Moderna Språk*, 74 (1980), 113–20

Imhof, Rüdiger, 'Minimal Fiction, or the Question of Scale', *Anglistik & Englischunterricht*, 23 (1984), 159–68

'The International Symposium on the Short Story', *Kenyon Review*, 30 (1968), 443–90; 31 (1969), 57–94, 449–503

Kafka, Franz, *Letters to Friends, Family, and Editors*, translated by Richard and Clara Winston (London, 1978)

Kostelanetz, Richard, 'Notes on the American Short Story Today', in *Short Story Theories*, edited by Charles May, pp. 214–25

Leibowitz, Judith, *Narrative Purpose in the Novella* (The Hague, 1974)

Lohafer, Susan, *Coming to Terms with the Short Story* (Baton Rouge, 1983)

Marcus, Mordecai, 'What is an Initiation Story?', in *Short Story Theories*, edited by Charles May, pp. 189–201

May, Charles E., 'The Nature of Knowledge in Short Fiction', *Studies in Short Fiction*, 21 (1984), 328–38

ed., *Short Story Theories* (Ohio, 1976)

'The Unique Effect of the Short Story: A Reconsideration and an Example', *Studies in Short Fiction*, 13 (1976), 289–97

O'Connor, Frank, *The Lonely Voice* (1962; reprinted, London, 1963)

O'Faolain, Sean, *The Short Story* (1948; reprinted, Dublin and Cork, 1983)

Peden, William, 'Realism and Anti-Realism in the Modern Short Story', in *The Teller and the Tale*, edited by W. Aycock, pp. 47–62

Poe, Edgar Allan, 'Review of *Twice-Told Tales*', *Graham's Magazine*, May 1842, reprinted in *Short Story Theories*, edited by Charles May, pp. 45–51

Porter, Katherine Anne, 'An Interview', *Paris Review*, 29 (1963), 87–114

Pratt, Mary Louise, 'The Short Story: The Long and the Short of It', *Poetics*, 10 (1981), 175–94

Pritchett, V. S., *Collected Stories* (1982; reprinted, Harmondsworth, 1984)

Propp, Vladimir, *Morphology of the Folktale*, translated by Laurence Scott (second edition, 1968; reprinted, Austin, 1988)

Reid, Ian, *The Short Story* (London, 1977)

Scheer-Schaezler, Brigitte, 'Short Story and Modern Novel: A Comparative Analysis of Two Texts', *Orbis Litterarum*, 25 (1970), 338–51

Schorer, Mark, ed., *The Story: A Critical Anthology* (New York, 1950)

Scott, Virgil and David Madden, eds., *Studies in the Short Story* (1968; fourth edition, New York, 1976)

Shapard, Robert, and James Thomas, eds., *Sudden Fiction: American Short-Short Stories* (1986; reprinted, Harmondsworth, 1988). (Brief theoretical notes by divers hands in the 'Afterwords' (pp. 227–58))

Shaw, Valerie, *The Short Story: A Critical Introduction* (London and New York, 1983)

Sherrill, Anne, and Paula Robertson-Rose, *Four Elements; A Creative Approach to the Short Story* (New York, 1975)

Szávai, János, 'Towards a Theory of the Short Story', *Acta Litteraria Academiae Scientiarum Hungaricae*, 24 (1982), 203–24

Vannatta, Dennis, ed., *The English Short Story, 1945–1980* (Boston, Mass., 1985)

Wain, John, 'Remarks on the Short Story', *Les Cahiers de la Nouvelle: Journal of the Short Story in English*, 2 (1984), 49–66

Walker, Warren S., *Twentieth-Century Short-Story Explication: Interpretations 1900–1975, of Short Fiction Since 1800* (Hamden, Connecticut, 1977)

Warde, William B. (Jr.), 'The Short Story: Structure of a New Genre', *South Central Bulletin*, 36 (1976), 155–7

Welty, Eudora, 'The Reading and Writing of Short Stories', in *The Atlantic Monthly*, 183 (February and March 1949), 54–8 and 46–9, reprinted in *Short Story Theories*, edited by Charles May, pp. 159–77

OTHER SECONDARY MATERIAL

Adams, Robert Martin, 'What Was Modernism?', *Hudson Review*, 31 (1978), 19–33

Alcock, Peter, 'An Aloe in the Garden: Something Essentially New

Zealand in Miss Mansfield', *Journal of Commonwealth Literature*, 11 (1977), 58–64

Alpers, Antony, *Katherine Mansfield* (London, 1954)

The Life of Katherine Mansfield (London, 1980)

Althusser, Louis, *Essays on Ideology* (London, 1984)

and Etienne Balibar, *Reading Capital*, translated by Ben Brewster (1970; rep. London, 1986)

Anderson, Walter E., 'The Hidden Love Triangle in Mansfield's "Bliss"', *Twentieth Century Literature*, 28 (1982), 397–404

Baker, James R., and Thomas F. Staley, eds., *James Joyce's 'Dubliners'* (Belmont, 1969)

Bakhtin, M. M., *The Dialogic Imagination*, edited by Michael Holquist, translated by Caryl Emerson and Michael Holquist (Austin, 1983)

Problems of Dostoevsky's Poetics, edited and translated by Caryl Emerson (Manchester, 1984)

Bakhtin, M. M., and P. N. Medvedev, *The Formal Method in Literary Scholarship*, translated by Albert J. Wehrle (Cambridge, Mass., and London, 1985)

Balibar, Etienne, and Pierre Macherey, 'On Literature as an Ideological Form', *Oxford Literary Review*, 3 (1978), 4–12, reprinted in *Untying the Text: A Post-Structuralist Reader*, edited by Robert Young (1981; reprinted, London, 1987), pp. 79–99

Bareham, Tony, *Malcolm Lowry* (London and Basingstoke, 1989)

Beja, Morris, ed., *'Dubliners' and 'A Portrait'* (London, 1979)

Epiphany in the Modern Novel (London, 1971)

'One Good Look at Themselves: Epiphanies in *Dubliners*', in *Work in Progress: Joyce Centenary Essays*, edited by Richard F. Peterson, Alan M. Cohn and Edmund L. Epstein (Carbondale, 1983), pp. 3–14

Bell, Michael, ed., *1900–1930* (London, 1980)

Bennett, Tony, *Formalism and Marxism* (London and New York, 1986)

Benstock, Bernard, 'The Kenner Conundrum: Or Who Does What With Which to Whom', *James Joyce Quarterly*, 13 (1975–6), 428–35

Berkman, Sylvia, *Katherine Mansfield: A Critical Study* (London, 1952)

Berman, Marshall, *All That is Solid Melts Into Air: The Experience of Modernity* (1982; reprinted, London, 1987)

Blayac, Alain, '"After the Race": A Study in Epiphanies', *Les Cahiers de la Nouvelle: Journal of the Short Story in English*, 2 (1984), 115–27

Booth, Wayne C., *The Rhetoric of Fiction* (second edition, Chicago and London, 1983)

Bowen, Zack, 'Joyce and the Epiphany Concept: A New Apporoach', *Journal of Modern Literature*, 9 (1981), 103–14

Bowen, Zack, and James F. Carens, eds., *A Companion to Joyce Studies*, (Westport and London, 1984)

Bowlby, Rachel, *Virginia Woolf: Feminist Destinations* (Oxford, 1988)

Boyle, Robert, 'A Little Cloud', printed in *James Joyce's 'Dubliners': Critical Essays*, edited by Clive Hart (London, 1969)

Bradbury, Malcolm, *Possibilities: Essays on the State of the Novel* (Oxford, 1973)

and James McFarlane, eds., *Modernism* (Harmondsworth, 1981)

Brandabur, Edward, *A Scrupulous Meanness: A Study of Joyce's Early Work* (Urbana, 1971)

Brown, Homer Obed, *James Joyce's Early Fiction: The Biography of a Form* (Cleveland, 1972)

Brugaletta, John J., and Mary H. Hayden, 'The Motivation for Anguish in Joyce's "Araby"', *Studies in Short Fiction*, 15 (1978), 11–17

Campbell, SueEllen, *The Enemy Opposite: The Outlaw Criticism of Wyndham Lewis* (Athens, Ohio, 1988)

Chadwick, Joseph, 'Silence in "The Sisters"', *James Joyce Quarterly*, 21 (1983–4), 245–55

Cianci, Giovanni, ed., *Wyndham Lewis: Letteratura/Pittura* (Palermo, 1982)

Clark, Katerina, and Michael Holquist, *Mikhail Bakhtin* (Cambridge, Mass., and London, 1984)

Cork, Richard, *Vorticism and Abstract Art in the First Machine Age* (London, 1976)

Corrington, John William, 'Isolation as a Motif in "A Painful Case"', *James Joyce Quarterly*, 3 (1965–6), 182–91

Costa, Richard Hauer, 'The Northern Paradise: Malcolm Lowry in Canada', *Studies in the Novel*, 4 (1972), 165–72

Cross, Richard K., *Malcolm Lowry: A Preface to His Fiction* (London, 1980)

Daiches, David, *New Literary Values: Studies in Modern Literature* (Edinburgh and London, 1936)

Daly, Saralyn R., *Katherine Mansfield* (Boston, 1965)

Dasenbrock, Reed Way, *The Literary Vorticism of Ezra Pound and Wyndham Lewis: Towards the Condition of Painting* (Baltimore and London, 1985)

Daugherty, Beth Rigel, 'The Whole Contention Between Mr Bennett and Mrs Woolf Revisited', in *Virginia Woolf: Centennial Essays*, edited by Elaine K. Ginsberg and Laura Moss Gottlieb (New York, 1983), pp. 269–94

Davies, Alistair, *An Annotated Critical Bibliography of Modernism* (Brighton, 1982)

Davis, Lennard J., *Resisting Novels: Ideology and Fiction* (New York and London, 1987)

Day, Douglas, *Malcolm Lowry* (Oxford and New York, 1973; reissued, 1984)

Day, Robert Adams, 'Joyce's Gnomons, Lenehan, and the Persistence of an Image', *Novel*, 14 (1980–1), 5–19

Dolch, Martin, 'Eveline', in *James Joyce's 'Dubliners'*, edited by James R. Baker and Thomas F. Staley (Belmont, 1969), pp. 96–101

Dowling, William C., *Jameson, Althusser, Marx: An Introduction to 'The Political Unconscious'* (London, 1984)

Durman, Michael and Alan Munton, 'Wyndham Lewis and the Nature of Vorticism' in *Wyndham Lewis: Letteratura/Pittura*, edited by Giovanni Cianci (Palermo, 1982), pp. 101–18

Eagleton, Terry, *Against the Grain: Essays 1975–1985* (1986; reprinted, London, 1988)

Criticism and Ideology (1976; reprinted, London, 1986)

Edmonds, Dale, 'The Short Fiction of Malcolm Lowry', *Tulane Studies in English*, 15 (1967), 59–80

Elliott, Gregory, *The Detour of Theory* (London and New York, 1987)

Ellmann, Richard, *James Joyce* (revised edition, Oxford, 1983)

Fabian, David R., 'Joyce's "The Sisters": Gnomon, Gnomic, Gnome', *Studies in Short Fiction*, 5 (1968), 187–9

Farrington, Jane, *Wyndham Lewis* (London, 1980)

Feshbach, Sidney, '"Fallen on His Feet in Buenos Ayres": Frank in "Eveline"', *James Joyce Quarterly*, 20 (1982–3), 223–7

Forster, E. M., *Aspects of the Novel* (1927; reprinted, Harmondsworth, 1981)

Foster, Hal, ed., *Postmodern Culture* (1983; reprinted, London and Sydney, 1987)

Frank, Joseph, *The Widening Gyre* (New Brunswick, 1963)

French, Marilyn, 'Missing Pieces in Joyce's *Dubliners*', *Twentieth Century Literature*, 24 (1978), 443–72

Freedman, Ralph, ed., *Virginia Woolf: Revaluation and Continuity* (Berkeley, Los Angeles and London, 1980)

Friedrich, Gerhard, 'The Gnomonic Clue to Joyce's *Dubliners*', *Modern Language Notes*, 72 (1957), 421–4

Frow, John, *Marxism and Literary History* (1986; reprinted, Oxford, 1988)

Fullbrook, Kate, *Katherine Mansfield* (Brighton, Sussex, 1986)

Garrison, Joseph M., Jr., 'The Adult Consciousness of the Narrator in Joyce's "Araby"', *Studies in Short Fiction*, 10 (1973), 416–17

Genette, Gérard, *Narrative Discourse*, translated by Jane E. Lewin (1980; reprinted, Oxford, 1986)

Gifford, Don, *Notes for 'Dubliners' and 'A Portrait of the Artist as a Young Man'* (second edition, Berkeley, 1982)

Ginsberg, Elaine K., and Laura Moss Gottlieb, eds., *Virginia Woolf: Centennial Essays* (New York, 1983)

Goode, John, *Thomas Hardy: The Offensive Truth* (Oxford, 1988)

Gordon, John, *James Joyce's Metamorphoses* (Dublin, 1981)

Guiguet, Jean, *Virginia Woolf and Her Works*, translated by Jean Stewart (London, 1965)

Hankin, C. A., 'Fantasy and the Sense of an Ending in the Work of Katherine Mansfield', *Modern Fiction Studies*, 24 (1978), 465–74

Katherine Mansfield and Her Confessional Stories (1983; reprinted, London and Basingstoke, 1988)

Hanson, Clare, 'Katherine Mansfield and Symbolism: The "Artist's Method" in *Prelude*', *Journal of Commonwealth Literature*, 16 (1981), 25–39

Hanson, Clare, and Andrew Gurr, *Katherine Mansfield* (London and Basingstoke, 1981)

Harmon, Maurice, 'Little Chandler and Byron's "First Poem"', *Threshold*, 17 (1962), 59–61

Hart, Clive, 'Eveline', in *James Joyce's 'Dubliners'*, edited by Hart, pp. 48–52

ed., *James Joyce's 'Dubliners'* (London, 1969)

Head, Dominic, 'Expanding Circles: Inductive Composition in *Hear Us O Lord From Heaven Thy Dwelling Place*', in *Malcolm Lowry Eighty Years On*, edited by Sue Vice (London and Basingstoke, 1989), pp. 70–91

Hendry, Irene, 'Joyce's Epiphanies', *Sewanee Review*, 54 (1946), 449–67

Herring, Phillip F., *Joyce's Uncertainty Principle* (Princeton, 1987)

Hyman, Suzanne Katz, '"A Painful Case": The Movement of a Story Through a Shift in Voice', *James Joyce Quarterly*, 19 (1981–2), 111–18

Jameson, Fredric, *Fables of Aggression: Wyndham Lewis, the Modernist as Fascist* (1979; reprinted Berkeley, Los Angeles and London, 1981)

The Ideologies of Theory: Essays 1971–86, 2 vols. (London, 1988)

The Political Unconscious: Narrative as a Socially Symbolic Act (1981; reprinted, London, 1986)

'Postmodernism and Consumer Society', in *Postmodern Culture*, edited by Hal Foster, pp. 111–25

Joyce, Stanislaus, *My Brother's Keeper*, edited by Richard Ellmann (1958; reprinted, London, 1982)

Kenner, Hugh, *The Pound Era* (1972; reprinted, London, 1975)

Kermode, Frank, *The Genesis of Secrecy: On the Interpretation of Narrative* (Cambridge, Mass., 1979)

The Sense of an Ending (1967, reprinted, Oxford, 1968)

Kleine, Don W., 'Katherine Mansfield and the Prisoner of Love', *Critique*, 3 (1960), 20–33

'Mansfield and the Orphans of Time', *Modern Fiction Studies*, 24 (1978), 423–38

Kobler, J. F., 'The Sexless Narrator of Mansfield's "The Young Girl"', *Studies in Short Fiction*, 17 (1980), 269–74

Lafourcade, Bernard, 'The Taming of the Wild Body', in *Wyndham Lewis: A Revaluation*, edited by Jeffrey Meyers (London, 1980), pp. 68–84

Lawrence, D. H., '*Fantasia of the Unconscious*' and '*Psychoanalysis and the Unconscious*' (Harmondsworth, 1971)

Leigh, James, 'The Gnomonic Principle in *Dubliners*', *The Lamar Journal of the Humanities*, 9 (1983), 35–40

Lentricchia, Frank, *Criticism and Social Change* (Chicago and London, 1985)

Lukács, Georg, *The Meaning of Contemporary Realism*, translated by John and Necke Mander (London, 1963)

Lunn, Eugene, *Marxism and Modernism* (1982; reprinted, London, 1985)

MacCabe, Colin, *James Joyce and the Revolution of the Word* (London, 1983)

MacDonald, R. D., 'Canada in Lowry's Fiction', *Mosaic*, 14 (1981), 35–53

McLaughlin, Ann L., 'The Same Job: The Shared Writing Aims of Katherine Mansfield and Virginia Woolf', *Modern Fiction Studies*, 24 (1978), 369–82

Macherey, Pierre, *A Theory of Literary Production*, translated by Geoffrey Wall (1978; reprinted, London, 1986)

Macherey, Pierre, and Etienne Balibar, 'On Literature as an Ideological Form', *Oxford Literary Review*, 3 (1978), 4–12, reprinted in *Untying the Text: A Post-Structuralist Reader*, edited by Robert Young (1981; reprinted, London, 1987), pp. 79–99

Magalaner, Marvin, *The Fiction of Katherine Mansfield* (Carbondale and Edwardsville, 1971)

Materer, Timothy, *Wyndham Lewis the Novelist* (Detroit, 1976)

Meyers, Jeffrey, 'Katherine Mansfield: A Bibliography of International Criticism, 1921–1977', *Bulletin of Bibliography*, 34 (April–June 1977), 53–67

'Katherine Mansfield: A Selected Checklist', *Modern Fiction Studies*, 24 (1978), 475–7

'Murry's Cult of Mansfield', *Journal of Modern Literature*, 7 (1979), 15–38

Michel, Walter, *Wyndham Lewis: Paintings and Drawings* (London, 1971)

Miller, D. A., *Narrative and its Discontents: Problems of Closure in the Traditional Novel* (1981; reprinted, Princeton, 1989)

Minow-Pinkney, Makiko, *Virginia Woolf and the Problem of the Subject* (Brighton, 1987)

Molesworth, Charles, *Donald Barthelme's Fiction: The Ironist Saved From Drowning* (Columbia and London, 1982)

Morrissey, L. J., 'Joyce's Narrative Strategies in "Araby"', *Modern Fiction Studies*, 28 (1982), 45–52

Munton, Alan, 'Fredric Jameson: Fables of Aggression', in *Blast 3*, edited by Seamus Cooney (Santa Barbara, 1984), pp. 345–51

Murry, John Middleton, *The Letters of John Middleton Murry to Katherine Mansfield*, edited by C. A. Hankin (London, 1983)

Nebeker, Helen, 'The Pear Tree: Sexual Implications in Katherine Mansfield's "Bliss"', *Modern Fiction Studies*, 18 (1973), 545–51

Nyland, A. C., 'Malcolm Lowry: The Writer', in *Malcolm Lowry: Psalms and Songs*, edited by Margerie Lowry (New York and Scarborough, Ontario, 1975), pp. 139–84

Ortega y Gasset, José, 'The Dehumanization of Art', translated by Helene Weyl, in '*The Dehumanization of Art' and Other Essays on Art, Culture, and Literature* (Princeton, 1948; reprinted, 1972), pp. 1–54

O'Sullivan, Vincent, 'The Magnetic Chain: Notes and Approaches to Katherine Mansfield', *Landfall*, 29 (1975), 95–131

Parrinder, Patrick, *James Joyce* (Cambridge, 1984)

Peterson, Richard F., Alan M. Cohn and Edmund L. Epstein, eds., *Work in Progress: Joyce Centenary Essays* (Carbondale, 1983)

Purdy, Richard Little, *Thomas Hardy: A Bibliographical Study* (1954; reprinted, Oxford, 1979)

Richter, Harvena, 'Hunting the Moth: Virginia Woolf and the Creative Imagination', in *Virginia Woolf: Revaluation and Continuity*, edited by Ralph Freedman (Berkeley, Los Angeles and London, 1980), pp. 13–28

Scholes, Robert, 'Further Observations on the Text of *Dubliners*', *Studies in Bibliography*, 17 (1964), 107–22

'Grant Richards to James Joyce', *Studies in Bibliography*, 16 (1963), 139–60

'Joyce and the Epiphany: The Key to the Labyrinth?', *Sewanee Review*, 72 (1964), 65–77

Scholes, Robert, and Richard M. Kain, eds., *The Workshop of Daedalus* (Evanston, 1965)

Scholes, Robert, and Florence L. Walzl, 'The Epiphanies of Joyce', *PMLA*, 82 (March 1967), 152–4

Showalter, Elaine, *A Literature of Their Own: British Women Novelists From Brontë to Lessing* (revised edition, 1982; reprinted, London, 1988)

Skerl, Jennie, 'A New Look at Vladimir Propp's Narrative Grammar: The Example of Joyce's "Eveline"', *Essays in Literature*, 8 (1961), 151–71

Sprinker, Michael, *Imaginary Relations: Aesthetics and Ideology in the Theory of Historical Materialism* (London, 1987)

Stead, C. K., 'Katherine Mansfield and the Art of Fiction', *The New Review*, 4 (1977), 42, 27–36

Stengel, Wayne B., *The Shape of Art in the Short Stories of Donald Barthelme* (Baton Rouge and London, 1985)

Tomalin, Claire, *Katherine Mansfield: A Secret Life* (London, 1987)

Tomlinson, Sophie, 'Mans-Field in Bookform', *Landfall*, 39 (1985), 465–89

Vásquez, Adolfo Sánchez, *Art and Society: Essays in Marxist Aesthetics*, translated by Maro Riofrancos (1973; reprinted, London, 1979)

Vice, Sue, ed., *Malcolm Lowry Eighty Years On* (London and Basingstoke, 1989)

Voelker, Joseph C., '"Chronicles of Disorder": Reading the Margins of Joyce's *Dubliners*', *Colby Library Quarterly*, 18 (1982), 126–44

Vološinov, V. N., *Marxism and the Philosophy of Language*, translated by Ladislav Matejka and I. R. Titunik (1973; reprinted, Cambridge, Mass., and London, 1986)

Walker, Warren S., 'The Unresolved Conflict in "The Garden Party"', *Modern Fiction Studies*, 3 (1958), 354–8

Walzl, Florence L., 'Dubliners', in *A Companion to Joyce Studies*, edited by Zack Bowen and James F. Carens (Westport and London, 1984), pp. 157–228

Wilde, Alan, *Horizons of Assent: Postmodernism and the Ironic Imagination* (Baltimore and London, 1981)

Williams, Raymond, *Marxism and Literature* (1977; reprinted, Oxford and New York, 1985)

Young, Robert, ed., *Untying the Text: A Post-Structuralist Reader* (1981; reprinted, London, 1987)

Index

allegory, 197–8
Althusser, Louis, 26–31
  aesthetic effects, 27–31
  relative autonomy, 26–31
  symptomatic reading, 28–9, 77, 186–7
Amis, Martin
  'Bujak and the Strong Force', 197–9
  Einstein's Monsters, 36, 196–9
Ancient Mariner, The, 182
Anderson, Walter, 24–5
apocalypse, 36, 195–6, 199
Aristotle, 12
Austen, Jane
  Emma, 5

Bader, A. L., 13
Bakhtin, Mikhail, 33–4, 67–8, 76, 95–9,
  102, 115, 202
  centripetal and centrifugal forces,
    67–8, 95, 97
  dialogics, 33–4, 67–9, 95–9, 102
  heteroglossia, 96, 97, 102, 202
Baldeshwiler, Elaine, 13, 16–17, 79
Balibar, Etienne, 29, 77
Barth, John
  'Frame Tale', 11
Barthelme, Donald, 36, 200–5
  'Balloon, The', 200–5
  Snow White, 202
Bayley, John, 22, 122–3
Beckett, Samuel
  Unnamable, The, 162
Beja, Morris, 49, 51
Bennett, Arnold, 33, 34, 81–2, 83–4, 88,
  89, 94, 107
Berman, Marshall, 204
Bergonzi, Bernard, 167–8
Booth, Wayne, 20
Bowen, Elizabeth, 4, 18

Bowen, Zack, 49
Bradbury, Malcolm, 165, 184
Brandabur, Edward, 44–5
Burgess, Anthony, 4

Campbell, SueEllen, 163
Chapman, Michael, 7, 193
Chekhov, Anton, 16, 22
closure and non-closure, 13–14, 36,
  189, 193–5, 198–203
Coleridge, Samuel Taylor
  Ancient Mariner, The, 182
Conrad, Joseph, 17
Coppard, A. E., 12
Cortázar, Julio, 21, 43–4, 58, 176
Cross, Richard, 168
Cubism, 141
Curran, Constantine, 38

Daly, Saralyn, 109
Davis, Lennard, 192
Day, Robert, 43
Death in Venice, 7
Didion, Joan, 192–3, 194, 195
disarmament, 197–8
Dolch, Martin, 66
Dollerup, Cay, 12
Dostoevsky, Fyodor, 97–9, 115
  'Double, The', 98–9
  Eternal Husband and Other Stories, The,
    97, 99
Doyle, Arthur Conan
  Sherlock Holmes stories, 4
Dubliners, 21, 32, 33, 37–78, 87–8, 110,
  144, 148; *see also* Joyce, James

ecology, 172
Einstein, Albert, 198–9
Einstein's Monsters, 36, 196–9

Eliot, T. S., 82
Emma, 5
Erskine, Albert, 167
Eternal Husband and Other Stories, The, 97, 99

Falconer, John, 46
Ferguson, Suzanne, 16–17
Fleishman, Avrom, 10, 104–5
Forster, E. M., 4
Friedman, Norman, 4
Friedrich, Gerhard, 42
Fullbrook, Kate, 122, 189
Futurism, 141

Galsworthy, John, 82, 107
Garnett, Constance, 97
Genette, Gérard, 58
Gerlach, John, 13, 14, 22
Goode, John, 27
Gordimer, Nadine, 92, 190–1
Gordon, John, 50

Hankin, C. A., 30
Hanson, Clare, 14, 16–17, 19, 20, 23, 80
Hardy Thomas, 4, 26
    Jude the Obscure, 26
    Under the Greenwood Tree, 5
Hart, Clive, 66
Hartley, L. P., 1, 2
Hear Us O Lord From Heaven Thy Dwelling Place 35, 165–84, 189; *see also* Lowry Malcolm
Hedberg, Johannes, 10
Hegelian dialectic, 12
Hemingway, Ernest, 22
Herring, Phillip, 46, 47–8, 66, 76
Hyman, Suzanne, 74

Imhof, Rüdiger, 11
implied author, 20
Impressionist art, 9
Irish Homestead, 44

Jacob's Room, 6, 105
James, Henry, 4, 17, 23
James, William, 23
Jameson, Fredric, 28–9, 93, 131, 134, 159, 161–2, 186, 204
jazz, 21, 172, 175–6
Joyce, James, 2, 10, 14, 16, 17, 18, 31, 32, 33–4, 35, 37–78, 81, 82, 87–8, 109, 113, 139, 141, 144, 148, 161, 163, 168, 169, 173, 185, 187–8

correspondence with Grant Richards, 39–41, 46–7
Dubliners; ambiguity, 37, 38, 41, 44, 45–6, 53, 59, 61, 65, 76–7; dialogized narrative, 67–9, 72–3, 74–6, 77; dissonant and disruptive effects, 38, 48, 53, 58, 64–5, 73, 77–8; ellipsis, 37, 44, 48; epiphany/revelation, 21, 32, 37, 38–9, 48–51, 53, 54–8, 62, 69–70, 74, 75, 110; focalization, 58, 73; gnomon, 32, 42–8, 87–8, 144; historical determinants/ideological restraints, 48, 65, 73, 76–7; immanent author, 51, 55–6, 58; initiation plot, 64–6, 187; narrative grammar, 71–2; non-epiphany principle, 32, 60, 62, 70, 75; paralysis, 32, 37–43, 65, 66, 73, 77; rebuilding approaches, 32, 37–49; relative autonomy, 48, 65, 68; romance fiction, 70–1, 73; symbolic effects, 37, 38, 56, 57; tri-part structure, 64–6; vacillation, 51–3, 58, 75–6; visual metaphor, 32, 37, 43–4, 87–8
Portrait of the Artist, A, 45
Stephen Hero, 54
Ulysses, 5, 6, 43, 45

Stories: 'After the Race', 56–8; 'An Encounter', 53; 'Araby', 50–3; 'Boarding House, The', 38; 'Clay', 54, 55–6, 57, 70; 'Counterparts', 40, 46–7, 54, 55–6; 'Dead, The', 10, 37–8; 'Eveline', 38, 44, 66–73, 77; 'Little Cloud, A', 38, 58–65, 187–8; 'Painful Case, A', 53, 73–6; 'Sisters, The', 32, 42, 53, 56; 'Two Gallants', 43, 45, 54, 55–6, 57
Joyce, Stanislaus, 39
Jude the Obscure, 26

Kafka, Franz
    'Before the Law', 15–16
    'Metamorphosis', 14
Kenner, Hugh, 44, 69
Kermode, Frank, 15, 195–6
Kipling, Rudyard, 80
Kostelanetz, Richard, 191, 192

Lawrence, D. H., 13, 34–5, 82, 122–3, 131
    Women in Love, 34

Index   239

Stories, 'Blind Man, The', 34; 'Fox,
The', 122–3; 'Horse Dealer's
Daughter, The', 34; 'Man Who
Died, The', 34; 'Man Who Loved
Islands, The', 34; 'New Eve and
Old Adam', 34; 'Prussian Officer,
The', 34; 'Woman Who Rode
Away, The', 34
Leibowitz, Judith, 6, 7
Lewis, Percy Wyndham, 2, 31, 35,
139–64, 168, 186, 187, 195
art/life dichotomy, 35, 141–4
automatism, 144–9, 159–60
circumscribed action/pattern, 35,
144–9, 153–4, 157–64, 168
commitment and detachment, 148–9,
152–63
dehumanization, 152–3
detachment, 35, 141–6, 150–2, 161
dialogic failure, 160–3
dynamic form, 141–5, 157, 161
formal disjunction/dissonance, 35,
140, 148, 159, 161, 163
fragmentation, 160–4
inferior religion, 146–7, 150, 161
'Inferior Religions', 142, 144–5
'Meaning of the Wild Body, The',
142–3
Penseur, Le, 142
physician, 152–3, 158
pseudo-couple, 162
reversal/perepeteia, 145, 147–9, 161
satire, 143, 148–9, 151–2, 156, 158–9,
161
solitary experience, 164
Tarr, 141
unified/conventional short story, 35,
145, 163
visual metaphor, 142
vortex, 141–5, 154, 158, 161
Vorticism, 35, 140–6, 148, 151–2, 153,
158, 161, 164, 165
Vorticist, The, 142
Wild Body, The, 35, 139–64, 165, 168,
179
Workshop, 142

Stories: 'Beau Séjour', 143; 'Bestre',
154; 'Brobdingnag', 148–9;
'Brotcotnaz', 145–9, 154, 161;
'Death of the Ankou, The', 149–52,
161; 'Soldier of Humour, A',
154–61

Lohafer, Susan, 2, 3, 13–14, 193–4
Long Story Short, 4, 5
Lowry, Malcolm, 2, 31, 35, 165–84, 186,
189, 199
anagnorisis, 176, 179
closure and non-closure, 35, 166,
168–70, 174–5, 176, 181, 186
epiphany/revelation, 36, 166, 169,
172–3, 175–6, 180
expanding circle motif, 35, 166,
169–70, 173–4, 178–9, 182–3, 184
formal dissonance/disruption, 36, 166,
168–9, 174–6, 181, 183
fragmentation, 167, 183
Hear Us O Lord From Heaven Thy
Dwelling Place, 35, 165–84, 189
in British Columbia, 168
inductive composition, 168
isolation, 35, 167–8, 171, 177, 179
jazz break, 172, 175–6
private and public issues, 36, 166,
170–2, 175, 177, 180, 181, 182, 184,
186
self-consciousness, 165, 182–3
single effect techniques, 175, 182
symbolism, 36, 166, 169, 172, 173,
174–5, 177, 179–81
Under the Volcano, 166

Stories: 'Bravest Boat, The', 181;
'Elephant and Colosseum', 176–81,
183, 184, 199; 'Forest Path to the
Spring, The', 36, 166, 168–76, 179,
183; 'Gin and Goldenrod', 181;
'Present Estate of Pompeii', 181;
'Strange Comfort Afforded by the
Profession', 181–2; 'Through the
Panama', 182–3
Lukács, Georg, 31

Macherey, Pierre, 29, 77, 186
Mann, Thomas
Death In Venice, 7
Mansfield, Katherine, 2, 12, 14, 16, 17,
19, 20, 24, 29–30, 31, 33–4, 35, 65,
79, 108, 109–38, ,139, 141, 148,
161, 168, 169, 185, 186, 188, 189
ambiguity, 30, 33, 109–10, 119, 136–8
dialogized narrative, 115–22, 132–8
epiphany/revelation, 109–10, 111,
135–6, 138
fantasy, 122–4, 127–8
female victimization, 119, 125, 127–8

formal dissonance/disruption, 29–30, 33, 110, 111, 113, 127–8, 130, 137–8
historical determinants/ideological restraints, 29–30, 113, 119–22, 124, 127–8, 130–1, 132–8
'mystery', 122–3, 137
reversal, 111–13, 130
romance fiction, 121–2
symbolism, 20, 24–6, 30, 117, 124–8, 134–7, 188

Stories: Aloe, The, 117; 'Bain Turcs', 30; 'Birthday, A', 113; 'Black Cap, The', 117; 'Bliss', 24–5, 29–30, 65, 109, 138, 187; 'Daughters of the Late Colonel, The', 114; 'Escape, The', 19; 'Festival of the Coronation, The', 117; 'Garden Party, The', 131–8, 186, 188; 'Her First Ball', 128–30; 'Honeymoon', 123–8; 'In Confidence', 117; 'Je ne Parle pas Français', 114–17, 139; 'Late at Night', 117; 'Married Man's Story, A', 114; 'Millie', 111–13, 130; 'Miss Brill', 110–11, 130; 'Modern Soul, The', 30; 'New Dresses', 113; 'Ole Underwood', 113–14; 'Pic-Nic, A', 117; 'Prelude', 117–22, 130–1; 'Psychology', 114; 'Something Childish but Very Natural', 114; 'Stay Laces', 117; 'Swing of the Pendulum, The', 113; 'Tiredness of Rosabel, The', 122; 'Two Tuppenny Ones Please', 117
Marxism, 27, 186
Materer, Timothy, 149, 151
Maugham, W. Somerset, 80
Maupassant, Guy de, 16, 86
  'Idyll', 86
metafiction, 8, 36, 80, 83, 86–7, 165, 182, 200
Miller, D. A., 199–200
Molesworth, Charles, 202
Morrissey, L. J., 50, 52
Mrs Dalloway, 5, 6, 105
Munro, H. H. (Saki), 80, 86
  'The Mouse', 86
Murry, John Middleton, 115

novella, 6, 7
nuclear weapons, 195–9

O'Connor, Frank, 167, 189–90, 191–2
Ortega y Gasset, José, 152–4

parable, 15–16
Poe, Edgar Allan, 2, 9, 11, 35, 49, 151, 175
  'Tale of the Ragged Mountains, A', 151
poetry, 21, 25, 96
pop modernism, 204
Porter, Katherine Anne, 12
Portrait of the Artist, A, 45
postmodernism, 36, 165, 200–5
Pratt, Mary Louise, 3, 5
Pritchett, V. S., 190
Propp, Vladimir, 71
Proust, Marcel, 173

Reid, Ian, 12–13, 23
Richards, Grant, 39–41, 46–7
romance fiction, 70–1, 73, 121–2

Saroyan, William, 193
Scholes, Robert, 40, 46–7, 49
Schorer, Mark, 18
Shaw, Valerie, 9, 20, 190
short story, the
  ambiguity and paradox, 2, 8, 14, 15, 22
  and the novel, 1, 3–9, 16, 17–18, 96, 191–2
  and the visual arts, 9–10
  dissonant and disunifying effects, 2, 10–11, 20, 21–31, 33–4, 139, 186–9
  ellipsis, 2, 23, 31
  epiphany/revelation, 18–19, 20–1, 24, 29, 32, 33, 36
  fantasy, 122–3
  initiation plot, 64–6, 187
  isolation, 164, 167–8, 189–92
  modern, 1, 13, 21
  'mystery', 23, 30, 31, 122–3, 137
  'single effect' doctrine, 2, 9, 35, 48–9, 166, 175, 182, 185
  symbolism, 14, 20, 23–6, 127–8
  two types, 16–17, 79–80
  unifying theories, 9–24, 35, 37, 42, 96, 106, 175
  visual metaphors, 10–12, 14, 21, 37, 43–4, 87–8
Showalter, Elaine, 128
Skerl, Jennie, 71
Snow White, 202

Stengel, Wayne, 201
Stephen Hero, 54
Stern, G. B.
  Long Story Short, 4
  'The Uncharted Year', 5
Stevenson, Robert Louis, 80
Symbolism, 19
symptomatic reading, 28–9, 77, 186–7
Szávai, Janos, 22

Tarr, 141
Tennyson, Alfred
  'The Lady of Shalott', 87

Ulysses, 5, 6, 43, 45
Under the Greenwood Tree, 5
Under the Volcano, 166
Utopia, 186–7, 189

Voelker, Joseph C., 45
Vološinov, V. N., 76, 102
Vorticism, 35, 140–6, 148, 151–2, 153, 158, 161, 164, 165

Wain, John, 11, 21, 43
Walzl, Florence, 39, 49
Wells, H. G., 82, 107
Welty, Eudora, 23
Wild Body, The, 35, 139–64, 165, 168, 179; *see also* Lewis, Wyndham
Wilde, Oscar, 30, 106
  'Sphinx Without a Secret, The', 106
Women in Love, 34
Woolf, Virginia, 2, 10, 16, 17, 20, 21, 31, 32–4, 35, 78, 79–108, 109, 131, 139, 141, 148, 161, 168, 186, 188
  adaptation/subversion of convention, 79–81, 84, 85, 89–90, 96–7, 104–8
  ambiguity, 88–9, 103
  dialogized narrative, 95–9, 100–4, 108
  formal dissonance/disruption, 32–3, 79–81, 83–4, 89–90, 94, 95, 105–6, 108
  fragmentation, 93–5, 188
  framing structures, 91, 96, 97, 103–5
  heteroglossia, 96, 102, 103, 108
  historical determinants/ideological restraints, 84, 89, 94
  Jacob's Room, 6, 105
  metafiction, 80, 83, 86–7
  'Modern Fiction', 33, 34, 81, 90, 103
  moth image, 90–1
  'Mr Bennett and Mrs Brown', 33, 34, 81–2, 83–4, 88, 89, 94, 107
  Mrs Dalloway, 5, 6, 105
  narrative voice/fallibility, 33, 90
  reversal, 83, 85, 89, 96
  symbolism, 85, 86, 88, 89, 90–1, 104
  To the Lighthouse, 105
  visual metaphor, 87–9
  wave imagery, 91, 94–5
  Waves, The, 95
  Stories: 'An Unwritten Novel', 80, 81–2, 84–6, 87, 89; 'Blue and Green', 80, 90, 105; 'Duchess and the Jeweller, The', 80; 'Evening Party, The', 80, 90–9, 103, 105, 188; 'Haunted House, A', 80, 90; 'Kew Gardens', 80, 90, 99–103, 105; 'Lady in the Looking-Glass, The', 10, 80, 82, 86–9; 'Lappin and Lapinova', 80; 'Mark on the Wall, The', 106–8; 'Moments of Being', 10, 20, 21, 80, 82–4, 86; 'Monday or Tuesday', 80, 90, 103–5; 'Shooting Party, The', 89

Lightning Source UK Ltd.
Milton Keynes UK
21 December 2009

147833UK00001B/20/P